Choosing Sides

American Controversies Series
Series Editor: Douglas R. Egerton, Le Moyne College

Students love debate. They love contention, which they see all about them in modern society. Yet too many monographs or biographies erase the controversies that existed in earlier decades. Slavery and institutionalized sexism, for example, strike modern readers as being so clearly wrong that they cannot understand why rational Americans endorsed slavery or thought it foolish to enfranchise women. How could a politician as brilliant as Thomas Jefferson believe that forced assimilation was the best policy for Native Americans? Why did Americans allow Hitler to become so powerful before confronting him? Why were many of the so-called Greatest Generation indifferent to social justice at home? How did the Vietnam War become such a political and cultural powder keg? Hindsight is often the enemy of understanding, and what strikes us as obvious was often anything but simple to earlier generations.

This series deals with major controversies in American history. The events depicted in this series were either controversial at the time (such as militant abolitionism) or have sparked modern historiographical controversies. (Did slave conspiracies actually exist, for example? Why did witch trials in Salem spiral out of control in 1692?) Each volume in the series begins with an extensive essay that explains the topic, discusses the relevant historiography, and summarizes the various points of view (contemporaneous as well as modern). The second half of the volume is devoted to documents, but each is annotated and preceded by a brief introduction. By contextualizing each document, this series pulls back the curtain, so to speak, on the process of writing history, even as the essays, letters, laws, and newspaper accounts that follow allow important American actors to speak in their own voices. Most of all, by examining both sides in these debates, and by providing documents that see each issue from different angles, the American Controversies Series will bring history alive—and enliven history classrooms.

Volumes Published

Slavery and Sectional Strife in the Early American Republic, 1776–1821
Gary J. Kornblith

Antebellum Women: Private, Public, Partisan
Carol Lasser and Stacey Robertson

Witchcraft in Early North America
Alison Games

Choosing Sides: Loyalists in Revolutionary America
Ruma Chopra

Choosing Sides

Loyalists in Revolutionary America

Ruma Chopra

ROWMAN & LITTLEFIELD
Lanham • Boulder • New York • London

To Mona Sahadeo and Rakhee Chawla, in utmost admiration

Published by Rowman & Littlefield
A wholly owned subsidiary of The Rowman & Littlefield Publishing Group, Inc.
4501 Forbes Boulevard, Suite 200, Lanham, Maryland 20706
www.rowman.com

Unit A, Whitacre Mews, 26-34 Stannary Street, London SE11 4AB,

British Library Cataloguing in Publication Information Available

Library of Congress Cataloging-in-Publication Data

The hardback edition of this book was previously cataloged by the Library of Congress as follows:

Chopra, Ruma.
  Choosing sides : loyalists in revolutionary America / Ruma Chopra.
    pages cm — (American controversies series)
  Includes index.
  1. American loyalists. 2. United States—Politics and government—1775-1783.
I. Title.
  E277.C545 2013
  973.3—dc23   2013005789

ISBN: 978-1-4422-0571-0 (cloth : alk. paper)
ISBN: 978-1-4422-0572-7 (pbk. : alk. paper)
ISBN: 978-1-4422-0573-4 (electronic)

∞™ The paper used in this publication meets the minimum requirements of American National Standard for Information Sciences—Permanence of Paper for Printed Library Materials, ANSI/NISO Z39.48-1992.

Printed in the United States of America

Contents

Acknowledgments

This volume highlights the cross-spectrum of voices that defined loyalist persuasions in British North America in the late eighteenth century. It recognizes the aspirations and hopes of American loyalist families—free, enslaved, and Indian. It asks students and scholars to consider carefully how ideological and pragmatic motivations intersected and collided as colonists chose sides. For patriots as much as for loyalists, time and space influenced the evolution of allegiances, and the experience of war altered initial commitments.

This project has benefited from funding by San Jose State University, and from support by colleagues and friends. It was initiated with encouragement from Gary Kornblith and Douglas Egerton, and was improved with sharp commentary from Robert Middlekauff. Bob and Beverly Middlekauff have become precious friends. My indebtedness to my advisors, Alan Taylor and Clarence Walker, remains.

This year, I have learned much about history-telling from opportunities to lecture to lively and thoughtful audiences at the Clements Library, the David Library of the American Revolution, the American Revolution Roundtable (Richmond, Virginia), and at the Fraunces Tavern Museum in New York City where, remarkably, a talk on the loyalists was sold out! New York City served as British headquarters and loyalist haven during the revolutionary war. That New Yorkers of 2013 came in such numbers to honor the loyalist experience of 1776–1783 was fantastic. The loyalists, no doubt, would have found it most bizarre.

For the "unbearable joy of being," I thank Gucci and Juicy. Dr. Kamlesh Masi's grace anchors and inspires. To my remarkable sisters, I dedicate this book.

Introduction

Most eighteenth-century Euro-Americans began their life as Britons. The most influential imaginary community that anchored their social, political, and economic life was the British empire. They regarded Britain as their mother country, even if they were several generations removed from British birth. Although many never had any direct contact with Britain, they shared the same imperial myths and pride. Through their use of the English language, their faith in Protestant religious orders, and their adherence to British notions of liberty and justice, they celebrated their place as assimilated subjects of the British Atlantic community. They copied British fashions and books, trusted British constitutionalism, followed British politics, and along with fellow Protestant Britons in Europe, regarded England as the center of their cultural identity. During the twenty-year revolutionary struggle, half the colonies of British America and a substantial minority—20 percent—in the thirteen rebellious colonies remained loyal to Britain. This volume describes the context that led Euro-Americans in the British Atlantic to defend their society and their empire, and explores the circumstances that led most Native Americans and African Americans (slaves and free) in the thirteen mainland colonies to choose the British side. No sharp divide differentiated rebels from loyalists; a combination of principles, interests, location, and social attitudes influenced initial choices, the exigencies of war modified decisions, and losses sometimes reversed initial commitments.

The Americans who chose allegiance to the empire did not share character traits, patrons, or parishes. Those who remained loyal comprised the native and foreign born, those in backcountry areas as much as in cities, and those who worshiped in Anglican churches as well as those who were Quakers and Congregationalists. The average loyalist might come from any walk of life: he may be a British merchant or an innkeeper or a cartman, a farmer who used the revolution to resist his rebel landlord, or a tenant who reacted against the rebel mandate for militia enlistment. He may be a recently immigrated Scot who imagined his future in an integrated empire. The loyalist may be an American-born slave or a Mohawk Indian. Many colonial women took sides that sustained their marital ties.

The dominant interpretation of the revolution has downplayed the diversity and potential of the loyalists. They are depicted as imperial placemen solely motivated by a desire to maintain position and fortune, or as backward-looking conservatives.[1] In contrast to virtuous rebel farmers who bravely stood for liberty, the loyalists emerge as colonial aristocrats who selfishly pursue wealth and position. This reading misses the fact that both loyalist and rebel included constituents from the privileged circles and also people in the margins of colonial society. Of course, the well educated, cosmopolitan, wealthy, and ambitious comprised the loyalist elite. But founding fathers such as George Washington, Thomas Jefferson, and John Adams were not inferior in social rank to prominent loyalists such as the royal governor of Massachusetts, Thomas Hutchinson; Pennsylvania assemblyman Joseph Galloway; or the Indian superintendent, Sir William Johnson. Indeed, the most disadvantaged in the colonies—the African-American slaves and the Native Americans—mostly sided with the British.

The character of the loyalists has endured deep scrutiny even as loyalist choices have been caricatured. The loyalists appear as hidebound conservatives or as political lackeys lacking ideological commitment, motivated by fear to maintain the status quo. When the loyalist choice has been acknowledged, the decision toward allegiance to the empire has been framed as an aberrant and individual one. Written more than thirty years ago, Bernard Bailyn's intellectual biography of the royal governor of Massachusetts, Thomas Hutchinson, has defined the general understanding of loyalists.[2] Bailyn portrayed Hutchinson as "political, not philosophical," and described his arguments against patriots as "bland in content and blandly told."[3] Unlike John Adams, Hutchinson felt "no inner promptings" to "follow a wayward course."[4] Bailyn's Hutchinson stands for the "losers," one of many lone figures who could not understand the progressive passion of the revolutionaries.

But the loyal Americans were as passionate as their adversaries and resiliently defended their vision of liberty within the empire. A deep ideological commitment and a sentimental attachment to the empire determined the allegiance of this courageous minority. The loyalists continued to trust the British government, labeled the rebels as tyrants, and opposed what they repeatedly called the "unnatural rebellion."[5] They worried about an American future under the reign of power-hungry demagogues who conspired against the true freedoms of the British government. They assumed a grimmer picture of human nature, a greater concern with the consequences of a disordered society, and a deeper sense of indebtedness to Great Britain. They celebrated their birthright as Britons and fought hard to preserve their precious link to the empire. Like the rebels, the loyalist leaders struggled to rally the undecided and to create a winning coalition despite differences in opinions and strategies.

More than ideological commitments, the proximity of the British army and the threat of local coercion dramatically affected people's choices. Protection from British troops could drive the wavering to embrace reunion, but evacuation of the same troops could lead the abandoned to accrue grievances against the empire. Likewise, patterns of violence affected the direction of political choices as much as heartfelt allegiance. When colonists refused or hesitated to choose rebellion, they risked physical harassment, social isolation, and legal ostracizing from local enforcement agencies, known as the Committees of Safety. These punishments stifled loyalists' utterance of their political inclinations. Many chose sides to maintain the security of their kin and property, not necessarily out of deep political convictions.

As much a war of political independence between colony and empire as a civil war between Euro-Americans, the rebellion was a struggle by slaves for emancipation and a war by Indians for survival. Like Euro-Americans, slaves and Indians chose sides based on a mixture of local considerations and ideological commitments. Many plantation slaves answered the British administration's desperate need for military manpower to find a path to freedom. A few urbanized northern slaves who served actively with the British military considered themselves British allies in a war that could end the rule of slave owners. Some felt the voice of God called upon them to end the rebellion. Most Indian communities, like others in the colonial population, tried to avoid choosing a side until the war actually touched their localities, and sometimes their very homes. Many communities distrusted the settlers' yearning for Indian land and put their faith in the British government. Some such as the Mohawks who long benefited from a close bond with British agents and Anglican clergymen saw no reason to abandon the relationship. Internal disagreements divided Indian communities as they divided Euro-American neighbors.

In the turmoil of the rebellion, self-interest and idealism informed one another, and political allegiances did not stay firm. Some examples highlight the volatility of loyalties, even among the most prominent rebel ideologues. Recognized rebel politicians such as New York attorney John Jay remained undecided for years before choosing independence. Indeed, Jay was identified as a conservative in the First Continental Congress in September 1774. Of non-English stock, sometimes described as vain and stuffy, Jay hoped to raise his stature through securing land grants and to advance his legal career through connections to friends in London. Denied access to both land and a judgeship, Jay committed to the rebel side by marrying the daughter of William Livingston, a prominent rebel leader who became governor of New Jersey after the loyalist governor, William Franklin, was forced to give up his seat. As late as October 1775, Jay hoped to restore peace and prosperity in an "Empire now rent by unnatural convulsions."[6] But by 1776, Jay "inched towards over resistance" and transformed himself into a "hardline insurgent." Jay led a committee to root out loyalists; hung Thomas Hickey, accused of a plot against General George Washington; and threw the loyal mayor of New York City, David Mathews, into jail.[7]

New York merchant Isaac Low rejected rebellion for loyalism only in 1775. His unwillingness to break with the empire was as sudden as John Jay's decision to support rebellion. Low headed many rebel committees during the late 1760s and early 1770s. One of the founders of the New York Chamber of Commerce in 1768, Low was also a member of the First Continental Congress and signed the Continental Association that promoted the boycott of British goods.[8] In a meeting held on April 29, 1775, Low called George III a "Roman Catholic tyrant" who had "broken his coronation oath."[9] But by the end of 1775, Low drew the line at the idea of independence. A merchant who enthusiastically supported imperial reform, Low advocated orderly and legal methods of protest; he drew the line at violent revolt against the empire. For his support, the British appointed Low president of the revived Chamber of Commerce in New York City in 1779. Four years later, when the state of New York passed anti-loyalist legislation that confiscated the property of inhabitants defined as traitors, Low confronted the monumental consequences of his allegiance. His earlier leadership of rebel committees cost him a second time. Having lost his colonial possessions, Low turned to the British for compensation for his losses on behalf of the empire. But, as questions arose about his late turn to loyalism, he received only a small fraction of the losses he claimed.[10]

Unlike Isaac Low, William Franklin steadfastly remained loyal to Britain. In 1762, at the age of thirty-two, William Franklin had sworn fidelity to the

Crown when he became governor of New Jersey, and he did not deviate from his oath. Son of Benjamin Franklin, the politician who, after spending fourteen years in England, emerged belatedly as a spokesman for the American rebellion, Franklin's decision to side with the British was not a foregone conclusion. Born in the colonies, cultivated to be as much an American politician as an English gentleman, Franklin did not blindly follow imperial dictates. He understood colonial political reasoning, supported the rights of colonial assemblies, and denounced parliamentary taxation as unconstitutional. However, Franklin opposed a violent break with empire and regarded the instigators of rebellion with suspicion. He lamented that "principal demagogues oppose everything which may have been the remotest tendency to conciliate matters in an amicable way, & to omit nothing which may have any chance of widening the breach."[11] In January 1775, Franklin hoped the New Jersey assembly would follow the right road, the middle path toward "peace, happiness, and the restoration of the public tranquility," and not the route to "anarchy, misery, and all the horrors of a civil war."[12] Franklin never subscribed to the radical notion that England harbored some secret design to enslave the colonies.

The last royal governor of New Jersey, William Franklin spent—humiliatingly—the first three years of the war in a rebel prison. He lost full political authority in New Jersey by May 1775 as the rebel de facto government usurped his authority and raised troops in preparation for violent resistance (see document—Inflamed Rebels and Scattered Friends). A year later, Franklin was interrogated, arrested, and sent under guard to Connecticut until 1778, when he finally reached the British headquarters of New York City. Until 1782, Franklin hoped to gain the trust of British officials and lead the loyalist military opposition in the colonies. Ironically, the man who had earlier pledged to do everything to promote peace encouraged pillaging and murderous raids against nearby rebel strongholds. Like Isaac Low, William Franklin was treated skeptically by the British authorities. His pedigree—as Benjamin Franklin's son—never left him. When he petitioned the British government for compensation, he was obliged to produce witnesses to provide proof of active loyalism. A bitter exile in England after the war, Franklin remained permanently estranged from his home and his famous father.

Unlike William Franklin, Governor John Wentworth of New Hampshire received substantial recognition for his steadfast loyalty to the empire. Also born in the colonies, Wentworth came closest to William Franklin in his desire to find some kind of accommodation between the extreme positions taken by radical colonists and a stubborn British administration on the other. Both men, experienced in colonial politics and attentive to the enduring role of colonial assemblies, emphasized pragmatic solutions that would reduce conflict in the future. Neither was a hard-line advocate of British authority sometimes associated with the term "loyalist." In fact, neither imagined himself in the category of "loyalist" because each believed that reasonable policies and sound government would soon be restored in the colonies without violence. Wentworth regarded the crisis as temporary and short sighted. Once Britain prevailed, he hoped the colonies could build a strong and integrated British Empire, "cemented by justice and reciprocation of interest with an evident attention to mutual rights."[13]

The Wentworths had already been in New Hampshire for a century and had deep—five generations deep—familial roots and mercantile ties in the colony. They had accumulated wealth through the timber trade and were long regarded as the elite in the province. Wentworth was of Anglican faith, and his family had long been connected to royal authority. His uncle, Benning Wentworth, had served as governor of New Hampshire for a quarter of a century, longer than any other governor in the history of the North American colonies. John Wentworth hoped the colonies would continue to play a vital role in the profitable and expanding empire.

In 1775, fearing the action of rebel mobs in New Hampshire, Wentworth fled to British New York City, hoping that the British would restore order and authority (see document—Hunting of the Tories). A group of trusted military recruits, "Wentworth's Volunteers," accompanied Wentworth. Only in 1778 when Wentworth realized the rebellion would not be easily suppressed did he sail for England. Unmarred by any earlier association with rebellion or rebels, Wentworth formed close-knit connections to British politicians; after the war, he earned an appointment as surveyor general of His Majesty's Woods for the reduced British Empire in North America. Nova Scotia served as a substitute, if not a replacement, for the home he had lost in New Hampshire. In 1791, Wentworth continued to believe that the revolution could have been avoided if only "true, wise and open measures had been embraced on both sides."[14] His appointment as governor of Nova Scotia in 1792 underscored the political rewards available to a select few trustworthy subjects untainted by rebellion. No other revolutionary royal governor served again as head of another British North American colony.

Like William Franklin and John Wentworth, New York's lieutenant governor, Cadwallader Colden, did not waver in his support for the empire. Yet, Colden stands apart because loyalism was so firmly grounded in his experience that loyalist identity during the rebellion involved no agonizing decision. Born of a Presbyterian minister in southeastern Scotland, Colden arrived in New York in 1718 under the patronage of Governor Robert Hunter, converted to Anglicanism, and served in prominent political positions in New York for almost four decades. Until his death in September 1776, at the age of eighty, Colden served as the most royalist of Crown officeholders in New York. Unlike Franklin and Wentworth, Colden had neither sympathy nor tolerance for the plight of the colonists. Whereas the two governors understood colonial grievances and hoped for imperial reform whereby Parliament better represented the interests of the faraway colonies, Colden believed Parliament adequately represented the outlying Atlantic dominions as well as constituencies within Britain. Impatient with colonial protests, Colden lamented the weakness of the British government and advocated tighter and more centralized royal control of the colonies. Whereas Benjamin Franklin's son, William, defied him to support the empire, Cadwallader's son, David Colden, followed his father's faith and actively supported the British during the rebellion (see document—Seeking Refuge in Britain).

Loyal Britons

Loyalty to the mother country was the colonial norm. As Peter Marshall has observed, "A sense of being British was never the exclusive property of the peoples of the British Isles."[15] Most eighteenth-century British colonists shared in the feeling of British patriotism, an alignment that emerged from the massive wars between 1689 and 1815, one that allowed diverse people to focus on what they had in common rather than on what divided them. During this time, seven different wars were fought with France, a country with a larger population, army, and landmass. In gaining victories over Catholic France, Britons across the Atlantic celebrated the Protestant culture they shared. The internal divisions within Protestantism were eclipsed by the pull of Protestant solidarity in the face of perceived Catholic threats from France. Protestantism, as Linda Colley observes, formed a "unifying and distinguishing bond" of British identity.[16] Because the colonists associated Catholicism with superstition and arbitrary government, illiteracy and starvation, they reveled at their own literacy, freedoms, and prosperity.

By mid-century, commerce as well as migration led to increased opportunities for Britons to exchange political culture, Protestant literature, prestige goods, and visits within Atlantic communities. The Atlantic became a bridge that integrated the American colonies to the British empire, and local elites drew power from the unity of the English Atlantic. Sea travel became safer, faster, and more frequent with increased navigational knowledge and more sophisticated maps. Models of gentility, modes of religious revivalism, and habits in soil cultivation were shared across British Atlantic communities. Through the medium of British shipping, not only was there a mixing of commodities and messages, but also people. Merchants, planters, officeholders, and their families crossed the Atlantic to collect debts, visit relatives, seek office, or even recover their health.[17] The American colonies became more multiracial and multicultural with the immigration of thousands of immigrants, voluntary and involuntary, European and African.

The more connected Atlantic also brought Britishness within reach of most colonists. A core group of glass, ceramic, and textile goods acquired a distinctive British identity, and their purchase further anglicized American consumer cultures. Colonists from Halifax to Barbados enthusiastically adopted British candlesticks, cutlery, framed looking glasses, mechanical toys, and teaware. In contrast to French silk, velvet, or satin coats, English plain clothing exemplified natural dignity and refined taste. Brass buckles and brass furniture became highly coveted. Made on the latest cylinder printing machinery, upholsteries and window hangings transformed Indian and Chinese landscapes into recognizable English floral designs. Ironically, Britishness came to be defined by fabrics of Asian origin.[18] Also imprinted in local newspapers, trade catalogs, and shipping orders, the British brand pointed to high status.[19]

New habits, which demanded a variety of new consumer goods, further integrated Britons across the Atlantic. The ritual of drinking tea, common to European elites early in the eighteenth century, became an expected part of middle-class behavior for both Britons and non-British European immigrants in the British colonies. As tea drinking became a shared American experience, along with the teacups came a demand for ceramic teapots, silver spoons, sugar bowls, sugar tongs, tea strainers, and tea tables.[20] In 1748, a foreign traveler commented that tea "is drunk here in the morning and afternoon, especially by women, and is so common at present that there is hardly a farmer's wife or a poor woman who does not drink tea in the morning."[21] Importantly, in the 1780s, when loyalist refugee women presented their claims to a British commission established to compensate them for property confiscated by the rebels, they recounted the loss of such beloved objects as "blue and white tea and Table China," "a silver tea pot," and "Mahogany Dining Tables."[22] The loyalist women, much as the men, mourned for goods that had marked their social acceptance and prosperity in the British empire.

In addition to the religious and consumer connections that tied the Atlantic world, constitutional culture proved a crucial means of integration. The American colonists spoke a constitutional vernacular of Britain. Although legal authority traveled below from the Crown, in practice it was flexible, layered with compromise and local adjustments derived from many areas of the British Atlantic.[23] The colonists cherished British political culture and the English liberties epitomized by the constitution such as trial by jury. They revered the "paper empire"—the mix of documents, political agreements, and traditions that made up the English constitution.[24] Not merely a description of the institutions and principles of government, the constitution was a repository of ideals and duties that could be invoked to make sense of the imperial-colonial political landscape, a relationship that defined an Atlantic political community.[25]

Until mid-eighteenth century, natural rights and English rights were interchangeable; and most colonists thought the English constitution embodied their natural rights. They believed they had inherited a flexible constitution that protected their cherished rights as Britons. The British political system, which balanced the power of the monarchy, the wisdom of the aristocracy, and the virtue of democracy, was the best means to secure the liberties of the people. Without proper checks, monarchy could become despotism, aristocracy could transform into oligarchy, and democracy would lead to anarchy and perpetual turbulence. Mixing the three regimes in one British system, they trusted, nullified the extreme tendencies of each one.

Colonists celebrated the British monarchy through feasts, illuminations, and toasts to mark royal birthdays as well as royal births. Throughout the eighteenth century, they regularly observed royal and ecclesiastical anniversaries that reminded them of their affection for the king and their special ties to one another. In addition to St. George's Day (April 23), St. Patrick's Day (March 17), and St. Andrew's Day (November 30), the colonists celebrated the coronation and accession of George III. Ritualistic observances cemented imperial bonds. The deeply sentimental attachment to the king that most colonists felt persisted into the years of the crisis. Until the eve of independence, George III's birthday continued to be celebrated with similar enthusiasm throughout the colonies.

Imperial Crisis

The expansion of the British empire at the close of the Seven Years' War was unprecedented in scale. The British gained the whole of inland North America from the Appalachians to the Mississippi River, Canada, new West Indian Islands, a new colony in West Africa, and from 1765, effective control over Bengal, India. In addition to authority over ten to twenty million people in Bengal, George III inherited 75,000 French Canadians and 100,000 Native Americans as new subjects in the Atlantic.[26]

The cultural diversity in the new Atlantic colonies brought a new sense of insecurity. It mandated political adjustments and new accommodations with non-British subjects to lower the risks as much as the costs involved in ruling over alien people. The British hoped to enforce rule over immense new territories with 10,000 soldiers (although only 4,500 arrived).[27] The soldiers were intended to mitigate possible aggression from unknown subjects, not loom as a threat to colonial liberties.

To assimilate French Catholics in Quebec into the imperial structure required unprecedented policy shifts. Quebec posed a strategic anomaly because the large Catholic population already had established religious and civil institutions. The compromise chosen after ten years of uneasy rule antagonized English subjects in the British Isles and in North America. The 1774 Quebec Act extended the boundary of Quebec by putting the area from the Great Lakes to the Ohio River under Quebec, gave political rights to Catholics, and recognized non-British systems of government. Most problematically, the Quebec Act precluded governance through a representative assembly. The British attempt at integration flew in the face of existing tradition of Catholic exclusionism and led to outrage and disillusionment. Britons on both side of the Atlantic held no sympathy for the claim that Catholicism was tolerable because it posed no threat to state security. Many American colonists viewed the Act as one in a legislative program meant to deprive them of their cherished liberties.[28]

The British were not entirely sure how to incorporate large numbers of Native Americans into their empire. Linda Colley has observed that the British empire, paradoxically, shared similarities with the Native Americans in 1763. Both sides "worried about the ever-growing expansion and power of white colonists."[29] Given the condescension British military officers showed, many Indians suspected that the British would not be generous allies like the French. Clashing interpretations between British administrators and Indians generated a devastating Indian war, Pontiac's Rebellion, which encompassed many more groups than those directly led by the Ottawa leader, Pontiac. Identifying colonist-Indian tension over land as a major cause of the war, the British hoped to pacify the frontier by establishing a boundary that forbade white settlement west of the Appalachian Mountains. The 1763 Proclamation Line, which brought the trans-Appalachian West Indian territory under the direct authority of Britain, also put the British government in an unusual position of being a relatively pro-Indian mediator. When the revolution broke out a decade later, the British had the upper hand with most Indians. Unable to control the ambitions of squatters and speculators despite the Proclamation Line, most Indians imagined more security in allying with the British.

Effective defense and commercial regulation of Britain's newly acquired colonies required active and expensive oversight by the British Parliament. The government was also burdened by the tremendous debt incurred during the Seven Years' War. Attempting to bring the colonies into tighter economic and political control, Parliament passed the Currency and Sugar Acts in 1764, the Stamp and Quartering Acts in 1765, the Townshend Acts in 1767, and the Tea Act in 1773. This presumption of Parliament's power was in accordance with Parliament's increasing confidence in its ability to regulate domestic affairs. The government did not have overarching designs for suppressing colonial liberties. The British perceived that many colonists made insufficient contributions to the war effort and smuggled extensively outside the imperial system. The government's policies, hence, moved from a fluid economic environment, characterized by salutary neglect, to a much more structured and constraining environment.

Unforeseen by the British government, the extension of the bureaucratic state led to increased tensions in the American colonies. As the British established policies designed to rule over new subjects, manage new territories, and raise money, many colonists became disillusioned and felt that the empire had not lived up to its ideal, namely, that the colonists were not offered the true rights of Englishmen. These Americans wanted the British to treat the prerogatives of their assemblies as virtually equal to Parliament. Their rhetoric focused overwhelmingly on the unprecedented and "unconstitutional" nature of parliamentary taxes. A new question had emerged: Could the Parliament represent colonial interests better than colonial assemblies?

The resistance of colonial assemblies to British legislation was less a progressive fight for democracy than a defense of long-accrued local privileges against a government perceived as interventionist. It arose from disillusionment and resentment rather than an abiding desire for separation. During the eighteenth century, the colonial assemblies grew in power and self-confidence. Through the assemblies, an emergent group of colonial leaders resisted imperial initiatives and integrated their own power within each colony. They claimed the right to frame revenue measures, and guarded their position from the intrusions and instructions of royal governors. Simultaneously, the colonial assemblies maintained reverence for Parliament and the British constitution, and upheld the Crown as a stabilizing symbol. The ambiguities of negotiating between the distant empire and the local realities did not produce great upheaval. The political elites understood themselves simultaneously as beneficiaries of the empire and as colonial leaders, as Englishmen and assemblymen.

The polarization between American rebels and the British administration happened only gradually, after a decade of ferocious debate. In 1763, the colonists celebrated British victory over the French and showed enthusiasm about their membership in the empire. Their excitement arose not only from greater expectations of profit, but from an attachment to the cultural heritage and outlook shared with the mother country. The celebratory sermons of New England churchmen testify to a belief in a shared spiritual mission. The Reverend Thomas Barnard rejoiced that the war had "served to fix liberty more firmly" so the children of New England should behold the triumph of George III who "gives peace to Half the world." For many, this sense of belonging persisted well into the actual years of warfare; for others, the attachment never died.

Between 1765 and 1774, most colonists regarded the Parliament's actions as excessive and arrogant, capricious and conspiratorial. Although they resented the arrogance that seemed to drive British measures, few colonists imagined permanently severing ties with the empire. By the mid-1770s, those who chose the rebellion interpreted British actions as a tyrannical ploy meant to subjugate the colonies, and those who stayed loyal interpreted Britain's hard-line stance as a tragic miscalculation. Still, most colonists continued to work for a solution within, not outside, the empire. They wanted reform, not revolution. It was only in 1774 that the Intolerable Acts, which punished Boston and Massachusetts for the destruction of the taxed tea, alienated many Americans and led some to organize an aggressive and systematic resistance toward independence. Indeed, if the two sides had quickly and sharply distinguished themselves into competing sides, the revolution would have occurred in the mid-1760s instead of the mid-1770s.

Revolutionary affiliations cannot be projected backward upon the prerevolutionary years. Early America was composed of rapidly expanding and highly diverse societies that did not share a single ideological worldview. Our knowledge that the United States would emerge from thirteen disunited and diverse colonies has flattened the political world of the late-eighteenth century. American colonists flourished in a contentious political world that debated the nature of society, the role of government, and the right of revolution. The colonists were also accustomed to occurrences of episodic violence—riots in seaports, tenant protests in rural districts, backcountry rebellions, and slave uprisings. Few imagined that these tensions would become the broader context for a colonial war of independence.[30] As historian Ian Steele has noted, "Despite the well known centrifugal tendencies that operated in this period, colonial fathers could die in 1740 without hearing a whisper of the coming of the American

Revolution." He cautions historians from making "colonial grandfathers into veterans of their grandsons' revolution."[31]

A violent and unprecedented rebellion gave birth to the United States. Most rebels and loyalists experienced the collapse of imperial authority from 1774 to 1776 as sudden and traumatic. Those who remained loyal opposed the violent separation that mutinous colonists advocated and hoped to remain oriented within an imperial and constitutional order. They denied that the king's actions had forfeited colonial loyalty. They also challenged the legitimacy of demanding allegiance and coercing loyalty from those who were unwilling participants in the struggle for independence.

In the absence of political compulsion, people had avoided choosing a single political side. But between 1774 and 1776, rebel neighborhoods ostracized loyal Americans and cast them as enemies of independence, as traitors, and as sycophants or puppets of empire. Overt pressure from hostile rebel neighbors and militia committees undermined the rights of individuals to make a free choice (see document—Guilty until Proven Innocent). Forced to endure the mortification of a public obloquy, colonists were forced to make a choice. Those "convicted" of disloyalty could repent by enlisting in the Continental Army. An unprecedented test oath became a qualifier for American citizenship, for voting, and for holding property. The rebel tactics of tarring and feathering, imprisonment, and banishment employed to suppress opposition forced people to abandon a neutral stance (see document—Confronting Mobs). The practice of confiscating the property of suspected loyalists kept the wavering in line, created revenue at the expense of those who refused support for the rebel cause, and dislodged and expelled committed loyalists (see document—Confronting Confiscation Laws). Together, the oaths, violence, and property confiscations eroded the middle ground between loyalism and rebellion.

Compelling the undecided to commit to a political side, the rebels challenged the concept of allegiance as natural and perpetual. Forced to choose sides in a world where loyalty had served as the norm, many colonists developed a hatred for the rebel cause. If the rebellious Americans imagined the British as enemies of their cherished rights as Englishmen, the loyal Americans dismissed the rebels as hypocritical schemers who practiced a greater infidelity to American liberty by resorting to violence to suppress political disagreement. In their eyes, the "spirit" of 1776 did not represent American liberty. It meant persecution, vindictiveness, and wantonness.[32]

New York printer Hugh Gaine's political decisions between September and November of 1776 provide a useful paradigm for conceptualizing the contingency of political allegiance during the war. Gaine's maneuvering reflects a strand of political decision making opened by the war, a process that cannot be understood outside the local military context. When historian Stephen Conway considers the moment in which the British government transformed its regard for the colonies, when Americans went from being fellow nationals to becoming foreigners, he observes "no smooth and uninterrupted transition in the way in which Britons from Britain looked on Americans." He calls this change in British consciousness a "jagged broken and faltering move- ment—like a drunkard lurching forward and then tottering back."[33] In the same manner, no single defining moment determined political allegiance for most colonists. There were many stages in the process of choosing sides, and many quite different reasons for committing to the decision. The process was unplanned and reactive, sensitive to the changing local context and the proximity of military troops. As Peter Onuf has written, the colonists were not Americans on the inside, just waiting to shed their British identity to get out.[34] Hugh Gaine's crossing—and re-crossing—of the Hudson in 1776 highlights how the proximity of the British army and British victories led to an initial "lurching" toward rebellion and then a turn to loyalism.

Hugh Gaine lived in New York City, a commercial port in which colo- nists faced eastward, where they had kinship and trading connections in Bris- tol, London, or Glasgow. Trade meant long-distance commerce across the Atlantic, not local exchange within communities. Conditions of legality and stability the empire provided were necessary for New Yorkers' survival and growth. Their reliance on credit and loans could be defended in the courts and under a stable legal system. In the context of his status and his city, Hugh Gaine's initial "lurching" toward rebellion was extraordinary.

Hugh Gaine found it impossible to remain politically neutral in the fall of 1776 when he, along with thousands of other New Yorkers, confronted the imminent threat of a British invasion. In September, Gaine sought to avoid military battle, to follow his rebel sympathies, and to preserve his hard-earned social position by moving to rebel-controlled Newark, New Jersey.[35] Gaine had not fled New York City in panic. It had taken him too long—more than two decades—to establish himself as printer gentleman of New York province. Born into a working-class family in Ireland, he served a five-year apprenticeship in Belfast before landing in New York City in 1745 at the age of eighteen. He then served as journeyman for James Parker, official printer of New York province, for six years before establishing his own newspaper. The rewards of his hard work and ambition stood apparent in 1757 when Gaine moved his printing operations to prestigious Hanover Square: this east side location near the markets and wharves represented wealth and fashion in eighteenth-century New York. In 1768, Gaine became the official printer to the colony and city of New York.[36]

When prerevolutionary tensions escalated between the colonies and the mother country, Gaine strictly avoided taking a partisan role. He strove to provide balanced accounts and keep his paper unbiased.[37] Indeed, his focus on acquiring leadership roles and his measured land speculation consolidated his status in New York. He served as a vestryman of Trinity Church, joined the St. Andrews Society, and became the treasurer and vice president of the St. Patrick's Society. In 1770, he purchased six thousand acres of land in Albany County; and in 1774, to prevent his dependence on paper supplies from England, he established a partnership at a paper mill in Long Island. Thus, in the fall of 1776, Gaine was not just a tradesman printer but a proprietor of a large printing establishment and a noted gentleman in the city.[38]

From Newark, Gaine's alternate newspaper put forth news favorable to the rebel side.[39] Gaine's rebel sympathies were apparent. Although the Newark paper did not explicitly criticize the British government in London or New York City, it contained news that supported rebel recruitment and rebel government. On September 28, the paper listed the number of battalions each colony needed to provide for the Continental Amy and promised awards in order of military appointment: a colonel would receive 500 acres of land, a lieutenant colonel 450 acres, and a noncommissioned officer just 100 acres. Gaine's political inclinations became explicit when he referred to the rebel Congress as the "Honorable Continental Congress," and denigrated the British forces as "the piratical fleet."[40]

Yet, in the last months of 1776, Gaine was among thousands of other New Jerseyans who chose loyalism by taking advantage of the British offer of amnesty.[41] Gaine's decision to return to New York City must be situated within a broader revolutionary context in which American colonists—even those as informed and enlightened as Gaine—doubted rebel victory over the British. Indeed, the military and ideological forces in support of reunion also appeared invincible to the British commanders. On December 22, the British commanders in chief would report the good news to London:

A very considerable number of persons who had been active in the rebellion, particularly in this province, and in that of the Jerseys, have already subscribed the declaration of allegiance. The whole of the Jerseys, except a very inconsiderable part which we think must of course, follow, has submitted; and of the province of Pennsylvania, which his majesty's forces have not yet entered, several persons of property . . . have subscribed the declaration.[42]

Gaine's physical crossing across the Hudson River, from New York City to Newark and back again, demonstrates the pragmatic considerations that shaped political calculations during the war. His flip-flopping highlights the limited role that ideological inclinations played in determining many colonists' political choices: local on-the-ground realities exerted greater pressures than staunch convictions. Hence, the larger explanation for Gaine's return to British-held New York City lies in the strength of the British-loyalist coalition in November 1776: the military defeat of George Washington's Continental Army in New York and the growing ideological strength of the British-loyalist coalition in New York City during the first months of the war.

Gaine's switch to loyalism, however, came too late. His absence during the first months of British occupation and his publication of the Newark paper had raised doubts about the authenticity of his allegiance. Valued for his printing skills, Gaine was permitted to return to New York City and to resume *The New York Gazette and Weekly Mercury*. But he did not regain his former eminence: James Rivington, who had stayed staunchly loyal, would receive appointment as King's printer when he returned to the city in October 1777.

In contrast to loyalists such as Isaac Low, William Franklin, John Wentworth, and Cadwallader Colden, who made political choices with less consideration for the local military context, Gaine defines a different movement toward loyalism. Gaine's maneuvering reflects a strand of political decision-making opened up by the civil war context of the colonies. His case illustrates the conflicted, inconsistent, and reluctant movement toward political identification in the mainland. He underscores the extent to which political choices were made and remade based on the proximity of military forces, and, particularly, on colonists' faith in British military strength. His circumstantial "lurching" also cautions against a globalizing history of loyalism in the British Atlantic.

Loyal Colonies

There were twenty-six British colonies in North America in 1776. Aside from the rebellious thirteen colonies, the British managed the following administrative units: Nova Scotia, Quebec, and St. John (Prince Edward Island) in Canada; the Bahamas and Bermuda; East Florida and West Florida; and Jamaica, Barbados, the Leeward Islands, Grenada, St. Vincent, and Dominica.[43] Staying loyal did not entail the same symbolic or practical experience for Britons in all the Atlantic colonies. In the case of the thirteen mainland colonies, we distinguished between two kinds of loyalism: a long-held form of allegiance to the empire many Britons shared in the North

American colonies (epitomized by Franklin, Wentworth, and Colden); and a second form of loyalism, which emerged in the thirteen colonies during the traumatic moments between 1774 and 1776 (and during the military years of the war) when colonists felt compelled to make startling political choices, as seen with Hugh Gaine. The ideological polarization of Anglo-America after the Intolerable Acts in 1774 and the battles of Lexington and Concord in 1775 did not extend to the Caribbean, to Florida, or to the Canadian colonies.

The Caribbean colonies shared similar political developments and were closely associated with the mainland colonies through proximity and trade, but they did not rebel from the empire. The Caribbean elite wanted autonomy and self-government but within the British empire. Unlike the mainland elite who straddled an Atlantic world along with a vast continental interior, the planter elite depended on Britain for its political power, economic wealth, and military protection. Whatever the course of the war in the Caribbean, the islands could not maintain an independent existence and would remain colonies of one power or the other. As significantly, the islands were truncated societies that lacked many of the factors that made rebellion thinkable in the thirteen colonies. They were overseas extensions of the empire rather than mature societies: they had no history of a dissenting religious tradition, had few Britons of middling stature who felt constricted by the political opportunities in the islands, and lacked a politically informed constituency who inquired about the political meanings of imperial measures in representative assemblies.

Members of the Jamaican assembly initially resisted the implications of British taxation and debated the need to resist conspiracy and protect liberty. But living in a colony with 94 percent slaves, the slaveholders did not dare to risk the disruption of a rebellion. They relied on British naval protection to defend themselves externally from foreign attack and internally from slave revolts. The very nature of their society had required a centralized government to provide slave-catching institutions and jails, but fewer schools, churches, or other cultural centers. Although many Jamaican planters were genuinely concerned about the constitutional implications of the new taxes, their fears did not lead to a frenzied attack on imperial policies. Their best future prospects, they believed, lay within the British empire.

The Leeward Islands, with a higher percentage of slaves and more dependence on salted fish and corn from the mainland colonies, reacted more stringently against the Stamp Act than Jamaica. Like the inhabitants in the mainland colonies, the colonists in St. Kitts and Nevis rioted in opposition: they led ceremonial processions, burned effigies, and destroyed stamps. More than loss of constitutional status, these islanders feared mainland merchants would blacklist them if they supported the Stamp Act. But their resistance was short lived. No Caribbean-wide opposition formed to the Stamp Acts, and no printers produced bold essays debating the subject of imperial taxation. Significantly, after 1767, the island colonies were sometimes immune or exempted from the new imperial policies.[44]

Interestingly, the loyalty of the Caribbean colonies may have influenced Britain's policy toward the thirteen colonies in the early stages of the rebellion. The lack of opposition by the Caribbean assemblies may have led Britain to underestimate the opposition from the mainland colonies. British interests in the Caribbean also played a part in the last years of the war. Colonies such as Jamaica were strategically, politically, and economically key to British interests. The subtropical products of the West Indies fit much better into British economy than the products of North American farms and fisheries. In 1778, Britain's greater interest in protecting the sugar islands led to a diversion of military and naval resources from the mainland colonies and helped to seal the combined French and rebel victory at Yorktown, Virginia, in October 1781.

Unlike the rebels in the thirteen colonies who broke with tradition and launched a revolt against the mother country, East Florida followed the colonial norm and remained loyal to the mother country. Acquired from Spain after the Seven Years' War, the colony of East Florida, like the Caribbean colonies, contained more blacks than whites. By the time of the signing of the Declaration of Independence, some loyalists from Georgia and South Carolina had already fled to East Florida. They predicted the rebel government would fail and hoped to take advantage of the restoration of British dominion on the edge of the frontier. Included in the loyalist immigrant stream were members of the council, attorneys, plantation owners and their slaves, and some poor farmers. The numbers of blacks increased sixfold, from two thousand in 1775 to more than twelve thousand in 1783. Slaves built plantation homes, worked as skilled artisans, operated sugarhouses and indigo vats, and boxed pine trees for turpentine collection. As they had served in South Carolina's militia during its founding years in the late seventeenth century, they served in East Florida loyalist militias.[45] They were armed and trained to defend the lands of their loyalist masters.

The rebellion was not compelling for the new territories the British had acquired in Acadia after the Treaty of Utrecht in 1713 and in Quebec after the Seven Years' War. The colonies of Quebec and Nova Scotia together stretched from the Mississippi River in the west to Cape Breton in the east.[46] These northern-most British colonies—in today's Canada—shared a harsh northern climate, minimal slavery, and a reliance on the metropolitan political culture. None of these colonies were founded as colonies of settlement. Instead, British sovereignty in these colonies came through conquest, commercial occupation, or diplomatic agreement with other Europeans. These territories were economically and strategically valuable but remained politically and demographically weak.[47]

By 1775, the Canadian territories had acquired a distinct political structure founded on strong executives and weak assemblies, and dependent on Crown funding for colonial development. Most famously, the Quebec Act of 1774 established imperial supervision and restricted representative government in a manner unknown to the southern colonies. Because these northern-most colonies developed under greater state control, the populations lacked the political expectations that fostered fears of Crown conspiracy in the rebellious colonies. They had a far greater toleration for executive measures undertaken to integrate the Atlantic colonies to the imperial realm.[48]

The case of Nova Scotia is illustrative. Ceded to Britain by France, Nova Scotia—the first British colony after Pennsylvania in 1681—followed a different trajectory from the colonies founded in the seventeenth century.[49] Founded in the eighteenth century, Nova Scotia did not benefit from the salutary neglect that had permitted the earlier colonies to develop autonomously. The British directly controlled the colony and buttressed it through providing military and civil expenditures. Indeed, Nova Scotia had more in common with Georgia than with Massachusetts or Barbados. Just as Georgia was formed to defend South Carolina from the Spanish in Florida, Nova Scotia was established to protect Massachusetts from France.[50] Both colonies received infusions of British public spending to sustain them. Halifax, like Savannah, was built at the cost of British taxpayers. Nova Scotia and Cape Breton, in fact, would receive £152,300 sterling in the sixty years between 1756 and 1815.[51] Nova Scotians depended on the state for rewards and promotion and for their revenues. Accustomed to the intervention of the state, the Nova Scotians did not resist the implications of taxation—the extension of a bureaucratic state—because they were newly born products of this state.[52]

More than seven thousand land-hungry New Englanders migrated to Nova Scotia during the 1750s; and two decades later, at the eve of the revolution, they comprised a majority of the population.[53] Legally British since 1713, the Nova Scotian population in fact included mostly French and Indians until the early 1750s after the construction of Halifax in 1749 had drawn settlers from England and from New England.[54] Significantly, despite their shared background, and their connections to kin and friends from the rebellious colonies, the New England communities in Nova Scotia did not join the rebels in New England. Outside of Halifax, local settlements were isolated, scattered, and lacked autonomous merchant communities. As remote townships confronted American privateers who raided less-defended areas looking more for spoils than bloodshed, the naval and economic power in Halifax made the benefits of imperial attachments all too apparent (see document—Rejecting Violence).

The North American colonies—Florida, Quebec, and Nova Scotia—were too dependent on British goods and defense, and too little developed politically to join the resistance. They lived in an economically marginal world, both commercially and militarily dependent on the empire. Choosing rebellion mandated risks not confronted by their kin in the rebellious colonies, and most would opt to remain neutral. Importantly, each region—at the rim of the empire, and dangerously dominated by large numbers of non-English settlers—was defended by British troops after the Seven Years' War. Four British regiments were in the Floridas, four in Quebec, and three in Nova Scotia.[55]

Loyalist Convictions and Proposals

A broad cross-spectrum of colonists found greater stability in imagining a community within the empire. They continued to uphold the ideals of British patriotism established in the early eighteenth century. They associated Britain with Protestantism, commercial prosperity, naval power, and freedom; and saw themselves as heirs to a political tradition premised on constitutional rights such as trial by jury. These colonists believed that ties of kinship and common culture as much as commerce and protection bound the American colonies inextricably to Britain. Linking colonial success with empire, they saw no conflict between being loyal simultaneously to their local communities and to the empire.

The outbreak of war in 1775 was incomprehensible and shocking to thousands of common people in the rebellious colonies. Those who remained loyal resisted violence and separation. They wanted to preserve their prosperous world, their constitutional government, and their imperial liberties. They felt a deeper threat from rebel leaders who justified the legality of revolution than from the restrictive legislation the British ministry imposed. Like the rebels, they interpreted the revolutionary crisis as a conspiracy of self-interested men to destroy liberty. For the loyalists, however, the danger was internal, emanating from below rather than above. The loyal, in fact, regarded the rebellious Americans as traitors guilty of the ultimate crime, a breach of allegiance.

The loyalists differed in the strength of their convictions, in the timing of their loyalty, and in their methods of opposing the rebellion. However, they shared similar fears about the unleashing of violence that threatened to annihilate any sense of reason, about the blindness and provincialism of rebel leaders who awoke the passions of the mob on a utopian vision that had no historical backing, and about the appalling prospect of an unbalanced society. In short, they feared the rebellion would lead to the anguish and miseries associated with a state of nature, one in which might makes right. They preferred to be ruled by one tyrant three thousand miles away than be ruled by three thousand tyrants in their localities.

Like rebel leaders, loyalist spokesmen comprised a politicized minority in the thirteen colonies. They included royal governors, lieutenant governors, councilors, judges, and attorneys, men who were accustomed to elections, public gatherings, and debate. Men from the northern colonies—New England and the mid-Atlantic—most fully articulated loyalist opposition. These ideologues were moderates, cosmopolitan men who saw no reason to risk everything secure and constitutional in a violent insurrection. Frustrated at Parliament's unwillingness to think creatively about colonial needs, they also wanted change but within, not outside the imperial state. These Americans did not equate imperial integration with imperial subordination. They wanted to find a way to share the benefits of Britain's expanded trade and growing political reach. Whereas the rebels advocated a break with the empire, these Americans hoped for a long-lasting relationship within a reformed empire and revitalized colonial institutions. Foremost, the loyalists thought that strengthening the nonelective branches of colonial governments and establishing mechanisms for a larger colonial contribution to imperial decisions could solve the underlying imperial problems. They looked to Parliament to impose unity and order on colonial societies incapable of attaining harmony on their own. The liberty they sought necessitated protection from above.

Loyalist visionaries promoted arguments for preserving union with Britain in the highest government circles in England. Optimistic about the potential of the colonies, these moderates believed the colonies were and should remain integral parts of the British state. A long-established imperial government was more stable than rule by heterogeneous colonies with differing and conflicting interests. Ambitious schemers, they worried, would replace constitutional and orderly rule with anarchy. They proposed a legislative union (a Continental Parliament) that would unify the colonies and provide a way for Americans to shape and improve the empire. In their scheme, the

British Parliament would continue to provide the order and unity to ensure American stability and success.

Joseph Galloway held a seat in the Pennsylvania Assembly for almost ten years during the 1750s and 1760s, and served as speaker from 1766 to 1775. Galloway rejected radical measures and, in the First Continental Congress, proposed a revised constitution that would allow colonial autonomy within empire.[56] Galloway's Plan of Union drew upon Benjamin Franklin's 1754 Albany Plan, proposed during the eve of the Seven Years' War between Britain and France (see document—Albany Plan). Inspired by the necessity of common defense against the French and Indians, the Albany Plan supported a union of contiguous colonies in a local confederation. Emanating from the directives of the Lords of Trade, the Albany Plan suggested the creation of an in-between authority that would mediate between the Crown and the colonies for the purpose of protecting the colonists against the Natives and the British against the French. A Crown-appointed president general and a grand council of delegates elected by the colonial assemblies could bridge the realities of the colony and the interests of the Crown. Far from the harbinger of an American national identity, the proponents of the Albany Plan envisioned a future in which Britain would establish a stable and secure system for long-term imperial governance in North America.

Most colonial assemblies refused to even consider the Albany Plan because they were unwilling to compromise their own autonomy. Too suspicious about the repercussions stemming from a unification of the colonies, the British government also tabled the plan. The failure of the plan on both sides of the Atlantic signified the colonies' disinterest in uniting under an independent coalition and the government's unwillingness to sanction an intercolonial legislature. In 1774, when Parliament tightened its jurisdiction over the colonies, moderates such as Galloway returned to the Albany Plan—a proposal that had proposed colonial union without challenging the sovereignty of the Parliament or the legitimacy of imperial governance in the colonies. But two decades after the Albany Plan, after the formation of an intercolonial radical organization in the form of the Continental Congress, the British government remained unwilling to consider an alternate political arrangement with the colonies. Galloway had hoped a vision based on loyal and constitutional principles would counter the radicalism of the Continental Congress. Foremost, he wished to avoid a violent collision that would sever the empire (see document—Joseph Galloway's Plan).

Along with local politicians such as Galloway, educated and middling Scottish immigrants—ministers, doctors, and merchants—participated in the opposition to American independence. Coming from a community that viewed sojourning and emigration as an extension of culture, Scots preserved and valued commercial and kin networks that crisscrossed the Atlantic. They were loyal to the empire that facilitated these networks. Deeply involved in colonial life and in the trans-Atlantic networks of culture, trade, and science, they believed in preserving ties with a powerful empire that promoted commercial expansion. They approached the question of allegiance pragmatically and anticipated that the colonies would continue to benefit from imperial connections. Moderates such as New York Councilor William Smith Jr. had close ties to these Scottish-American elite.[57]

At the eve of rebellion, Smith lived in style at 5 Broadway. A first-generation New Yorker and a graduate of Yale College, Smith was well established at the eve of the revolution. Although appointed New York councilor in 1767, Smith was by no means blindly subservient to the Crown or the Parliament. In the 1760s, he had launched a crusade against the appointment of an Anglican bishop because he supposed a bishop would unduly expand royal power and limit colonial authority in New York.

In the mid-1760s and early 1770s, Smith denied Parliament's right to tax the colonies but upheld its legislative supremacy. Driven by the upheaval in the mainland, Smith proposed to create a middle way that would maintain the political and economic system created by colonization during the previous two centuries. During the years of the revolution, Smith continued to correspond with decision makers in the British government, hoping to use his influence to reshape British policies in the colonies. The empire served as his focal point.

Between 1765 and 1775, Smith proposed the creation of a continental Parliament comprised of a Crown-appointed lord lieutenant and a bicameral legislature for the colonies as a whole (see document—William Smith Jr.'s Proposal). Smith's framework paralleled the contours of Galloway's proposal. The legislature would include a Council, comprised of twenty-four elites, who would hold offices for life, as well as a House of Commons that would be elected at regular intervals. The assemblies would choose the deputies for the Council and House of Commons. This American Parliament would stabilize and unify the colonies. It would assume jurisdiction over provincial matters and taxation while the British Parliament retained sovereign power. According to Smith, the imperial Parliament alone could impose the unity and order necessary to ensure a permanent establishment of the colonies with the mother country.

Importantly, the vision of federal empire that Smith and Galloway proposed did not die with the revolution but survived in British North America (in what became Canada). Jonathan Sewell, former attorney general of Massachusetts, was among another eight thousand loyalists who sought refuge in England between 1775 and 1784.[58] Sewell diagnosed the reasons for the unnatural rebellion. He observed that "nothing" contributed more to the war than the distance of the colonies from Great Britain. He noted that the replies from Britain had taken so long that small issues had turned into "real evils." Indeed, "local circumstances shifted so suddenly and violently between the giving information and receiving instructions how to act" that the government was powerless to avoid acting on "erroneous principles." When an immediate remedy was necessary to stop disorders, it could not be constitutionally procured in sufficient time. The "lapse," he thought, gave "full scope for such disorders to increase and rage so universally" as to "render the intended remedy ineffective." To guard against this in the future, Sewell proposed the appointment of a lord-lieutenant or governor general who would have authority, on any emergency, to make final decisions (see document—Joseph Sewell's Plan).[59]

In 1785, Sewell returned to loyalist-supported plans initially proposed in the 1750s and 1760s. He proposed "one general form of government for all natural born British subjects in His Majesty's colonies on the Continent of America." As Benjamin Franklin had offered suggestions for a unification of the colonies in 1754 in his "Short Hints towards a scheme for Uniting the Northern Colonies," Sewell offered "some general hints on the subject."[60] Like Franklin in 1754, William Smith Jr. in 1767, and Galloway in 1774, Sewell proposed a Crown-appointed executive and a legislative council with the power to tax. The Albany Plan had proposed "one general government" for North America to guard against the French and their Indian allies; Sewell proposed one general act such as the Magna Carta for all the North American colonies to guard against encroachment from the United States.[61] The creation of a new American republic made union of the British North American colonies—Nova Scotia, New Brunswick, Prince Edward Island, Upper Canada, and Lower Canada—necessary.

Significantly, forty years later, Sewell's son, the younger Jonathan Sewell, along with John Beverly Robinson, son of Virginia loyalist Christopher Robinson, also emphasized that the empire faced no threat from the union of the British North American provinces. In their 1824 proposal to the British government, they argued that union of the British North American colonies would lead neither to separation nor revolt. Somewhat sharply, the loyalist sons reminded the British that intercolonial union and rebellion had no connection. The late American revolt had not arisen because of the consolidation of the colonies. The colonies had separate governments at the time of the revolt and, in fact, the "violence of particular states would have been moderated by the more steady counsels of the whole united."[62]

Like the loyalists of the American war, Sewell and Robinson hoped that the territories of British North America would rise to become "parts rather than dependencies of Britain."[63]

Loyalist persuasions extended beyond British politicians in London. In addition to private proposals aimed at decision makers, loyalist spokesmen sought to sustain and build their coalition by circulating pro-British papers in British garrisons. During the course of the war, the British occupied in various periods and for varying lengths of time the six largest colonial cities: Boston, (1776), New York City (1776–1783), Newport (1776–1778), Philadelphia (1777–1778), Savannah (1778–1782), and Charleston (1780–1782). Loyalist newspapers included *The Newport Gazette* in Rhode Island from 1777 to 1779; *The Pennsylvania Evening Post, Pennsylvania Ledger*, and the *Royal Pennsylvania Gazette* in Philadelphia for varying parts of the British occupation of Philadelphia from October 1777 to May 1778. Papers also appeared in Charleston, Savannah, and Florida.[64] The regular publication of James Rivington's *Royal American Gazette* and Hugh Gaine's *The New York Gazette and Weekly Mercury* ensured New York's refugee loyalists—the largest in any colonial city—regular coverage of the rebellion. Most importantly, the papers provided a forum for circulating loyalist arguments and promoting loyalist perceptions (see document—Loyalist Persuasions). Publicly offering their allegiance and military assistance, the loyalists pushed Britain to intensify its struggle against the rebels.[65]

In long essays published in loyalist newspapers, the loyalists articulated their sense of moral estrangement and described themselves as victims of a cruel, unnecessary, and unnatural rebellion. Like the revolutionaries, the loyalists perceived themselves as patriots who defended American colonists against the ambitions of a dangerous faction. If the rebels defended the colonies from the threat of British enslavement, the loyalists considered "American slavery and American independence" synonymous terms. [66] The loyalists, in fact, mocked rebel claims for liberty by pointing to the institution of slavery. In an essay published in March 1777, "Integer" mocked the rebel assertion that "all men are created free." "If all men are created free, what about blacks?," the essayist asked. Do the colonies "justly expect to have, in little time, a black Assembly, a black Council, a black Governor, and a black Commonwealth?" Such a polity, the essayist wrote, "would shine like a shoe."[67]

Loyalist essays defended British decisions and minimized British losses. In direct response to rebel accusations that the British tyrannically employed Hessian troops to subdue their own people, an anonymous writer asserted that the employment of German troops was a sign of "true wisdom and good policy" at this juncture, because the deluded colonies who are "running wildly after the shadow of liberty have lost their substance." Other spokesmen minimized the Trenton defeat in December 1776 as a mere "skirmish" and emphasized the "sickly" condition of Washington's soldiers, allegedly dying of smallpox in great numbers and facing the "scourge of famine." Ragged, hungry, and diseased, Washington's troops, they emphasized, posed no threat to the large numbers of well-equipped British troops.[68]

Loyalists praised the historical stability of the British constitution and faulted rebel leadership as unstable and violent. If the rebels associated tyranny with the king, the loyalists feared more the anarchy that would result from rebel greed and rebel power. Whereas the rebels painted a glorious republican future unshackled by imperial demands, the loyalists dwelled on the fearful consequences of a future ruled by the rebel congress. They imagined a "puny divided state," created in a "sea of blood," utterly without order or law. They argued that the threat to colonial freedom came not from external British tyranny or corruption but from the internal anarchy promoted by the selfish schemes of self-interested men who promoted the "unjust and precarious Cause." These "self-created bodies," they asserted, "violated all the sacred ties of civil society," including "personal liberty and freedom of speech." They contrasted the frenzy of the rebel leaders with the rationality and conservatism of the "British law, British protection and British union." Only the British constitution provided the perfect balance of liberty with order.[69]

Members of the Quaker faith, who shunned any form of extremism, shared the loyalist focus on moderation. Torn by their loyalties to the Crown, and to friends on both sides of the conflict, most Quakers hoped to remain loyal to their pacific principles and retain a neutral position during the war. In a public letter circulated in a New York City loyalist newspaper in February 1777, some Quakers declared their objection to rebel coercion: "Thus we may with Christian firmness and fortitude withstand and refuse to submit to the arbitrary injunctions and ordinances of men who assume to themselves the power of compelling others, either in person or by their assistance, to join in carrying on war and of prescribing modes of determining concerning our religious principle, by imposing tests nor warranted by the precepts of Christ, or the laws of the happy constitution under which we and others long enjoyed tranquility and peace."[70] As they witnessed the destruction of property, the silencing of dissent, and the displacement of hundreds of people, some Quakers felt alienated by the growing violence and experienced a moral crisis about toppling a legitimate government.[71]

In northern Virginia, some Quakers faced suspicion and incarceration because of their image as Indian sympathizers and antislavery proponents. As much as region and religion, timing influenced Quaker persecution. Significantly, Quakers in northern Virginia endured the most scrutiny when the colony felt most vulnerable and the rebel cause appeared most fragile—during 1777 when fighting in Pennsylvania threatened the Chesapeake area and again after 1780, when Virginians faced British invasion.[72]

Neither Anglican clergymen nor Anglican colonists were uniformly loyal to Britain during the rebellion. If the Church of England supplied more loyalist spokesmen than any other single denomination, it must also be observed that the signers of the Declaration of Independence included more men of Anglican faith than any other.[73] Religious denominations, like colonial assemblies, flourished from the salutary neglect that characterized British attitude toward its seventeenth-century colonies. Although members from the Society for the Propagation of the Gospel (SPG) were sent to the colonies in the early eighteenth century to promote Anglicanism, the British government was less interested in imposing Anglicanism than in expanding the colonial population and securing commercial gains; it hoped that loyalty would follow prosperity. Hence, by the time of the revolution, more than 75 percent of Americans were non-Anglicans in comparison with the English population where less than 10 percent were dissenters from the Church of England.[74]

The repercussions of the British focus on population and commerce were especially obvious in the southern colonies. During the eighteenth century, the British—along with the southern gentry—hoped to increase the white populace to serve as a buffer against the Indians, and to counterbalance the large slave population in the South. The incentive of inexpensive land drew thousands of settlers into the backcountry between the 1750s and 1770s. These immigrants shared a desire to acquire fertile land but were otherwise heterogeneous in nationality and religion. Few were Anglican. The arrival of diverse immigrants weakened an already weak Anglican presence in the southern colonies. Although the Church of England was the establishment in every colony in the South, the southern laity and legislature had long curbed the authority of the Anglicans. Wealthy planters protected their political and economic interests by acting as vestrymen and keeping the power of the Church. The clergymen, in turn, saw their salaries and standing best protected by an alliance with the planters.[75]

Anglican ministers varied greatly in the intensity of their involvement with the war effort. Dependent on the British government for their livelihood, and loyal to the Church from which they derived their sense of meaning, some Anglican clerics in the northern colonies associated loyalty to the Church as synonymous with loyalty to the empire. They equated the rebel argument for the natural rights of man with the state of nature and painted a picture of terrifying, unbridled, and unending social chaos. These loyalist writers expressed fear, hatred, and a rising hysteria about the effects of rebellion. They feared not the loss of British constitutionalism but the disruption of the social fabric. The American rebellion represented disloyalty to the Crown and disobedience to God.

The active persecution of Anglicans did not play a central role in the revolution. Indeed, the reputation Anglican clerics earned—their association with moderation—meant a general escape from revolutionary persecution. The Anglicans—both clergy and laity—who did not loudly and publicly assert their loyalty or participate actively in the cause of reunion were left unharmed. Others like Reverend Charles Inglis of New York City did not go unnoticed. Inglis described the rebellion as "one of the most causeless, unprovoked, and unnatural that ever disgraced any country . . . a rebellion marked with peculiarly aggravated circumstances of guilt and ingratitude."[76] When Inglis responded to Thomas Paine's *Common Sense* with *The True Interest of America Impartially Stated*, his pamphlet was seized from the printer and burned. The rebels also plundered his house. Addressing himself to the "passions of the populace," Inglis warned that Paine's "scheme" of a republican empire was as "new as it is destructive." It invited "uncommon phrenzy" and would prove ruinous to America. By rashly inviting the Continental Congress to move toward a "romantic and untried scheme," argued Inglis, Paine furthered the breach between Great Britain and the colonies. Instead of proposing reconciliation with Britain on "solid constitutional principles," the fanatical Paine proposed "cutting off a leg because the toe happened to ache." Insisting that he belonged to no party and cared only about the welfare of America, Inglis pleaded for the avoidance of "blood and slaughter."[77] (See document—Preaching to Loyalist Soldiers.)

Although Anglicans were reputed for their moderation, the revolutionary divide was not between evangelicals and anti-evangelicals. Evangelicals gave overwhelming support to the revolution, but anti-evangelicals were by no means a loyalist phalanx. They could be found all along the political spectrum of the era from Thomas Paine and Thomas Jefferson on the left to George Washington in the center, and to Joseph Galloway and Thomas Hutchinson on the right. Importantly, except in Connecticut and New Jersey, evangelicals seldom achieved positions of political leadership. Anti-evangelicals directed events on both sides of the revolutionary divide.

Loyalist Potential

The population of the thirteen rebellious colonies was about 2.5 million of all races, growing to about three million by the end of the war. The best estimate is that half a million Euro-Americans opposed the revolution, approximately 30,000 of them in arms.[78] Another half million were African Americans with limited opportunities for military service on the rebel or loyalist side. There were approximately 100,000 Indians in eastern North America.[79] Of the remaining fewer than two million rebellious whites, half were women, at least another half too old, too young, or incapable of serving. This left rebel manpower at roughly half a million.

Unlike previous wars, the British government had no foreign allies to share the burden of suppressing the American rebellion. Still, the British did not devise a formal policy for joining their three sources of potential strength: arming white loyalists, supporting powerful natives along the Appalachian border, and freeing the large African-American population along the southern coast. These loyalists would have strengthened the force of 30,000 Americans who served during the rebellion.[80] For the most part, individual commanders and leaders acted independently, depending on local circumstances. No systematic attempt was made to assess loyalist military capacity, and no unified policy guided loyalist mobilization during the war.[81] Still, approximately 19,000 men in forty-one loyalist regiments fought on the British side during the war.[82]

The British army's rootedness in European traditions influenced their unwillingness to recruit American loyalists (see document—Recruiting Loyalist Regiments). Like European officers, British officers promoted an aristocratic ethos associated with chivalry and honor, cultivated French manners, and attended foreign military academies. Qualities essential to command were understood to be the preserve of gentlemen. Like European troops, British regiments employed similar muskets, bayonets, and artillery pieces; organized their men in the familiar organizations of companies, battalions, and regiments for the infantry; and most importantly, shared military legal etiquette—convictions about upholding the laws of war derived from treaties, practice, and pronouncements of leading lawyers who established guides to military conduct, including principles of restraint.[83]

Given the commonalities with European military traditions, the British preferred to depend on foreign troops instead of American-born loyalists. When additional military manpower was needed, the British commander in chief, Sir Henry Clinton, favored "drawing over from the Rebels the Europeans in their service."[84] But Clinton relied most upon Hessian troops. Hired from the princes of German principalities, the Hessians formed between one-quarter and one-third of the British army. Rented soldiers with no ideological commitment to His Majesty's cause who faced a bleak future on their return home would pursue opportunities in colonies with abundant land. Still, the British preferred the mercenaries to ideologically committed American loyalists who were too amateurish to be regarded as a core part of the British effort.[85] Some officers also worried that personal animosities drove loyalists to fight with their neighbors; these loyalists would not bend to British discipline. Always significant in the British effort to suppress the American rebellion, the Hessians made up 37 percent of the British army by 1781.[86]

Drawing on their experience with Americans during the Seven Years' War, British officers regarded loyalist soldiers as outside the European military fraternity and dismissed them as undisciplined and untrustworthy.[87] High-ranking officers such as General Charles Cornwallis, head of British operations in the south, also worried that loyalists would switch sides and desert at the most crucial moment. Common British soldiers looked down on loyalist militiamen. The rebel poet Philip Freneau captured the British unwillingness to equip loyalist regiments in favor of using them as laborers. Freneau referred to the loyalists as Tories, a common epithet of the time.

> Come, gentlemen Tories, firm, loyal and true,
> Here are axes and shovels and something to do!
> For the sake of our king,
> Come labor and Sing.[88]

In the early part of the war, British officers underestimated the potential strength of the rebels, and anticipated a quick and decisive war. Expecting to suppress the rebellion with a few well-chosen military blows, the British saw no reason to organize a systematic campaign to enlist and create a corps of formidable loyalist regiments. During the first three years of the war, when military battles concentrated in the North, the British commanders in chief did not focus on large-scale loyalist recruitment and did not consider that loyalist military capacity could affect the outcome of the war. Influenced by previous biases and narrow financial considerations—hoping to avoid unnecessary military expenses—they were unwilling to make the preparations required to train loyalist soldiers into an efficient and dependable army. Instead, the British offered ad hoc concessions to known elites.

Influential and wealthy gentlemen were granted warrants to raise loyalist regiments. When the leaders mustered enough men, they were awarded a commission. The commanders of loyalist regiments were wealthy and influential men, not always with military experience, who recruited locally, bore all expenses, and drew full salaries only after their companies attained three-quarters strength. Led by New Jersey's Brigadier General Cortlandt Skinner, attorney general under Governor William Franklin, the New Jersey Volunteers was the largest single loyalist regiment, consisting of six battalions and a total of 3,300 soldiers. Loyalist regiments were armed, paid, disciplined, and provisioned like the British army but were not initially eligible for half-pay, which British officers could draw for life.[89] Loyalists were ranked junior to regular officers within each grade. Most of the loyalist corps conducted desultory raids against rebel-governed areas in New York, New Jersey, and along the New England coast. Only five loyalist regiments—Queen's Rangers, Volunteers of Ireland, New York Volunteers, the King's American Regiment, and the British Legion—were eventually raised to the level of the British establishment.[90]

French alliance with the rebels in 1778 led the British to reconsider the military role of the loyalists. Beset by financial problems, threatened by France in Europe and in the West Indies, and lacking adequate troops to suppress the rebellion in the mainland colonies, the British anticipated a larger role for loyalist militias in the southern backcountry. Unlike loyalist regiments, which served when ordered, enlisted for long periods, and fought far from their neighborhoods, the militia would serve temporarily and locally, leaving British regulars free for military duty elsewhere. But rallying loyalists in the southern colonies, especially in the backcountry regions, proved difficult.

More than a million people lived in the backcountry regions, from the Shenandoah Valley in Virginia to the Savannah River in Georgia. There were 15,000–20,000 Catawba Indians, 80,000 African-American slaves. Of the 900,000 Euro-Americans, many had already been on the move for three or four generations.[91] The contestations between the ethnic yeoman farmers—Highland Scots, Germans, and English—created a high level of social instability. Lacking a powerful and long-standing leadership, some regions in the backcountry engaged in intense rivalries and were more likely to follow local leaders than big causes. The bonds of social deference that fused long-standing communities in the Chesapeake tidewater regions were not easily carried to more recently settled backcountry regions. These transient communities were more dismissive about newspaper appeals or loyalty oaths, and did not share the same ideological fervor as northern colonists along the Hudson Valley. The communities' principal tactics against militia service and the draft reveal their local orientation. Most commonly, they issued anonymous threats against leaders, stole livestock, and fired on houses at night. Only rarely did they respond with open and armed insurgency.[92]

Winning and sustaining loyalty in the backcountry required a different kind of political mobilization than in the North. Gaining the "hearts and minds" of the backcountry residents proved a formidable—indeed, impossible—task for the British. Jack Greene has suggested that the concept of loyalty implies "a degree of certainty and levels of long-term commitment" that do not apply to the southern backcountry.[93] The "disaffected" people, those who resisted supporting either cause, bristled with local resentments and committed to a side based on personal and community vendettas rather than ideological convictions.[94]

In communities such as Kettle Creek, in northwest Georgia, a long-standing tension between colonial governments and backcountry families became mapped into political divisions. Southern frontier families who opposed the social power of the rebel coastal planters petitioned in favor of reunion with the empire. They also supported the king because they expected the British government would protect them from Indian attacks.[95] In the North Carolina backcountry, the aftermath of the Regulator Rebellion in 1771 left farmers hostile to the eastern elite who had crushed the rebellion. Loyalist leaders such as North Carolina Governor Josiah Martin competed with rebel leaders for the allegiance of these disaffected farmers.

The consequences of guerrilla warfare in the backcountry regions of the South after 1778 reshaped allegiances among frontiersmen as much as the presence of formal naval and army officers had influenced choices in cities such as New York in 1776. Without a majority consensus or long-standing political elite who could mobilize the frontiersmen, coercion through force became the only mechanism for local regions to preserve their authority. The British soldiers and loyalist militia functioned as a scapegoat against which to focus otherwise centrifugal social energies of the backcountry. To control the rural interior, rebel militias isolated loyalists and punished them violently. The early zeal of some southern loyalists turned to cynicism and timidity while others drew strength from British support and retaliated viciously in kind, hoping to settle old scores. The bitterness of persecution helped to shape the allegiance of colonists who might otherwise have avoided choosing between the king and their neighbors. When militant committees and military battles touched lives, colonists made choices to preserve their safety, not to advance their ideals.

Loyalist Women

Some women openly and audaciously supported reconciliation with Britain. On September 15, 1776, women jubilantly welcomed British troops and administration into New York City, and asserted their heartfelt attachment to Britain. A newspaper reported:

The King's Forces took Possession of the Place, incredible as it may seem, without the Loss of a Man. Nothing could equal the Expressions of Joy, shewn by the Inhabitants, upon the arrival of the King's officers among them. They even carried some of them upon their Shoulders about the Street, and behaved in all respects, Women as well as Men, like overjoyed Bedlamites. One thing is worth remarking; a Woman pulled down the Rebel Standard upon the Fort, and a Woman hoisted up in its Stead His Majesty's Flag, after trampling the other under Foot with the most contemptuous Indignation.[96]

Most women followed the political choices their husbands and fathers made, but saw the plight of their families in more personal terms. In contrast to the rebel committees, which instigated violence and coerced consent, the empire—even in military uniform—represented order and stability. Less concerned with constitutional issues around taxation and sovereignty, the prolonged rebellion probably sapped many women's enthusiasm not only for war, but for empire.

E. P. Thompson, in writing about eighteenth-century riots in Britain, noted that women "were proto-nothing: they were not bugged by notions of equality, in a competitive sense, since they were deeply habituated to the acceptance that men's and women's roles were different, and that neither was more nor the less for that."[97] In turbulent circumstances, trusting the patriarchal order—honoring choices that husbands, fathers, and sons made—may have anchored many women.[98] But, during this period of suspicion, a wife's loyalty to her husband, once a private commitment, transformed into a political act. Loyalist wives became guilty by association. Determined to strike a blow against enemies who supported the British cause, every colony passed laws confiscating loyalist property. Indeed, the confiscation acts are testimony to the chronic loyalist problem. In 1779, the state of New York declared fifty-nine persons guilty of felony and ordered them to forfeit their property to the state. Included were three women, all wives of prominent loyalists. The Reverend Charles Inglis's wife was listed. Given the limited autonomy of women in public life and their circumscribed role in church structure, it is surprising that any women were included. Although women participated in family worship and religious education, men dominated as church leaders (with the exception of women in the Quaker faith). Yet, during the rebellion, as Mrs. Inglis's case illustrates, women became politicized through their association with loyalist husbands. Revolutionary statutes that defined treason spoke of "persons" instead of men alone (see document—Confronting Confiscation Laws).

Accompanying their loyalist husbands, some women fled to nearby British strongholds and lived as refugees during the war. Mothers pleaded to take sons who were more than twelve years old; some rebel communities forbade this because older boys were considered capable of bearing arms against rebellion. Women who lacked a means of support when their husbands were drawn into service followed after them. They cared for their men, earning their subsistence as seamstresses, laundresses, nurses, and cooks. Cramped in garrisons with British troops, loyalist refugees, runaway slaves, and established residents, women struggled to keep their world intact. Burdened with large families but having no marketable skills led some to steal, sell alcohol, and commit fraud.[99] Others undoubtedly attached themselves to loyalist regiments because they feared to lose track of men with whom they had developed relationships, or because they feared to stay on in a loyalist area after it had returned to rebel control. They sought to avoid the intensifying rebel hatred that compromised their troubled lives even further.

Some loyalist women from high-ranking families remained in their homes. They hoped their long-standing ties to the neighborhood would keep them safe. Other women stayed to preserve their husband's estate for their children. They calculated that their presence would shield the property from confiscation or worse, total destruction. But as women managed farms, estates, and businesses, they faced suspicion from rebel neighbors who considered them surrogates for their offending husbands who had left to join the British. Considered traitors because they were married to loyalist men, they became victims of politicized communal outrage on the least provocation. Women were sometimes arrested and imprisoned for harboring or helping raiding parties, and for providing intelligence information to the British. Family prestige and even personal ties to rebel leaders did not always protect them.

Grace Galloway, wife of prominent loyalist Joseph Galloway, stayed in Philadelphia while her husband left to serve in the British administration. In 1778, Grace Galloway fell from her pinnacle as the wife of one of Philadelphia's most influential politicians to the depths of powerlessness. After the First Continental Congress rejected her husband's plan for reconciliation, he became a leading spokesman for the loyalists. Joseph Galloway joined the British in New York in December 1776 and returned to Philadelphia with them in September 1777. Galloway served as superintendent of police until June 1778 when the British evacuated Philadelphia. Four months later, he sailed for England. Joseph Galloway was deemed an attainted traitor, considered "civilly dead," and his property confiscated.[100]

Grace Galloway's worst nightmare was confirmed. Unprepared for the traumatic reversals of a lifetime, the fall from status was unbearable for her. She felt publicly humiliated when her carriage was confiscated and she, a lady of great status and influence, was compelled to walk the streets of Philadelphia like a common laborer. Mrs. Galloway stayed to protect the land inheritance she had brought into the marriage as the daughter of a wealthy man. Due to property laws of the time, wives who fled with their husbands could not claim dower in confiscated property. Mrs. Galloway could have renounced her loyalty to the British and secured the safety of the estate. But the idea of rebellion against the familiar monarchy was reprehensible, and she refused to be a traitor to the empire (see document—A Mother's Advice). Mrs. Galloway's gamble proved successful. After the war, when she willed her property to her son-in-law, the Supreme Court of Pennsylvania upheld her claim.[101]

Some women drew on their religious faith to draw judgments about the rebellion. Quaker women noted and condemned rebel violence against loyalist neighbors. In the midst of their discourse on fashion and tea ceremonies, on personal meditation and spiritual renewal, they dwelled on the injustices committed during the war. Hannah Griffitts celebrated women's private space at the tea table and thought tea-drinking rituals promoted politeness in men and sociability in women: "Blest Leaf whose aromatic Gales dispence. . . . To Men, Politeness, & to Ladies Sense."[102] But Griffitts also wrote verses about the violence of the rebellion because she feared that moderate voices were being drowned out by hard-liners. In her poetry, she denounced Thomas Paine, the radical author of *Common Sense*, as a "Snake beneath the Grass" and an ensnaring "Serpent." Although raised on the Quaker principles of his father, Paine called for violent resistance in ways abhorred by the pacifist Friends who instead sought to achieve their ends by personal example. Above all, many Friends avoided violating their principles of nonparticipation in militarism. Paine's arguments against monarchy and the tyrannical king were specious, Griffitts countered, because "sixty as well as one can tyrannize."[103] Here, she referred to the violent acts of rebel committees against colonists who wished to remain neutral.

Griffitts expressed her sadness and anger at the "unnatural Contest" at Long Island in August 1776, the first sustained battle of the revolution, one in which the rebels lost.[104] In a poem, she conveyed her horror at the execution of two Quakers, John Roberts and Abraham Carlisle, on November 4, 1778, hung by the rebels for their alleged collaboration with the British (see document—Mourning Loyalist Execution). Both Quakers had shown great zeal for reunion when the British army was in Philadelphia. As gatekeeper, Carlisle had issued passes to those entering or leaving the city; Roberts had recruited men and furnished supplies for the British. After British evacuation, both men faced rebel retribution. They were tried, then hung for treason. More than four thousand Philadelphians attended the burial procession of the two men. Philadelphia loyalists worried that the two Quakers' execution, gone unpunished by the British, led to loyalist withdrawal and disappointment. They hoped the British would take the execution as an opportunity to turn people's wrath against tyrannical rebel leaders. But the British were not worried about the fate of two unknown Quakers.[105]

Benjamin Franklin's cousin, Kezia Folger Coffin of Nantucket, defied her Quaker faith and actively chose loyalism. With the outbreak of war in Lexington and Concord in 1775, Mrs. Coffin, like many Nantucketers, saw no reason to disrupt the imperial relationship. A well-connected businesswoman of means, Mrs. Coffin achieved success within the empire. She benefited tremendously from the rapid profitability of the Anglo-American whaling industry and spermaceti candle manufacturing in Nantucket. She also took advantage of connections established by her husband, John Coffin, a wealthy owner of whaling vessels, and her brothers, two of whom were whaling captains. When the Nantucket Society of Friends demanded stricter adherence and absolute neutrality, Mrs. Coffin rejected her Quaker faith and identified with the British cause.

Mrs. Coffin's decisions were the logical extension of her success since the 1750s. Her loyalism was not born anew during the imperial crisis but persisted through the crisis. Unencumbered by heavy maternal responsibility (she had only one child), Mrs. Coffin operated confidently in the patronage-based culture that was still organized around "houses" instead of "firms" and hence allowed female participation in mercantile operations.[106] Choosing the British side meant protecting the family whose interests she had carefully cultivated for the past two decades. As described by Jane Mecom, Benjamin Franklin's sister, she took the "wrong side & Exerted her Self by Every method she could devise Right or Wrong to Accomplish her Designs, & Favour the Britons, went in to Large Traid with them, & for them."[107]

A total of 3,225 loyalists filed claims for compensation from the British government after the revolution. Unfortunately, Kezia Coffin missed the deadline for requesting restitution. Most claims tended to come from propertied, skilled, seaboard, and urban residents. More than one-third of the claims came from New Yorkers, half of the claims came from those born outside North America, and 468 of the claims were made by women.[108] In petition after petition, women strategically emphasized their weakness and helplessness, and their need for British benevolence. The appeals conceal the resilience through which women survived their multiple displacements and kept their families and properties intact. Loyalist wives and daughters suffered alongside their husbands; the revolution meant a permanent exile in

England, Canada, or the Caribbean. From Halifax, Nova Scotia, the daughter of a New England loyalist expressed her sadness in verse: "I am a young Exile from my native Shore. . . . Start at the Flash of Arms and dread the Roar."[109] The diversity of the colonial experience makes it difficult to assess how the paternalism of British monarchy situated loyalist women in Canada in relation to the emerging ideal of republican motherhood in the United States. But the revolution did not inaugurate a golden age for women, rebel or loyalist.

Slaves

Between 1775 and 1783, an estimated twenty thousand slaves escaped their masters, mostly from the southern colonies.[110] Although the Church of England enjoyed a virtual monopoly on missionary work in the colonies, the Anglican establishment played a modest role in drawing blacks to the British side. Despite British racism and support for slavery, the British were regarded as allies and associated with slave emancipation. Slaves expressed faith in the empire through their actions: They took advantage of revolutionary upheaval not to flee to the wilderness and establish maroon communities but to join British troops (see document—Escaping to the British). When the rebel army evacuated New York City in 1776, a British soldier saw "black children of slaves hugging and kissing each other" with relief.[111] One man who left rebel-governed New York for British Nova Scotia after the rebellion called himself "British Freedom," and in naming himself thus, revealed that he had greater faith that British monarchy rather than American republicanism would deliver African Americans from slavery.[112]

From 1775 onward, the British recruited rebel slaves as an expedient measure in an effort to weaken and fragment the rebel slaveholding community. British officers never authorized manumissions en masse; public opinion did not favor radical social equality, and the British did not wish to poison the American political context beyond recovery. As much as alienating the colonial populace, the British worried deeply about liberated slaves: Would they require relocation outside the empire? But local and immediate exigencies led British officers to consider slaves as important sources of manpower and slave emancipation as a valuable tactic against rebel slave owners.

Curiously, the British proclamations issued to the blacks paralleled those issued to white loyalists during the rebellion. Through protections offered to wavering white colonists and rebel-owned slaves, the British sought to weaken and fragment the rebel coalition. Beginning in July 1776 and repeated periodically until 1781, the British commanders in chief offered pardons to white colonists, "to all those who in the tumult and disorder of the times may have deviated from their just allegiance and who are willing by a speedy return to their duty to reap the benefits of his royal favour."[113] In November 1775, the governor of Virginia, Lord Dunmore, encouraged able-bodied black men bonded to rebel slave owners to enter British lines. His recruitment represented the first of several desperate attempts to buttress British weakness in the South and to simultaneously challenge the power of the rebel slaveholders. Dunmore anticipated that slave-owning rebels would be deprived of their workers and compelled to return home to manage their properties instead of carrying arms against the British. As importantly, Dunmore hoped to supply himself with badly needed manpower. Almost four years later, in preparation for the southern campaign, British commander in chief Sir Henry Clinton not only echoed but expanded Dunmore's proclamation. In June 1779, Clinton encouraged "every Negro [not only armed men but also women and children] who shall desert the Rebel standard, full security to follow within these lines any occupation which he shall think proper."[114] Neither the British ministers in London nor British officers in the colonies intended the proclamations to function as a first step toward ending slavery. The interests of British slave traders and of sugar planters in the Caribbean islands, along with worries about alienating loyalist slave owners, conspired against slave emancipation.[115]

Taking advantage of the route to manumission unavailable to black women, black men enlisted in British regiments. In 1775, one thousand were ready to serve on behalf of the empire and joined Lord Dunmore's Ethiopian Regiment. But their hopes for freedom and betterment—and perhaps honor and distinction—were short lived. Like many colonists, these blacks had no immunity to smallpox and suffered ghastly casualty rates. But unlike white Americans, they received neither inoculation nor hospitalization and perished in larger numbers.[116] When Dunmore was forced to retreat from Virginia, the surviving black loyalists accompanied him to New York City. In the first battle fought between British regulars and the Continental Army on Long Island, New York, in August 1776, the Ethiopian Regiment fought alongside the British against the rebels.[117]

From New Jersey's Monmouth County, 21-year-old Titus fled his owner, John Corlies, to fight with Dunmore's Ethiopian regiment. Despite his membership in the Society of Friends, Corlies did not perceive it was "his duty to give [the slaves] their freedom."[118] Serving the British under the honorary title of Colonel Tye, Titus fought bravely with white loyalists against rebel forces in the Battle of Monmouth on June 28, 1778. His title did not represent a formal British commission but bestowed respect and acknowledged

Titus's bravery and leadership. Soldiers who had served in the Caribbean oversaw his transformation from servant to warrior status. Taking advantage of his knowledge about the terrain around New York City, Colonel Tye led raids against rebels, kidnapped soldiers, and carried off cattle for British troops. Acting as "insurgent extensions of British power," his men exerted a destabilizing influence to protect the British hold over New York City.[119] Until September 1780, when Tye died from a fatal wrist wound, his unit was employed for reconnaissance and quick raids to protect British-held New York City.[120]

Although British military officers actively solicited black manpower, they tried to restrict black families from entering British lines. They did not want to waste precious resources on feeding and housing black women and children. When the exploits of Colonel Tye and interracial guerrilla bands posted in ferry landings in New Jersey encouraged black families to flee to New York City, some British officials fumed. In May 1780, Major General James Patterson wrote Cuyler that "not only male but female Negroes with their children take advantage of your port in New Jersey to run away from masters and come into the city where they must become a burden to the town. . . . Be so good as to prevent their passing the North [Hudson] River as far as it is in your power to do it." Some officers explicitly forbade black men to enter British lines with their families. On December 2, 1780, Lieutenant Colonel John Simcoe of the Queen's Rangers issued a proclamation from his station in Oyster Bay, Long Island. Addressing the "able bodied men slaves to those who are in arms against his Majesty's government," he announced that they "would have their liberty & be protected by King George provided they come without their wives & children who cannot be received or protected at present." In exchange for their own freedom, Simcoe demanded that black men abandon their families to face the rage of rebel masters.[121]

Colonel Tye was extraordinary. Few runaways served in a military capacity: The majority, recruited and deployed in a hurry, did strenuous and time-consuming work. They dug trenches, buried bodies, and served as orderlies in hospitals. Black women laundered and sewed, black pilots guided ships in and out of treacherous ports, black fiddlers provided entertainment for military officers, and black cooks and servants ensured the comfort of elite homes. Other slaves and free blacks cared for animals, hauled provisions, and chopped and collected firewood. The slaves who escaped from northern colonies were more cosmopolitan and sometimes more literate than southern slaves, and sought to use this to their advantage. Like Tye, these men acted as spies, or as an ancillary guerrilla force, and raided rebel homes in concert with white loyalist refugees.

The experience of war was less harrowing for slaves in British New York City where the British administration's behavior toward blacks compelled hope, perhaps even trust.[122] Some slaves who escaped to the city worshipped at the Anglican Church, got married, baptized their children, and worked for the British military administration. Surprisingly, in return for their labor, the blacks were sometimes treated legally as British subjects.

Two incidents illustrate British defense of invited black subjects in 1783. When a New York loyalist sought a quick profit by capturing and selling a black man who took refuge in the city, the British favored the black over the white loyalist. In May, Thomas Willis, employed in New York City's police department, captured Caesar, tied his hands behind his back, and forced him through the public streets of the city by beating him with a stick. Willis hoped to return the runaway Caesar to Elizabethtown, New Jersey, for a "piece of gold coin."[123] Having evidence that Caesar entered the lines legally, the British sentenced Willis to receive five hundred lashes but then revoked the sentence for his display of "good character" and mandated his transport out of the city.[124]

In July, when a slaveholder tried to reclaim his black property, the British used military law to override the owner's claims. In July, Jacob Duryee carried off Francis Griffin, a black loyalist under the protection of the British government in New York City. In his defense, Duryee insisted that as a citizen of the United States of America, he had a "right to his property whenever he could find it." He infuriated Deputy Judge Advocate Stephen P. Adye, who reminded Duryee that a "general commanding an army in a hostile country possesses powers beyond what even His Majesty himself enjoys!"[125] In these instances, British paternalism provided reason for New York's blacks to remain committed to the empire.

During the years of the American rebellion, some British officers and loyalist leaders recommended the creation of a large slave imperial army. Governor Dunmore and Joseph Galloway promoted black enlistment in the British military.[126] Dunmore anticipated that a force of ten thousand blacks would be the "most efficacious, expeditious, cheapest and certain means of reducing this country to a proper sense of their duty."[127] Galloway believed that drastic and emergency actions were required to suppress the rebellion. But the long-standing notion of slaves as agricultural and household laborers in the American colonies clashed with the idea of slaves as military labor. During the war, loyalist slave owners were intensely conscious of the value lost in runaway property. In December 1778, William Smith Jr. recorded that his black servant, Jack, had left him, to join a British privateering expedition. In his diary, he carefully recorded the amount he had lost in his runaway property.[128] Yet by the 1790s, the British had learned that armed slaves, promised honor, distinction, and status, could be trusted to defend slavery. The lessons of the American experience led to new practices and policy. Ten years after the American war, in 1795, slaves in red coats served British forces during the Haitian Revolution and its aftermath. The British government purchased more than thirteen thousand Africans between 1797 and 1808 to man its Caribbean forces, to defend slavery in the Caribbean and in West Africa.[129]

Indian Allies

The revolution escalated white-Indian land tensions of prerevolutionary colonial society. Frontier wars were fought in the Ohio River Valley, in Kentucky, and in the Mohawk Valley. Both British and rebel leaders advocated using friendly Indians to wage war against hostile ones. Caught between their economic dependence on trade goods and the manipulations of both rebels and loyalists who wanted Indian allies in strategic backcountry regions, neutrality was not an option. In 1775, many such as Samson Occom, a Mohegan Christian, wished the whites "would let the poor Indians alone, what have they to do with your Quarrels."[130] Occom feared the violent consequences of siding with the losers.

In the end, most Indian communities allied with the British. These Indians hoped the British would continue to protect Indian country as they had most recently against the American settlers in the Proclamation of 1763. Others hoped to recoup some of the losses of past generations with British victory.[131] One historian calls the scale of anti-rebel alliance during the revolution the "largest, most unified Native American effort the continent would ever see."[132]

However, the vicious warfare also generated division and confusion within Indian communities and created new fissures. In 1779, the Delawares allied with the British, but individuals inside the community chose the opposing side.[133] British-allied Shawnee communities along the Ohio Valley splintered and restructured as rebel invasions compelled migrations to Cherokee and Creek territories in the South, and to residence with the Delawares. Along with forced migrations, the Shawnees dealt with the disruption caused by burned fields, the killing of noncombatants, and the wartime promotion of war chiefs at the expense of longtime village chiefs. The war that terminated in 1783 for the British did not end for the Shawnees until the mid-1790s when the chiefs finally sought accommodation with the victorious Americans.[134]

As importantly, the revolution was a civil war for the Six Nations Confederacy just as it was for white colonists. The League of Six Nations—the confederacy of Mohawks, Oneidas, Tuscaroras, Onondagas, Cayugas, and Senecas—had managed to maintain their pivotal position in upstate New York by preserving neutrality and unity. But the outbreak of war split the confederacy. Whereas most of the Oneidas and Tuscaroras sided with the rebels, the Senecas, Mohawks, Cayugas, and Onondagas sided with the British.[135] Joseph Brant, the Mohawk leader who had already fought for the British during the Seven Years' War, pulled four of the Iroquois nations to the British side (see document—Mohawks Side with the British). Undoubtedly, his sister's twenty-two-year relationship with Sir William Johnson, northern superintendent of Indian affairs, contributed to the Mohawk attachment to Britain. Equally at home in an Indian war council or as the hostess of Johnson Hall, Mary Brant had great influence in the matrilineal Iroquois society (see mention of Mary Brant, housekeeper, in document—Relations with Indians). She provided intelligence information to the British and fostered ties of loyalty and self-interest that mobilized Indian warriors to support the cause.[136]

For some Mohawks, membership in the Anglican Church may have led to alliance with the British. In March 1770, New York's Rev. Charles Inglis voiced the implicit link between loyalty and religion. He explained that the most effective way of securing Iroquois loyalty was by "proselytizing them to Christianity, as professed by the Church of England."[137] If neglected, they would "naturally grow alienated from the Government."[138] The Church signified a critical middle ground, and the Church's continual presence represented the Iroquois' successful negotiation in preserving their homeland from colonial squatters. Both Joseph and Mary Brant grew up in the home of the Indian superintendent, William Johnson, of Anglican faith. Brant's faith may have been further reinforced under the missionary teachings of the Reverend John Stuart in the 1770s. Brant would translate the Book of Common Prayer and, in 1787, a doctrinal primer.[139] Significantly, when Mary Brant died in 1796, the bell in the tower of the local Anglican Church at Cataraqui (Ontario) tolled for her. The extent to which Mary Brant's loyalism was influenced by her faith in the Anglican Church is hard to determine: the Anglican Church however, clearly recognized her as an important ally.[140]

Most colonial wars had included Indians on both sides. But by the end of the Seven Years' War in 1763, white colonists were much less dependent on Indian aid than they had been in the preceding decades.[141] A combination of prejudice, hatred, and a long history of frightful intercultural warfare transformed Indians from savages, uncivilized in English ways, to barbarians, bent on cruelty and undeserving of restraint (see document—Accusing Savages of Scalping Europeans).[142] Worries about Indians' elusiveness and treachery condoned levels of violence unthinkable against white loyalists. Backcountry settlers took the law into their own hands, killing combatants and noncombatants alike, burning Indian crops, and destroying Indian villages.[143] In 1779, George Washington's policy against the Iroquois made it "essential to ruin their crops now in the ground and prevent them planting more."[144] Soldiers in the Continental Army destroyed easily accessible Iroquois homelands even as they eyed them as future possessions. Troops burned cornfields at the time of harvest and took Indian hostages as "security."[145] They marked their initials on landmarks, hoping to claim Indian land as private property after the war. Continental officers sometimes "chastened those [soldiers] who presumed to mark trees in the wood with initial letters and their names at large."[146]

Sadly, the Indians' overwhelming allegiance to the British side did not protect them from white loyalists who regarded the Natives as military pawns in the larger war. Rebels and loyalists alike equated the security and stability of colonial society with entitlement to Native land. Initially, both sides sought to keep Natives outside the "family" rebellion. But Indians' fear of losing land to rebel speculators denied them the neutrality they sought. Far from promoting a united loyalist union inclusive of the races, the white loyalists hoped that Indian terrorist tactics would intimidate rebels and move them toward neutrality or loyalism. In one particularly revealing letter written in December 1778, the loyalist governor of New York, William Tryon, urged the British to enlist the Indian Nations lying between Quebec and West Florida and "let [them] loose on the frontiers of the revolted colonies, unrestrained excepting to women and children."[147] Without normal subsistence and with unreliable access to trade goods, the Natives became increasingly dependent on their allies. By the end of the war, Indian country, from the Mohawk Valley to Florida, was a site of devastation and ruin.

The Peace Treaty and Its Aftermath

The warfare in Indian country was not decisive in shaping the outcome of the revolution; the outcome of the revolution, however, decisively affected the Indian world in North America. The Peace Treaty ceded to the United States all of the lands east of the Mississippi and south of the Great Lakes, and made no mention of the Indians who had fought and died on the empire's behalf and who inhabited the territory that now belonged to the United States. The British neglect of their Native allies closed the disputed "middle ground" of the Natives, preserved tenaciously for almost two hundred years. One Iroquois called the Treaty an "Act of Cruelty and injustice that Christians only were capable of doing."[148] The military raids as well as disease and malnutrition promoted by the war caused Iroquois numbers to fall by one-third after the revolution—from nine thousand to six thousand.[149] Indians such as the Iroquois Nations who had tried to prolong porous borderlands eventually became confined—and divided—within the borders of consolidated regimes.

Territorial disputes between Americans and Indian nations in thinly populated regions within the United States would be decided not by treaties and litigation but by the reality of settler occupation. By the early nineteenth century, the Cherokees, who had survived better than the Iroquois and established themselves as an autonomous republic associated with the United States but not subordinate to it, could not counter the expansive claims of Georgia's settlers. Frontier vendettas and backcountry violence continued unabated through the early nineteenth century. Facing east, toward Britain, the rebels had called themselves Sons of Liberty, but after the war, facing west, they declared themselves proprietors of a vast continent (see document—Indians as Beasts of Prey).

The terms of the Peace Treaty stunned white loyalists (see document—Dreadful Tidings). Those who had courageously fled their homes and their communities for British garrisons had faced neglect, suspicion, and derision; and competed for scarce wood, adequate shelter, and British patronage. Regarded as enemies and traitors, they had lived as refugees under the British military because they expected the imperial government to protect them and compensate them for their sacrifices. The preliminary treaty of November 1782 confirmed the loyalists' worst fears: the Treaty made no mention of loyal white Americans outside of a meaningless clause in Article V that required the rebel Congress to "earnestly recommend" that each state legislature "provide for the restitution of all estates, rights, and properties which have been confiscated belonging to real British subjects" and promised that all noncombatant loyalists should have "free liberty to go to any part or parts of any of thirteen United States" without molestation as they endeavored to secure their confiscated properties (see document—Loyalists in the Peace Treaty).

Throughout the war, colonial governments had enacted laws confiscating the property of prominent loyalists (see document—Confronting Confiscation Laws). Because the states and not the Congress had seized the property, Congress had no power to deal with the question of loyalist reparations. It could not enforce the restoration of seized loyalist property or compel liberal treatment of returning loyalists. This meant, as both loyalists and the victorious rebels understood, that the loyalists would receive no mercy. In most states, the loyalists were proscribed as traitors, and local committees refused to allow them to return to their former homes. More than four decades after the war, Stephen Allen remembered the loyalist reaction to the peace treaty: "This was dreadful news for the loyalists in the city [New York] and their countenances and expressions on the occasion betrayed the bitter and malignant passions working within them."[150] One commentator observed acidly that the peace treaty "licks the feet of Congress, and of their General, and only begs not to receive a kick."[151] If there were any compensation for loyalist losses, it would have to come from the empire and not from the American states.

Regarded as disloyal citizens of the new nation, the loyalists faced both the wrath of the state governments and the vengeance of former neighbors. In the short term, at least, colonists identified publicly as loyalists had little future in the revolutionary republic.[152] When known loyalists tried to return to their homes in 1782 and 1783, they faced insults, threats, and banishment. In both the southern and northern colonies, loyalists were accused of massacring neighbors, desolating lands, and starting fires.[153] In response to the demand for retributive justice, South Carolina's new government legitimated its authority by employing disfranchisement, confiscation, and banishment against the loyalists. In New York, the Trespass Act permitted returning rebels to file a lawsuit against any person in British-ruled New York who had used the property they had left behind. The loyalist victims could not sue in return. Gradually, by 1788, the state governments rescinded the penalties on a case-by-case basis and gained support of the wider community.[154]

Anti-loyalist activity went unpunished in local neighborhoods. Angry residents used every means in their power—intimidation, assault, tarring and feathering—to prevent the exiles from returning home. When the loyalist Joshua Booth tried to return to his home in Ulster County, New York, to visit his mother, a group pinioned him and carried him six miles to a larger group. His head was tarr'd and feathered, his hair was shorn, and his eyebrows shaved with a pen knife. A paper was affixed on his forehead with the inscription: "Look yo Tory Crew, and see what George your King can do." He was pulled by a party on horseback about four miles with a drum beating and fife playing before being delivered on a boat bound for New York City (see document—Retaliation from Rebels).[155] The rising tide of violence by rebel committees in combination with the abandonment of British troops from garrisons left the loyalists repeatedly unprotected and vulnerable to rebel assault. For Booth and others like him, safety lay in exile.

Yet, despite fierce opposition, the majority of loyalists remained in the United States. A few loyalists such as the Reverend Henry Addison abandoned England for the United States after the rebellion (see document—Forsaking

Britain). Printer Hugh Gaine brought down the Crown from his shop sign and quietly went on with his printing business. No bloody reign of terror followed the rebellion. Some families undoubtedly moved to different localities to avoid the social stigma of loyalism. The "Black List," which preserved the names of the loyalists in Pennsylvania, still circulated in 1802 during an election dispute; the debate hinged on whether attainted loyalists could vote if they had not been officially pardoned by the state. Loyalist assimilation happened gradually as the new republic framed political decision making as a protected individual right and not as a sinful betrayal of the larger virtuous community.[156]

The British government was more ready to recover slave property lost by loyalists than to retrieve landed property confiscated from loyalists. Loyalist-owned slaves had no chance of freedom because the government would not divest a British subject of his property without his consent. They comprised the largest departing group from the southern garrisons. Tragically, the same British officers who had offered slaves freedom during the rebellion now offered to protect the property of loyalists, including their right to their slave property. The former governor of New Hampshire, Sir John Wentworth, invested nineteen of his slaves in his cousin's plantation in Dutch Guinea. In his letter of February 24, 1784, Wentworth assured his cousin that the slaves "are all American born and well seasoned and all are perfectly stout, healthy, sober, industrious, and honest . . . the Women are stout and able, and promise well to increase their numbers."[157] Approximately fifteen thousand blacks left the United States as the property of white loyalists.[158]

The empire did not fully abandon the loyalists who wished to remain Britons. The government provided transportation to scattered destinations throughout the empire—to Britain, Quebec and Nova Scotia, and the Caribbean. It issued provisions, tools, medicine, clothes, and seeds. It provided military protection. Most of all, it surveyed and granted land free of charge. Finally, it appointed a commission to assess loyalist suffering and awarded compensation to those who could demonstrate their sacrifices on behalf of the empire (see document—Claiming Losses in Income, Property, and Slaves). By 1788, the British government had spent about £7.5 million on the loyalists, twice the interest on the national debt in 1763.[159] In the process of categorizing loyalists, the British commissioners underlined the volatility of choosing sides during the rebellion. They differentiated loyalists who bore arms in the service of Britain, and those who bore arms for the American states but later joined the British side; those who had remained uniform and zealous; and those who took oaths to the Americans but afterward joined the British.[160]

Of the 60,000 displaced loyalists, more than half dreamed of better lives in Nova Scotia and Quebec (divided into Upper and Lower Canada in

1791). Quebec received 6,000 loyalists and 500 Mohawks, and the Maritimes received the majority, more than 30,000 loyalists. Nova Scotia (which included the future New Brunswick) and its dependencies (Prince Edward Island, then known as the Island of St. John, and Cape Breton) proved especially attractive because the colony was thinly populated, and its capital, Halifax, was just six hundred miles from the loyalist haven of New York City. More than 1,400 loyalist heads of households—about 8,000 people—sought employment and position in England between 1775 and 1784. In London, a small number of talented and influential exiles worked behind the scenes to influence Britain's policy toward the colonies. Pennsylvania's Joseph Galloway struggled to establish himself as the resident expert on colonial affairs. But Galloway, along with other London exiles, did not receive serious political consideration from British government. As Thomas Hutchinson lamented in 1782, "We Americans are plenty here, and very cheap. . . . Some of us at first meeting are apt to think ourselves of importance, but other people do not think so, and few, if any of us are much consulted, or enquired after."[161]

As many as 3,000 white loyalists and 8,000 slaves entered Jamaica after the British evacuated their southern garrisons in 1782, Savannah in July, and Charleston in December. Most of the southern loyalists migrated to the West Indies because plantation agriculture offered exiled slaveholders a chance to rebuild their fortunes using slave labor. Other loyalist families migrated to Dominica, St. Lucia, and other sugar islands, and to East Florida.[162]

The loyalist exodus from East Florida—2,500 white loyalists with their 4,000 slaves—doubled the white population and tripled the black population in the Bahamas.[163] Their arrival promoted an economic transition in the Bahamas, from shipbuilding and other maritime activities to a plantation economy based on cotton plantations and slave labor. In April 1783, news of evacuation came as a shock to loyalists in East Florida who expected to remain within the British empire and who thought they had escaped the fate of other southern loyalists. By 1783, the influx of loyalists fleeing rebel control in the southern colonies had increased the population of East Florida to 12,000—5,000 whites and 7,000 blacks.[164] In addition to loyalist families and their slaves, East Florida included British troops, loyalist soldiers, and Native Americans. The first East Florida newspaper, the *East-Florida Gazette*, was printed in February 1783.[165] When the Peace Treaty returned East Florida to Spain, these loyalists confronted the same choices as those made earlier by Savannah's and Charleston's loyalists.

Surprisingly, the British upheld the promises of freedom made to rebel-owned slaves. On paper, the British statesmen committed to return all property the army had seized from the rebels. In Article VII of the Peace Treaty, Britain agreed to withdraw its land and naval forces "with all convenient speed, and without causing any destruction, or carrying away any Negroes or other property of the American inhabitants." But would slaves freed by British proclamations still be counted as rebel property? The British had followed no explicit policy regarding the status and treatment of slaves during the war years. But amid defeat and evacuations, decisions were made. An ex-slave in New York, Boston King, expressed the horror of those last months in 1783: "Many of the slaves had very cruel masters so that the thoughts of returning home with them embittered life for us. . . . For some days, we lost our appetite for food, and sleep departed from our eyes."[166] (See document—Escaping to the British.)

Despite the hostility from colonists who hoped to recapture their slaves from British garrisons, the British commander in chief, Sir Guy Carleton, honored his predecessors' proclamations that had promised freedom to rebel slaves who entered British lines. Carleton, in fact, distinguished between slaves who fled to the British in response to the proclamations and those who sought refuge previous to the proclamations or subsequent to the cessation of hostilities. Sensing the acute situation, General Washington met Carleton in a conference in Orangetown, New Jersey, in May 1783. Washington argued that the embarkations of blacks on British ships violated the stipulations of the Peace Treaty (see document—Negotiating Slave Return). Washington knew that some of his own slaves had escaped to British New York City and along with other rebel leaders such as Virginia's governor, Benjamin Harrison, hoped to find them. But Carleton did not think the clause applied to blacks in New York City for they were already free.[167] In the end, 8,000 blacks left the United States as free people. Of these, 5,000 sailed to England and another 3,000 sought a new life in Nova Scotia.[168] Of the 3,000 free blacks, 1,336 were men, 914 women, and 750 children. Notably, 40 percent were female (see document—Book of Negroes).[169] Despite British officers' attempts to prevent black women and children from burdening British resources, they failed to dissuade slave families from escaping slavery.

Of the forty-seven free blacks who applied in England for compensation, only one was awarded anything for his property losses (see document—Black Petitions). Half the blacks were denied assistance altogether.[170] The British officials thought the black men merited no entitlement because they were "very fortunate in being in a Country" where they can "never again be reduced to a state of slavery."[171] In 1787, hundreds of blacks were encouraged to seek another home outside of England. Although initial schemes included considerations of the Bahamas where blacks would reintegrate into a slave society, and of New Brunswick where slaves would become hard-working laborers by converting forests into farmlands, Sierra Leone in West Africa was finally the chosen destination. By the early 1790s, the colony, poorly supported from Britain, vulnerable to the depredations of local slave catchers, and regarded with hostility by local chiefs, struggled to survive. Only the arrival of more than one thousand disillusioned black Nova Scotians in 1792 buttressed their numbers and gave the first settlers in Sierra Leone a second chance.

Refugees in the Maritimes

Many free black Nova Scotians were southern slaves who had earned their freedom by joining the British troops.[172] For almost ten years, they endured mistreatment from British administrators and violent discrimination from loyalist exiles. The British administrators saw no gain in attending to the needs of emancipated and penniless blacks. Unlike white loyalists, they received no saws, hoes, hammers, or nails. Free blacks arrived only with a spade, an ax, some clothing and one pair of shoes, and received land with the poorest soil.[173]

Still, they established the largest settlement of free blacks in North America, in the segregated town of Birchtown, northwest of Shelburne. Unable to compete with white laborers and disbanded soldiers, they sank to the bottom as day laborers and indentured servants. Their attempts at establishing schools and churches met militant opposition. Boston King remembered the conditions that accompanied a dreadful famine in Nova Scotia in the late 1780s when "many of the poor people were compelled to sell their best gowns for five pounds of flour, in order to support life. When they had parted with all their clothes, even their blankets, several of them fell dead in the streets, thro' hunger. Some killed and eat [sic] their doge and cats, and poverty and distress prevailed on every side, so that to my great grief i was obliged to leave [Birchtown] because I could get no employment."[174] Unlike many disappointed white loyalists who made their way back to familiar neighborhoods in the United States, returning to a life of re-enslavement in their masters' homes was not an option for black Nova Scotians. Moving to Sierra Leone represented a third desperate transition.

In a letter to his sister from Halifax in 1783, the Reverend Mather Byles lamented the fate of the loyalist refugees "in the howling wilderness, among a people who I believe are as conscientious as the first settlers of New England and who have been more cruelly persecuted."[175] Impressions formed based on sources such as Byles's letter portray white loyalists as tragic exiles in the British peripheries, as trapped in an unknown and uncultivated forest. But for the Micmac population, these loyalists were invaders. These Indians, who had held out against French settlement in the 1600s and 1700s and the settlement of Germans and New Englanders in the 1750s and 1760s, could not survive the large influx of the loyalists. Their influx ended the Aboriginals' ability to negotiate in Nova Scotia. Prior to 1782, the Aboriginals had lived with multiple groups of immigrants—Acadians, British, New Englanders—but colonization had remained confined to defined areas. Arriving with military experience and loyal credentials, the refugees eclipsed Aboriginal claims to land and trade. As historian John G. Reid has observed, the fur trade, so crucial to Aboriginal economy and autonomy, "became the preserve of poor loyalists not Aboriginal hunters and trappers."[176]

Enslavers and imperialists in relation to blacks and Indians in Nova Scotia, the loyalists were true Britons in the eyes of empire. For a fortunate minority, government largesse included land, compensation for losses sustained by the war, and important government offices. Providing benevolent compensation and position served not only imperial interests but protected Nova Scotia for Britain (see document—Envisioning British Nova Scotia). As the British officer Brook Watson expressed in 1783, "the province will be at last settled, and that with good People of Property carrying in their hearts, the most settled love to the Constitution of England, they will form a barrier against those of opposite principle, and become the envy of all their Neighbors."[177] The 1785 Nova Scotia charter described the colony as "the pole star . . . [that would] gratify the true loyalists by fixing them in as free and advantageous a situation as the nature of the government can admit." The "paternal goodness" of Britain would not only encourage the zeal and ambition of true subjects, but would "operate most forcibly on the revolted Americans by proving . . . what they might have enjoyed on a reunion with their careful and gracious Sovereign, and fellow-subjects."[178]

In 1784, New England loyalist Edward Winslow procured the coveted position as secretary to Brigadier General Henry E. Fox in Nova Scotia. Winslow advocated the partitioning of Nova Scotia. He hoped a separate province on the north side of the Bay of Fundy would create new provincial offices for young and ambitious loyalist immigrants (see document—Loyalist Nova Scotia). In becoming an immigrant in a new land, Winslow did not leave behind his sense of privilege. There was no sense of sudden commonality with other loyalists who were also struggling to establish a foothold. He was equally contemptuous of the local inhabitants, the poor immigrants, and the black refugees. He saw the inhabitants as "languid wretches" who were not ready to be industrious unless induced through shame.[179] In a letter to his wife, Winslow described "board day" in Halifax. From eight in the morning, the yard in front of his house crowded with the "most miserable objects that were ever beheld." He called the poor arriving from the streets of London "miserable remnants . . . and such as are able to crawl are begging for a proportion of provisions at my door." The African Americans he referred to as "Blackies begging for Christ's sake that Masser would give 'em a little provision if it's only for one week."[180]

In 1787, the Reverend Charles Inglis, former rector of Trinity Church in New York, was appointed bishop of Nova Scotia. Inglis hoped to link Anglican theology with British constitutionalism. After the rebellion, the British government did not favor political amalgamation of its remaining North America colonies. In 1784, New Brunswick and Cape Breton were separated from Nova Scotia, and each was given its own government. In 1791, Upper Canada as an English-speaking province was set apart from Lower Canada, which remained French. But the British reconsidered the role of region in creating people's attachment to the state. Significantly, Inglis had jurisdiction not only over Nova Scotia, but also Canada, Newfoundland, and New Brunswick. In April 1789, Inglis requested the establishment of a seminary so Nova Scotian children could be educated in "constitutional principles."[181] The Church would foster loyalty and prevent a second rebellion in North America.

The British government did not hesitate to provide provisions and land to ordinary white loyalists in North America. Indeed, the 30,000 exiles fit neatly into the larger project of British recolonization of Nova Scotia in the eighteenth century.[182] Loyalist settlers fulfilled the empire's persistent need for trustworthy subjects in its northern-most Atlantic domain. The white loyalist influx significantly strengthened the British position in the Maritimes. In 1755, the population of Nova Scotia and Cape Breton was 25,000. By 1767, in spite of the New Englanders' migration, the population was only 11,800; and in 1775, 20,000. The arrival of the loyalist refugees between 1775 and 1784 raised the population, so by 1791 the peninsula had 55,500 people (along with 1,500 more in Cape Breton); and by 1811, 70,000.

The loyalist exiles were the largest group who received British incentives to settle in the Maritimes. But they were not the first. Between 1750 and 1752, the British government—inspired by Pennsylvania's earlier successful example—directly encouraged the migration of 2,500 "foreign Protestants"—German and Swiss immigrants—to balance the existing Acadian population in the Maritimes. Importantly, this was not done through a chartered company or other intermediaries but directly under the auspices of the government. These Germans settled in Lunenberg, just west of Halifax, in one of the more fertile lands on the Atlantic shore. Although intended to be a long-term policy, the hostility from the Indians and the Acadians precluded further migration into the area. Some settlers deserted to the more secure and fertile colonies to the south.[183]

During the Seven Years' War, as anxieties about the security of the Maritimes escalated, the local British government ordered the deportation of the Acadians. In the context of war, their long-term neutrality became associated with treason. By the 1760s, the British had removed most of the region's French inhabitants and overpowered much of the local Micmac population. In their stead, the government encouraged New Englanders to settle on lands previously inhabited by the Acadians—this was cheaper than recruiting, shipping, and settling foreign Protestants from Europe. More than 7,000 farmers and fishermen (about 2,400 families) from New England settled in the region; and by 1775, they comprised as much as two-thirds of the population of Nova Scotia. In 1782 and 1783, the British assumed the same connection between landholding and allegiance as they had during the settlement of "foreign Protestants" in the 1750s. Land and loyalty were intimately connected. Whereas the British promised land to Germans to create loyalty, they granted land to American loyalists to reward loyalty.

The British hoped that Halifax, with loyalist leadership, would serve as an "entrepot" for North Atlantic commerce. Although ranked below the British West Indies, the security of the Maritimes was associated with the control of the Newfoundland fisheries as well as the preservation of the West Indies. With its nontropical climate and its access to fisheries and lumber, Nova Scotia would provide provisions to the sugar colonies in the Caribbean. But-tressed with thousands of proven loyalists, it would serve a crucial geopoliti-cal role in the reconfigured empire: as supplier to the valuable Caribbean Islands, as a check on the ambitions of the independent American states, and as a military and naval base in times of British warfare with the Caribbean.[184]

But the foundations of British and loyalist optimism about loyalist Nova Scotia were fragile. The linkage of land to allegiance was weak in a region that lacked land for subsistence or competency. When the fertility of the newly cleared lands was exhausted and the bounty from the government ceased, the difficulties only grew. Already in 1784, a British proclamation reassured the loyalists that the government would continue rations, recogniz-ing the "impracticability of the procuring subsistence from their lands until they are further cultivated . . ."[185] Some disappointed loyalists turned back to the United States to reestablish old connections. More avenues existed for the American loyalists than for the Germans in Lunenberg because of com-mercial, familial, and social networks created and nurtured in decades prior to the rebellion.

Overwhelmingly, the American loyalists were men and women of modest circumstances: tradesmen, laborers, carpenters, cordwainers. Their skills did not match the needs of the Nova Scotian landscape. Arriving from urban towns, many of the new immigrants to the Maritimes were inexperienced farmers. Some looked down on agricultural labor. Local consumption left little for export in the first years after the war.[186] Fishing remained more profitable than cultivating crops, and the high cost of growing grain could not compete with the lower cost and higher profits of raising cattle. In addition, the Nova Scotians found it easy to import provisions from the coastal towns in United States, just thirty miles south, where the flour was superior—and perhaps also cheaper because of the United States' reliance on slave labor.[187] Many loyalists drifted from county to county in search of work and led unhappy lives without community or security.

The exiles had chosen the empire for a multitude of reasons: some because they felt a sentimental attachment to the empire, others trusted the stability of British legal protection, and undoubtedly many because the British garrisons did not mandate military service and provided a better livelihood. Inconsequential in British political or military strategy, the loyalists had struggled to build and sustain a coalition during the war. Instead, the potential threat of a competing loyalist alliance may have worked to unite the rebels. In the Maritimes, however, the loyalists had a second chance. In the aftermath of the rebellion, the potential danger of an American invasion and British concerns about the volatility of the slave regime in the sugar islands led the predominantly white, English-speaking Maritime colonists to play a special role in the British Atlantic.

Notes

1. Nancy L. Rhoden, "Patriots, Villains, and the Quest for Liberty: How American Film Has Depicted the American Revolution," *Canadian Review of American Studies* 37, no. 2 (2007): 205–38.

2. Bernard Bailyn, *The Ordeal of Thomas Hutchinson* (Cambridge: Belknap Press, 1974).

3. Ibid., 17.

4. Ibid., 23.

5. Ruma Chopra, *Unnatural Rebellion: Loyalists in New York City during the Revolution* (Charlottesville: University of Virginia, 2011).

6. Richard B. Morris, "The American Revolution Comes to John Jay," in *Aspects of Early New York and Politics*, ed. Jacob Judd and Irwin H. Polishook (New York: Sleepy Hollow Restorations, 1974), 109.

7. Morris, "The American Revolution Comes to John Jay," 110, 113.

8. John A. Stevens Jr., ed., *Colonial Records of the New York Chamber of Commerce, 1768–1784 with Historical and Biographical Sketches* (New York: John F. Trow & Co., 1867, reprint 1971), 3.

9. Jason K. Duncan, Citizens or Papists: *The Politics of Anti-Catholicism in New York, 1685–1821* (New York: Fordham University Press, 2005), 35.

10. Rick James Ashton, "The Loyalist Experience: New York, 1763–1789," (Ph.D. dissertation, Northwestern University, 1973), 69.

11. Quoted in Larry R. Gerlach, *William Franklin: New Jersey's Last Royal Governor* (New Jersey Historical Commission, 1975), 26.

12. Quoted in Willard S. Randall, "William Franklin: The Making of a Conservative," in *The Loyalist Americans: A Focus on Greater New York*, ed. Robert A. East and Jacob Judd (Tarrytown: Sleepy Hollow Restorations, 1975), 69.

13. Quoted in Paul Wilderson, *Governor John Wentworth and the American Revolution* (Lebanon: University of New Hampshire Press, 1994), 268.

14. Quoted in Wilderson, *Governor John Wentworth*, 275.

15. Peter Marshall, "The British Empire: 10 Big Questions," *BBC History Magazine* (February 2012).

16. Linda Colley, *Britons: Forging the Nation, 1707–1837* (New Haven and London: Yale University Press, 1992), 18.

17. Ian Steele, "Empire of Migrants and Consumers: Some Current Atlantic Approaches to the History of Colonial Virginia," *Virginia Magazine of History and Biography* XCIX (1991): 496–97.

18. Maxine Berg, *Luxury and Pleasure in Eighteenth-Century Britain* (Oxford: Oxford University Press, 2005), 313.

19. Berg, *Luxury and Pleasure*, 279–83, 302–3, 298.

20. Berg, *Luxury and Pleasure*, 305–6.

21. Quoted in Mary Beth Norton, *Separated by Their Sex: Women in Public and Private in the Colonial Atlantic World* (Ithaca: Cornell University Press, 2011), 165.

22. Quoted in Norton, *Separated*, 166.

23. Daniel J. Hulsebosch, *Constituting Empire: New York and the Transformation of Constitutionalism in the Atlantic World, 1664–1830* (Chapel Hill: University of North Carolina Press, 2005), 5, 17; Daniel J. Hulsebosch, "Imperia in Imperio: The Multiple Constitutions of Empire in New York, 1750–1777," *Law and History Review* 16, no. 2 (1998): 341.

24. Ian K. Steele, "The Empire and Provincial Elites: An Interpretation of some recent writings on the English Atlantic," *Journal of Imperial and Commonwealth History* 8 (1979): 11.

25. Hulsebosch, *Constituting*, 32, 40; Daniel J. Hulsebosch, "The Constitution in the Glass Case and Constitutions in Action," *Law and History Review* 16, no. 2 (1998): 398.

26. Christopher L. Brown, "Empire Without Slaves: British Concepts of Emancipation in the age of the American Revolution," *William and Mary Quarterly* 562 (April 1999): 281.

27. Linda Colley, *Captives: Britain, Empire, and the World, 1600–1850* (New York: Anchor Books, 2004).

28. Elizabeth Mancke, "Chartered Enterprises and the Evolution of the British Atlantic World," in *The Creation of the British Atlantic World*, ed. Elizabeth Mancke and Carole Shammas (Baltimore: Johns Hopkins University Press, 2005), 258, 262. Significantly, the British government did not establish sovereignty over Natives (i.e., non-Europeans) in the way it protected French Catholics in Quebec; Philip Lawson, *A Taste for Empire and Glory: Studies in British Overseas Expansion, 1660–1800* (Norfolk, GB: Variorum, 1997).

29. Colley, *Captives*, quote from p. 202, population on p. 200; see also p. 164.

30. John Shy, "American Society and its War for Independence," in *Reconsiderations of the Revolutionary War: Selected Essays*, ed. Don Higginbotham (London: Greenwood Press, 1978), 76.

31. Steele, "The Empire and Provincial Elites," 3, 13.

32. Nicole Eustace, *Passion is the Gale: Emotion, Power, and the Coming of the American Revolution* (Chapel Hill: University of North Carolina Press, 2008). If the rebels began the war to stop the encroachment of power and to preserve virtue, they may have won the war by successfully transferring the authoritarian connotations associated with power to the passionate and sympathetic nuances associated with the patriot "spirit."

33. Stephen Conway, "From Fellow-Nationals to Foreigners: British Perceptions of the Americans, circa 1739–1783," *William and Mary Quarterly* 59, no. 1 (2002): 67.

34. Peter S. Onuf, *Jeffersonian America* (Oxford: Blackwell, 2002), 11.

35. Hugh Gaine printed his last New York City paper on September 9, 1776.

36. Paul Leicester Ford, ed., *The Journals of Hugh Gaine, Volume I* (New York: Dodd, Mead & Company, 1902), 4, 52; Alfred Lawrence Lorenz, *Hugh Gaine: A Colonial Printer-Editor's Odyssey to Loyalism* (Carbondale: Southern Illinois University Press, 1972), 2–24; Douglas C. McMurtrie, *A History of Printing in the United States: The Story of the Introduction of the Press and of its History and Influence during the Pioneer Period in Each State of the Union, Volume II: Middle and South Atlantic States* (New York: Burt Franklin, 1969), 154–56.

37. Janice Potter McKinnon and Robert M. Calhoon, "The Character and Coherence of the Loyalist Press," in *The Press and the American Revolution*, ed. Bernard Bailyn and John B. Hench (Worcester: AAS, 1980), 232; Ford, *Journals, Volume 1*, 51–54. Gaine published the proceedings of the Continental Congress in 1774 and 1775, and he advertised Thomas Paine's *Common Sense* in 1776. However, he also printed angry responses against the pamphlet.

38. Lorenz, *Hugh Gaine*, 76–82; Isiah Thomas, *The History of Printing in America, Volume II* (New York: Burt Franklin, 1874; reprint 1964), 110. Thomas argues that Gaine desired to side with the successful side. I argue that his move from New York City to Newark and his return to New York City demonstrate his uncertainty about which side would eventually prevail.

39. The Newark paper was published weekly between September 21 and November 2, 1776. Gaine had issued the New York City paper on Mondays and issued the Newark paper on Saturdays.

40. Ford, *Journals, Volume I*, 55.

41. Ira D. Gruber, *The Howe Brothers and the American Revolution* (New York: Atheneum, 1972), 195. Gruber notes that 4,836 colonists took an oath of loyalty to the Crown before the British defeat at Trenton, New Jersey, in December 1776.

42. Commissioners to Germain, December 22, 1776, K. G. Davis, ed., *Documents of the American Revolution, 1770–1783, Volume XII* (Dublin: Irish University Press, 1976), 274.

43. Andrew Jackson O'Shaugnessy, *An Empire Divided: The American Revolution and the British Caribbean* (Philadelphia: University of Pennsylvania Press, 2000), 251f; T. R. Clayton, "Sophistry, Security, and Socio-Political Structures in the American Revolution: or, Why Jamaica did not Rebel," *The Historical Journal* 29 (June 1986): 319.

44. Andrew J. O'Shaugnessy, "The Stamp Act Crisis in the British Caribbean," *William and Mary Quarterly* 51, no. 2 (1994): 209–16, 223, 225.

45. J. Leitch Wright, Jr., "Blacks in British East Florida," *Florida Historical Quarterly* 54, no. 4 (1976): 427; Linda K. Williams, "East Florida as a Loyalist Haven," *Florida Historical Quarterly* 54, no. 4 (1976): 471–74.

46. In terms of present-day Canadian territory, the colony of Quebec covered the provinces of Ontario and Quebec, and the colony of Nova Scotia included the provinces of New Brunswick and Nova Scotia.

47. Elizabeth Mancke, "Another British America: A Canadian Model for the Early Modern British Empire," *Journal of Imperial and Commonwealth History* 25 (1997): 3, 14, 8.

48. Elizabeth Mancke, "Early Modern Imperial Governance and the Origins of Canadian Political Culture," *Canadian Journal of Political Science* 32, no. 1 (1999): 17.

49. Mancke, "Another British America," 26, 14.

50. Julian Gwyn, "Economic Fluctuations in Nova Scotia," in *Making Adjustments: Change and Continuity in Planter Nova Scotia, 1759–1800*, ed. Margaret Conrad (Fredericton: Acadiensis, 1991), 86.

51. Gwyn, "Economic Fluctuations in Nova Scotia," 73.

52. Elizabeth Mancke, *The Fault Lines of Empire: Political Differentiation in Massachusetts and Nova Scotia, ca. 1760–1830* (New York: Routledge, 2005), 17, 141, 162; Elizabeth Mancke, "Elites, States, and the Imperial Governance Conquest of Acadia," in *The "Conquest" of Acadia, 1710: Imperial, Colonial, and Aboriginal Constructions*, ed. John C. Reid, Maurice Basque, Elizabeth Mancke, Barry Moody, Geoffrey Plank, and William Wicken (Toronto: University of Toronto Press, 2004), 27, 46.

53. Graeme Wynn, "A Region of Scattered Settlements and Bounded Possibilities: Northeastern North America, 1775–1800," *Canadian Geographer* 31, no. 4 (1987): 319.

54. Graeme Wynn, "A Province too much Dependent on New England," *Canadian Geographer* 31 (1987): 108.

55. John Shy, *Toward Lexington: The Role of the British Army in the Coming of the American Revolution* (Princeton: Princeton University Press, 1965), 67; John Shy,

"Thomas Gage: Weak Link of Empire," in *George Washington's Opponents: British Generals and Admirals in the American Revolution*, ed. George Athan Billias (New York: William Morrow and Company, Inc., 1969), 11.

56. Robert M. Calhoon, *Loyalist Perception and Other Essays* (Columbia: University of South Carolina Press, 1989), 74. John Jay supported Galloway's Plan in 1774.

57. Ned Landsman, "The Legacy of British Union for the North American Colonies: Provincial Elites and the Problem of Imperial Union," in *A Union for Empire: Political Thought and the British Union of 1707*, ed. John Robertson (Cambridge: Cambridge University Press, 1995), 302–9.

58. Darrel Butler, "Ward Chipman Senior: A Founding Father of New Brunswick," in *Eleven Exiles: Accounts of Loyalists of the American Revolution*, ed. Phyllis R. Blakeley and John N. Grant (Toronto: Dundurn Press, 1982), 147–48.

59. Jonathan Sewell, Plan of Union, 1785, in *Anglo-American Union*, 158. This plan has been misattributed to Galloway and was written by Sewell.

60. Sewell, in *Anglo-American Union*, 157–58.

61. Sewell, in *Anglo-American Union*, 164.

62. Sewell and Robinson, 1824 Plan of Union, 38.

63. Sewell and Robinson, 1824 Plan of Union, 41.

64. Potter and Calhoon, "Character and Coherence of the Loyalist Press," 233.

65. Janice Potter-McKinnon and Calhoon, "Character and Coherence of the Loyalist Press," 234. Loyalist newspapers included the *Newport Gazette* in Rhode Island, the *Pennsylvania Evening Post*, and other papers in southern garrisons.

66. John Dyke Ackland to Richard Howe, January 6, 1778, Sir Henry Clinton Papers, Clements Library, Ann Arbor, Michigan.

67. "Integer," *New York Gazette and Weekly Mercury*, March 3, 1777.

68. *New York Gazette and Weekly Mercury*, January 13, 1777; October 7, 1776; February 3, 1777.

69. "Benevolus," *New York Gazette and Weekly Mercury*, October 7, 1776.

70. *New York Gazette and Weekly Mercury*, February 17, 1777.

71. Catherine Le Courreye Blecki and Karen A. Wulf, eds., *Milcah Martha Moore's Book: A Commonplace Book from Revolutionary America* (University Park: Pennsylvania State University Press, 1997), 39.

72. A. Glenn Clothers, "Northern Virginia's Quakers and the War for Independence: Seeing a Path of Virtue in the Revolutionary World," in Joseph S. Tiedemann, *The Other Loyalists: Ordinary People, Royalism, and the Revolution in the Middle Colonies, 1763–1787* (Albany: SUNY, 2009), 106; Blecki and Wulf, *Milcah Martha Moore's Book*, 40–41; Robert Scott Davis, "Children of Dissent and Revolution: Joseph Maddock and the Wrightsborough, George, Quaker Community," in *Quaker History* 99, no. 1 (2010): 9.

73. John Frederick Woolverton, *Colonial Anglicanism in North America* (Detroit: Wayne State University Press, 1984), 232; also see Robert Calhoon and Ruma Chopra, "Religion and Loyalism," *Faith and Founders of the American Republic* (Oxford: Oxford University Press, 2013)].

74. Schlenter, "Religious Faith and Commercial Empire,"145–46; in contrast, Roger Finke and Rodney Stark note that 85 percent were non-Anglicans. See *The Churching of America, 1776–2005: Winners and Losers in our Religious Economy* (New Brunswick: Rutgers Press, 2005).

75. S. Charles Bolton, *Southern Anglicanism: The Church of England in Colonial South Carolina* (Santa Barbara, CA: Praeger, 1982), 5–6, 13–14.

76. Charles Inglis, October 31, 1776, in *The Life and Letters of Charles Inglis: His Ministry in America and Consecration as First Colonial Bishop, from 1759 to 1787*, 159.

77. Charles Inglis, "The True Interest of America Impartially Stated, in Certain Strictures on a Pamphlet Intitled Common Sense," in *Common Sense: Thomas Paine*, ed. Edward Larkin (Toronto: Broadview Editions, 2004), 151, 155, 157, 152.

78. Paul Smith, "The American Loyalists: Notes on their Organization and Numerical Strength," *William and Mary Quarterly* 25, no. 2 (April 1968).

79. John Shy, "Introduction," in *War and Society in the American Revolution: Mobilization and Home Fronts*, ed. John Resch and Walter Sargent (Dekalb: North Illinois University Press, 2007), 13.

80. Robert M. Calhoon, *Tory Insurgents:The Loyalist Perception and Other Essays, Revised and Expanded Edition* (Columbia: University of South Carolina Press, 2010), 232.

81. Philip D. Morgan and Andrew Jackson O'Shaugnessy, "Arming Slaves in the American Revolution," in *Arming Slaves: From Classical Times to the Modern Age*, ed. Christopher Leslie Brown and Philip D. Morgan (New Haven: Yale University Press), 187.

82. Smith, "The American Loyalists," 269.

83. Stephen Conway, "The British Army, 'Military Europe,' and the American War of Independence," *William and Mary Quarterly* 67, no. 1 (2010).

84. Sir Henry Clinton, March 8, 1776, Clinton Papers, Clements Library.

85. Chopra, *Unnatural Rebellion*, 218.

86. Conway, "The British Army," 78.

87. Paul Smith, *Loyalists and Redcoats: A Study in British Revolutionary Policy* (Chapel Hill: Omohundro, University of North Carolina Press, 1964), 34.

88. Quoted in Claude Van Tyne, *The Loyalists in the American Revolution* (New York: Macmillan, 1902), 147.

89. Todd W. Braisted, "Bergen's Loyalists," in *The Revolutionary War in Bergen County: The Times that Tried Men's Souls*, ed. Carol Karels (Charleston: History Press, 2007), 66–73.

90. Robert S. Allen, *The Loyal Americans: The Military Role of the Loyalist Provincial Corps and Their Settlement in British North America, 1775–1784* (Ottawa: National Museum of Man/National Museums of Canada, 1983), 12.

91. Robert N. Calhoon, *Political Moderation in America's First Two Centuries* (New York: Cambridge University Press, 2009), 151–53.

92. Albert H. Tillson Jr., "The Localist Roots of Backcountry Loyalism: An Examination of Popular Political Culture in Virginia's New River Valley," *Journal of Southern History* 54, no. 3 (1988): 404.

93. Jack Greene, "Independence, Improvement and Authority: Toward a Framework for Understanding the Histories of the Southern Backcountry during the Era of the American Revolution," in *An Uncivil War: The Southern Backcountry during the American Revolution*, ed. Ronald Hoffman, Thad W. Tate, and Peter J. Albert (Charlottesville: University of Virginia Press, 1985), 34.

94. Hoffman, "Introduction," in *An Uncivil War*, xiv.

95. Calhoon, "Loyalism and Patriotism Askance," in *Tory Insurgents*, 230–31.

96. Edward H. Tatum Jr., ed., *The American Journal of Ambrose Serle, Secretary to Lord Howe, 1776–1778* (San Marino: The Huntington Library, 1940), 104.

97. E. P. Thompson, *Customs in Common* (New York: The New Press, 1991), 332.

98. Janice Potter-Mckinnon argues that loyalist women continued to live under a more patriarchal regime than rebel women. See Potter-MacKinnon, "Loyalists and Community: The Eastern Ontario Loyalist Women," in *Loyalists and Community in North America*, ed. Robert M. Calhoon, Timothy M. Barnes, and George A. Rawlyk (Westport: Greenwood Press, 1994).

99. Frederick Bernays Wiener, "The Military Occupation of Philadelphia in 1777–1778," in *Proceedings of the American Philosophical Society* 111 (1967): 310–11. During the British occupation of Philadelphia, the British court tried Mary Fygis for perjury and Mary Collins for receiving stolen goods.

100. Beverly Baxter, "Grace Growden Galloway: Survival of a Loyalist, 1778–79," *Frontiers: A Journal of Women's Studies* 3, no. 1 (1978): 62.

101. Baxter, "Grace Growden Galloway," 66–67; Linda K. Kerber, *Towards an Intellectual History of Women* (Chapel Hill: University of North Carolina Press, 1997), 278–79, 296n.

102. Cited in Norton, *Separated*, 167; also see Laurel T. Ulrich, "Daughters of Liberty: Religious Women in Revolutionary New England," in *Women in the Age of the American Revolution*, ed. Ronald Hoffman and Peter J. Albert (Charlottesville: University of Virginia Press, 1989), 213.

103. Blecki and Wulf, *Milcah Martha Moore's Book*, 42.

104. Blecki and Wulf, *Milcah Martha Moore's Book*, 84–86.

105. Ruma Chopra, *Unnatural Rebellion: Loyalists in New York City During the American Revolution* (Charlottesville: University of Virginia Press, 2011), 100.

106. Sarah C. Chambers and Lisa Norling, "Choosing to be a Subject: Loyalist Women in the Revolutionary Atlantic World," *Journal of Women's History* 20, no. 1 (2008): 39–44.

107. Quoted in Chambers and Norling, "Choosing to be a Subject," 39. The letter was written in August 1789 from Boston.

108. E. C. Wright, "Red, White, and Black Loyalists," in *1776: The British Story of the American Revolution* (London: National Maritime Museum, 1976), 129.

109. Eliza Byles, September 29, 1778, in MG 1, vol. 163, #4, in Nova Scotia Archives, Halifax.

110. Graham Russell Hodges, *The Black Loyalist Directory: African Americans in Exile after the American Revolution* (New York: Garland Publishers, 1996), xiv.

111. Quoted in Simon Schama, *Rough Crossings: Britain, the Slaves, and the American Revolution* (New York: HarperCollins, 2006), 112.

112. Schama, *Rough Crossings*, 5.

113. William Smith, July 1780, Sir Henry Clinton Papers, Clements Library.

114. James W. Walker, "Blacks as American Loyalists; The Slaves' War for Independence," *Historical Reflections* 2, no. 2 (1975): 54.

115. Christopher L. Brown, "Empire Without Slaves: British Concepts of Emancipation in the Age of the American Revolution," *William and Mary Quarterly* 562, no. 2 (1999): 274.

116. By the end of the revolution, smallpox took 130,000 American lives, mostly Indian. See Alan Taylor, *Writing Early American History* (Philadelphia: University of Pennsylvania, 2005), 32.

117. Schama, *Rough Crossings*, 113, 112. Christopher Leslie Brown also suggests that the chance to bear arms in some instances meant an opportunity for enslaved men to assert control over women, both slave and free. See "The Arming of Slaves in Comparative Perspective," in *Arming Slaves: From Classical Times to the Modern Age*, ed. Christopher Leslie Brown and Philip D. Morgan (New Haven: Yale, 2006), 341.

118. Graham R. Hodges, *Slavery and Freedom in the Rural North: African Americans in Monmouth County, New Jersey, 1665–1865* (Madison: Madison House, 1997), 91.

119. David J. Fowler, "Loyalty is Now Bleeding in New Jersey: Motivations and Mentalities of the Disaffected," in Tiedemann, *The Other Loyalists*, 59.

120. Hodges, *Slavery and Freedom in the Rural North*, 92–102.

121. Chopra, *Unnatural Rebellion*, 270.

122. Walker, "Blacks as American Loyalists," 56.

123. His Excellency Sir Guy Carleton's Orders, May 11, 1783, in Carleton Papers.

124. His Excellency Sir Guy Carleton's Orders, May 11, 1783, in Carleton Papers.

125. His Excellency Sir Guy Carleton's Orders, July 18, 1783, and July 22, 1783, in Carleton Papers.

126. Walker, "Blacks as American Loyalists," 60.

127. Dunmore to Secretary of State, February 5, 1782, cited in Ellen Gibson Wilson, *The Loyal Blacks* (New York: Capricorn, 1976), 27.

128. William Smith Jr., Diary, December 17, 1778, in "The Diary of William Smith, August 26, 1778, to December 31, 1779," ed. Arthur James Acton (Ph.D. dissertation, University of Michigan, 1970), 90.

129. Christopher L. Brown, "From Slaves to Subjects: Envisioning an Empire Without Slavery," in *Black Experience and the Empire*, ed. Philip D. Morgan and Sean Hawkins (Oxford: Oxford University Press, 2004), 133.

130. Quoted in Colin G. Calloway, *The American Revolution in Indian Country: Crisis and Diversity in Native American Communities* (New York: Cambridge University Press, 1995), 28.

131. Calhoon, *Tory Insurgents*, xiv; Calloway, *The American Revolution in Indian Country*, 26; Colley, *Captives*, 164, 202.

132. Quoted in Calloway, *The American Revolution in Indian Country*, 63.

133. Calloway, *The American Revolution in Indian Country*, 31.

134. Colin G. Calloway, "'We Have Always Been the Frontier': The American Revolution in Shawnee Country," *American Indian Quarterly* 16, no. 1 (1992).

135. Wayne E. Lee, *Barbarians and Brothers: Anglo-American Warfare, 1500–1865* (Oxford: Oxford University Press, 2011), 216–17; James Merrell, "Amerindians and the New Republic," in *A Companion to the American Revolution*, ed. Jack P. Green and J. R. Pole (Malden: Blackwell, 2000), 392. The Stockbridge Indians of New England served as scouts for the Continental army, and the Catawbas in the Carolinas supported the rebels.

136. Carol Berkin, *Revolutionary Mothers: Women in the Struggle for America's Independence* (New York: Knopf, 2005), 110.

137. Inglis, June 15, 1770, in *The Life and Letters of Charles Inglis*, 101.

138. Inglis, March 8, 1770, in *The Life and Letters of Charles Inglis*, 94.

139. Milledge L. Bonham Jr., "The Religious Side of Joseph Brant," *Journal of Religion* 9, no. 3 (July 1929): 403, 414.

140. Berkin, *Revolutionary Mothers: Women in the Struggle for America's Independence* (New York: Knopf, 1995), 114.

141. Lee, *Barbarians and Brothers*, 215.

142. Lee, *Barbarians and Brothers*, 226.

143. John Grenier, *The First Way of War: American War Making on the Frontier, 1607–1814* (Cambridge: Cambridge University Press, 2008).

144. Quoted in Calloway, *The American Revolution in Indian Country*, 51.

145. Lee, *Barbarians and Brothers*, 221.

146. Lee, *Barbarians and Brothers*, 230.

147. William Tryon to George Germain, December 24, 1778, in *Documents of the American Revolution* XV, ed. K. G. Davies (Shannon: Irish University Press, 1976), 297.

148. Quoted in Merrell, "Amerindians in the New Republic," 393.

149. Alan Taylor, "The Divided Ground: Upper Canada, New York, and the Iroqouis Six Nations, 1783–1815," *Journal of the Early Republic* 22 (2002): 58.

150. John H. Travis, "Memoirs of Stephen Allen," New York Historical Society (June 1826), 32.

151. *Royal American Gazette*, December 26, 1782.

152. Most states repealed laws against loyalists by 1788—New York was the last; see E. Wilder Spaulding, *New York in the Critical Period, 1783–1789* (New York: Columbia University Press, 1932), 119.

153. Spaulding, *New York in the Critical Period*, 117.

154. Edward Countryman, *A People in Revolution: the American Revolution and Political Society in New York, 1760–1790* (New York: W. W. Norton, 1981), 174, 238.

155. British Headquarters Papers, PRO 30/55/85, Kew, England.

156. Aaron N. Coleman, "Loyalists in War, Americans in Peace: The Reintegration of the American Loyalists, 1775–1800" (unpublished Ph.D. dissertation, University of Kentucky, 2008), 134, 232.

157. Quoted in Wilson, *The Loyal Blacks*, 41.

158. Maya Jasanoff, *Liberty's Exiles: American Loyalists in the Revolutionary World* (Vintage, 2012), 358.

159. Charles R. Ritcheson, "'Loyalist Influence' on British Policy Toward the United States After the American Revolution," *Eighteenth Century Studies* 7 (Autumn 1973): 10.

160. John Eardley-Wilmot, *Historical View of the Commission for Enquiring into the Losses, Services, and Claims of the American Loyalists, at the Close of the War Between Great Britain and her Colonies, in 1783*, ed. George Athan Billias (Boston: Gregg Press, 1972), 188.

161. Ritcheson, "Loyalist Influence," 6–7.

162. Jasanoff, *Liberty's Exiles*, 354.

163. Moore, *The Loyalists: Revolution, Exile, Settlement* (Toronto: McClelland & Stewart, 1994, 104; Jasanoff, *Liberty's Exiles*, 356–57).

164. Williams, "East Florida as a Loyalist Haven," 475; Jasanoff, *Liberty's Exiles*, 354. More than thirty years earlier, Williams estimated 17,000 refugees.

165. Williams, "East Florida as a Loyalist Haven," 474.

166. Quoted in Mary Louise Clifford, *From Slavery to Freetown: Black Loyalists After the American Revolution* (Jefferson: McFarland, 1999), 33.

167. Quoted in Wilson, *The Loyal Blacks*, 56. In a letter written to Carleton in August 1783, Lord North explained that the "The removal of the Negroes whom you found in possession of their freedom upon your arrival at New York . . . is certainly an act of justice due to them from us, nor do I see, that the removal of those Negroes, who had been made free before the execution of the preliminaries of peace, can be deemed any infraction of the treaty."

168. Jasanoff, *Liberty's Exiles*, 71.

169. Hodges et al., *Black Loyalist Directory*, xix.

170. Mary Beth Norton, "The Fate of Some Black Loyalists of the American Revolution," *Journal of Negro History* 58, no. 4 (1973): 404; Julain Gywn, "Economic Fluctuations," 69, 71. In 1755, Nova Scotia and Cape Breton had 25,000 inhabitants: of these, 14,000 were Acadians, fewer than 3,800 were English (including soldiers), 1,600 were Germans, and 2,000 were Micmacs.

171. Quoted in Norton, "Fate of Some Black Loyalists," 404.

172. Morgan and O'Shaugnessy, "Arming Slaves," 200.

173. Clifford, *From Slavery to Freetown*, 44; Jeffers Lennox, "Crossing Borders, Changing Worlds: Eighteenth-Century Nova Scotia's Atlantic Connections," *Journal of Canadian Studies* 42, no. 1 (2008): 217.

174. Quoted in Harvey Amani Whitfield, *Blacks on the Border: The Black Refugees in British North America, 1815–1860* (Burlington: University of Vermont Press, 2006), 20.

175. Mather Byles letter to his sisters, November 22, 1783, in MG 1, vol. 163, #1–7, PAC.

176. John G. Reid, "Pax Brittanica or Pax Indegena? Planter Nova Scotia (1760–1782) and Competing Strategies of Pacification," *Canadian Historical Review* 85, no. 4 (2004): 689.

177. July 12, 1783, Brook Watson to Joshua Mauger, Mauger Papers, Gilder Lehrman, NYHS.

178. Nova Scotia Charter, 1785, Halifax Public Archives, MG 23 C 20.

179. Edward Winslow to John Wentworth, November 27, 1784, in *Winslow Papers*, 251.

180. Edward Winslow to his wife, September 25, 1784, Halifax, in *Winslow Papers*, 233.

181. Inglis to Archbishop, April 20, 1789, Halifax Public Archives, MG1, vol. 479a, vol. 1.

182. The word "recolonization" comes from vol. 9 of Lawrence Henry Gipson's fifteen-volume study of the eighteenth century.

183. Stephen J. Hornsby, *British Atlantic, American Frontier* (Hanover, NH: University Press of New England, 2005), 208; Winthrop P. Bell, *The Foreign Protestants and the Settlement of Nova Scotia: The History of a Piece of Arrested British Colonial Policy in the Eighteenth Century* (Toronto: University of Toronto Press, 1961), 110.

184. Richard J. Uniacke, February 10, 1806, Halifax Public Archives, MG1, vol. 1769, File #4.

185. Major General John Campbell, March 30, 1784, Microfilm B-1035, PAC.

186. Wynn, "A Region of Scattered Settlements," 326.

187. Gerald S. Graham, *Sea Power and British North America, 1783–1820: A Study in British Colonial Policy* (New York: Greenwood Press, 1941), 149.

CHAPTER ONE

Loyalist Predicament

Defining Loyalists and Patriots

Introduction

One of the signers of the Declaration of Independence, Dr. Benjamin Rush of Pennsylvania, differentiated rebels (Whigs) from loyalists (also called Tories) based on their background, motives, and fears. In this excerpt, Rush helps us to see the range of motives, both personal and political, that drove colonists to choose sides. As importantly, Rush identifies a third group in the American colonies, the undecided majority who avoided making a definitive choice.

I had frequent reason to observe that the Tories and Whigs were actuated by very different motives in their conduct, or by the same motives acting in different degrees of force. . . . There were Tories (1) from an attachment to power and office. (2) From an attachment to the British commerce which the war had interrupted or annihilated. (3) From an attachment to kingly government. (4) From an attachment to the hierarchy of the Church of England, which it was supposed would be abolished in America by her separation from Great Britain. This motive acted chiefly upon the Episcopal clergy, more especially in the Eastern states. (5) From a dread of the power of the country being transferred into the hands of the Presbyterians. This motive acted upon many of the Quakers in Pennsylvania and New Jersey, and upon the Episcopalians in several of those states where they had been in possession of power, or of a religious establishment.

It cannot be denied, but that private and personal consideration actuated some of those men who took a part in favor of the American Revolution. There were Whigs (1) from a desire of possessing, or at least sharing, in the power of our country. It was said there were Whigs (2) from an expectation that a war with Great Britain would cancel all British debts. There certainly were Whigs (3) from the facility with which the tender laws enabled debtors to pay their creditors in depreciated paper money. (4) A few men were Whigs from ancient or hereditary hostility to persons, or families who were Tories. But a great majority of the people who took part with their country were Whigs (5) from a sincere and disinterested love of liberty and justice.

Both parties differed as much in their conduct as they did in the motives which actuated them. There were (1) furious Tories who had recourse to violence, and even to arms, to oppose the measures of the Whigs. (2) Writing and talking Tories. (3) Silent but busy Tories in disseminating Tory pamphlets and news papers and in circulating intelligence. (4) Peaceable and conscientious Tories who patiently submitted to the measures of the governing powers, and who shewed nearly equal kindness to the distressed of both parties during the war.

The Whigs were divided by their conduct into (1) Furious Whigs, who considered the tarring and feathering of a Tory as a greater duty and exploit than the extermination of a British army. These men were generally cowards, and shrunk from danger when called into the field by pretending sickness or some family disaster. (2) Speculating Whigs. These men infested our public councils, as well as the army, and did the country great mischief. A colonel of a regiment informed a friend of mine that he had made a great deal of money by buying poor horses for his waggon, and selling them again for a large profit after he had fattened them at the public expense. (3) Timid Whigs. The hopes of these people rose and fell with every victory and defeat of our armies. (4) Staunch Whigs. These were moderate in their tempers, but firm, inflexible, and persevering in their conduct. There was, besides these two classes of people, a great number of persons who were neither Whigs nor Tories. They had no fixed principles and accommodated their conduct to their interest, to events, and to their company. They were not without their uses. They protected both parties in many instances from the rage of each other, and each party always found hospitable treatment from them.[1]

Confronting Rage (1774)

Introduction

Henry Hulton came to Boston in November 1767 as an agent of empire, part of a five-man commission sent to prevent smuggling in the colonies. This excerpt, from September 1774, describes the spread of mob violence in towns around Massachusetts. When Hulton left for England, the rebel government confiscated his home and sold it at a public auction.

In most of the towns they had now erected very high Liberty poles, to serve as Beacons, or signals, and if any one was refractory, or did not submit to the demands of the People, it was usual to hoist him up on the pole till he complyed.

Mr. [Timothy] Ruggles of Hardwick, one of the Council, having sheltered himself in Boston, the people vented some of their resentment against him, on a fine Stallion of his, which was esteemed of great value. This horse they poisoned.

Colonel Gilbert, who was a friend of Governor Hutchinson's, and a reputed Tory, whilst he was in an Inn on a journey, and his horse was at the door, the people took off the saddle, and drove nails through it so that when he mounted, the nails pierced the horse which reared, and threw him off, whereby his Collarbone was broke.

A little boy belonging to the Admiral's Ship, was thrown down by a person who swore he would break his leg, and then he took it up, and wrenched it til it snap[p]ed.

Another little boy, a child of Captain Holland's, the Engineer, was seized at his own door by a man who with both his hands[,] squeezed his throat till he had almost throt[t] led him, saying, he was a tory child and should be served so.

Mrs. Oliver, the wife of the chief justice, was not allowed to come to Boston to her husband, nor suffered to write to him.

When the people visited Mr. [Daniel] Leonard's house, one of the Council, several shots were fired into one of the Chambers where he was suspected to be hid.

Dr. Russel of Lincoln, who had given offence, as being a reputed tory, had his chaise fired at one evening, when another person was in it, and the ball passed between the young Gentleman's legs who was in the Chaise.

It were endless to relate all the various modes of persecution, and torture, practised on those who were deemed by the People unfriendly to American liberty.

A poor aged person in Connecticut, who had been severely treated by his breech being pounded on a stone hearth, was in great danger of his life, from the severity of the blows. One Dr. Beiby, who was sent for to attend him, expressing himself with some warmth at the cruelty and inhumanity of the treatment, was seized by the people, strip[p]ed, had hot pitch poured over him, then he was taken into the swine sty, and there rolled in their filth, and had it cram[m]ed into his throat, and Eyes.

One Man was sowed up in the skin of an Ox, just fleed, with the entrails in it. Some were put upon long pieces of sharp wood, and hoisted up and let down again, and tortured for some time in this manner, to the diversion of the people; some were tied by the hair of the head to an horse's tail, and dragged along in this manner. One person was confined for several hours in a chamber with a smoky fire, and the chimney stopt at the top, so that he had near perished with the smoke; some were repeatedly doused out of a boat into the water, till they were near drowned, to make them renounce their opinions, and subscribe to the terms imposed upon them.

The Independant Ministers kept the people's passions ever in a flame, by their prayers and sermons: fast days, and days of prayer, were often held; they roused the people's resentment against the King, and Parliament, whom they charged with every thing tyrannical, and unjust; then expostulated with the Almighty, as being his chosen race, that he should not leave them, and urged the people to fight and die for their liberties. One of these pious Ministers concluded a prayer with "and we pray, O Lord, thou wouldst take all the Tories both here and at home, and bind them hand and foot, and cast them into the bottomless Pit, where the smoke of their torments may ascend for ever and ever."[2]

Forced into Exile (1775)

Introduction

George Chalmers, a lawyer from England, arrived in Maryland in 1763. He fled to England in 1775 when the outbreak of revolutionary hostilities made it impossible for prominent loyalists to remain in the colonies. Chalmers remained bitter about his losses and his treatment during the war, and resisted any alliance between the United States and Great Britain after the rebellion. This perhaps provides an account of his loyalty during 1774–1775.

21st Nov 1783.

George Chalmers Esq—the Claimant—sworn.

Says he went to settle in Maryland in Augt 1763 & says that in no one instance has he ever swerved from his Loyalty & that his whole Conduct from May 1774 has been one continued exertion on the behalf of Great Britain. With the view of assisting this Country he furnished the Loyalists with arguments to enable them to support the Cause of Britain as they used to apply to him when they were at a Difficulty to answer the arguments of their Opponents. He not only furnished them with Arguments but shew'd them by his own example that they ought not to yield any obedience to the usurped powers or to sign any Association against this Country.

At the first great meeting of Baltimore County in May 1774 (when he dates the commencement of the troubles in ye province of Maryland) He attended in concert with the principal friends of the British Govt in order to act as the principal Speaker in favor of the Govt in opposition to the endeavours of the rebels. When he went to this Meeting he found the leaders of the Opposition had brought the principal Lawyers from Anapolis to support them as they were apprehensive their own Numbers & Talents would be insufficient to carry the point they aim'd at. There were several inflammatory Speeches made by a Mr Alexander. Says that he retired to his own House which was near the Meeting in order to refresh himself it being very hot. On his return thither he met Mr Thompson who was bloody & dishevel'd & was by him informed that on his speaking in Opposition to Mr Alexander & his friends a Tumult had arisen & they had attempted to throw him out of the Window or over the Stair Case. In consequence of this Information Claimant abstain'd from going again to the Meeting which he says was very fortunate for him as he afterwards learned that there had been a Plot concerted to throw him out of the Court House Window in case he should make a Speech there And from the Violence he observed at the Meeting & their treatment of Mr Thompson he entertains no Doubt they would have carried their intentions into execution. From this time neither himself nor any of the friends of Govt attended any Meeting As they had tried alone what could be done & found great Danger & no benefit from it. Says that in consequence of the above tumult Challenges pass'd between the Parties & he himself carried one of the Challenges. From this time he thought it necessary whenever he went out to carry Pistols for his Defence & likewise to have them by his bed side at Night As he consider'd his Life to be in Danger from the violence of the Opposers of the British Govt owing to the decided part he had taken in its favor.

When he found the antient Govt was overturned he endeavour'd to promote at Baltimore Town an Association among the friends of Govt for their mutual protection. It was a part of this plan which he concerted with Mr Christie to bring about a Change in the Commission of the peace As the then justices were of the most inflammatory part of the people. By an application to the Govr this matter was brought about & better and abler Men were substituted in their Room. This made so great a Noise in the province that the Claimant is of Opinion had it been discover'd before he quitted the Province that he was the principal Promoter of the Plan he should have been massacred. This measure of changing the Commn of the peace was not meant merely to change the Men but as part of a plan whereby it was intended that the Associators should act as the posse comitatus in dispersing by force any Mob when they were called upon by the High Sheriff (who was a loyal Subject) so to do. He therefore was deputed to apply to the Govr for some stands of the Province Arms. The Govr highly approved of the Plan & furnish'd the Arms—but they were never sent—as he believes the Govr on considering the Matter more coolly was of opinion that if it should be discover'd that he had furnished the friends of Govt with Arms it would render him very unpopular throughout the Province. This was in the beginning of the Year 1775.

Says he considers himself as having been put to considerable Risque by giving his Advice to the Revd Mr Edmiston when he was brought to Baltimore Town by the Committee for his Opposition to the British Govt. And he likewise visited Mr Christie who was under the Custody of a Serjts Guard on acct of his having written a Letter (which was intercepted) which offended the Committee.

Says he acted as a Lawyer in the usual mode of practice in America in the double Capacity of an Attorney & Counsellor in the difft Courts & says that in the Year 1773 the emoluments of his profession were £354 Sterg And doubts not he would have made as much or more in the successive Years had not the Troubles broke out.

Says he left Maryland in Septr & arrived in Engd in Novr 1775 & in ye Year 1774 he recd from the Treasury an Annuity of £100 a Year (with a retrospect for one Year) which he still continues to receive. The Claimant requests that his Services may be compensated by an Annuity of £300 a Year but does not ask of Govt any other Compensation. He waves all other Claim for Losses but from his Loss of Profession.

The Revd Willm Edmiston—late of Baltimore County in Maryland—sworn.

Says he was very intimately acquainted with the Claimant & lived in the same County with him. Says the Claimant was a Man of distinguish'd Loyalty throughout the whole of the troubles And he apprehends he was of material Use to this Country by his exertions. He acted with great personal fairness & is of Opinion that his person was thereby endanger'd.

Says he remembers Mr Chalmers practising in the Commissary's Court. He remembers a Conversation he once had with Mr Dulany the Head of that Court who said Mr Chalmers came before him better prepared than any other Lawyer who attended the Court. And the Witness is of Opinion he was in a very rising Situation in his profession.

He says he is of Opinion that had not the troubles arisen the Claimant would have been one of the first Lawyers in the Province & has had frequent Conversations with the first people of the Province who all concurred in the same Sentiment. Witness says he has known the Claimant from 1769 & from that time has never known him do anything but what was perfectly honorable & just. He was a Man of excellent Character.

Witness says he was called before the Committee of Baltimore County who gave him two Hours to consider of the Answer he was to give to the Questions they had put to him. He sent on this Occasion to Mr Chalmers to advise with him as a friend but doubted whether he would come to him owing to the violence of the people. The Claimant however did come to him & he considers by so doing that he ran a great personal risque.

Says he has been informed by Mr Lawson with whom he had conversed on the Subject of the Claimant's professional Claims—that his Tobacco fees were about 60000 Weight of Tobacco And adds that his profession produced him a sufficient Income to maintain him in a very genteel Situation.

Being asked whether Mr Chalmers lived at the rate of £350 a Yr in Maryland He says certainly not that he could not spend so much. The Expences of living in Maryland were so very reasonable.[3]

Guilty until Proven Innocent (1776)

Introduction
Circulated in June 1776, the following excerpt from New York City high-lights the aggression loyalists faced after the battles of Lexington and Concord. Determined to root out "enemies" within their midst, rebel leaders identified and punished those who were neutral as well as those who were loyal. Those considered enemies were variously ridiculed, tarred and feathered, jailed, or banished from local communities.

To Oliver DeLancey, Esquire—by virtue of the authority vested in us by certain resolution of the Congress of the colony of New York of the fifth day of June in 1776—there are in this colony, divers persons, who by reason of their holding offices from the King of Great-Britain; from their having neglected or refused to associate with their fellow citizens for the defense of their common rights; from their having never manifested by their conduct a zeal for, and an attachment to the American cause; or from their having maintained an equivocal neutrality, have been considered by their countrymen in a suspicious light; whereby it hath become necessary, as well for the safety, as for the satisfaction of the people, who in times so dangerous and critical, are naturally led to consider those as their enemies, who withhold from them their aid and influence; that certain persons, in the said resolutions, named _____ who are generally supposed . . .

[We] summon you to appear—to shew cause why you should be considered as a friend to the American cause, and of the number of those who are ready to risque their lives and fortunes in defence of the rights and liberties of America, against the usurpation, unjust claims and cruel oppressions of the British Parliament; which rights and liberties, and which unjust claims and cruel oppressions, are, as aforesaid, specified and stated in divers Addresses, Petitions, and Resolutions of the present and late Continental Congress.[4]

An Affair among Citizens (1776)

Introduction
The excerpted account from New York loyalist Christopher Benson, written on June 16, 1776, describes attacks against those marked as enemies of American liberty. Benson notes that George Washington's army offered no protection to loyalist civilians.

That on Monday night last about eleven o'clock a number of people to the number of two hundred or upwards came in a riotous or tumultuous manner to the street door of the deponent's house in John's Street in the city of New York, that the deponent having been informed they were coming to attack

him and that they had threatened to put him to death stood at his door with
a sword determined to defend himself as well as he could that the said mob
having first called on the deponent to come out declaring they would kill
him for a damned Tory, began pelting him with stones, one of which struck
the deponent on his forehead . . . That on the evening of the next Day being
Tuesday . . . the deponent heard a great noise near Leary Street and plainly
distinguished a cry of "Now for Bensons" and was soon after informed that
the mob were coming again to the deponent's house . . . thereupon the deponent . . . escaped to a friend's house where he staid [sic] that night that
the next morning the deponent went home again, but about 12 o'clock that
day the deponent was informed that the Grenadiers were just coming to
take the deponent that the deponent immediately looked out at the front
door and saw some of the Grenadiers coming towards his house, whereupon
he immediately escaped out of his back door as before, and with very great
difficulty got into a place of safety, owing to several other bodies of people
who were parading the streets in search of others denominated Tories, that
the deponent having found means to secret himself till the next morning being Thursday, when he returned again to his own house, where he received
a message from the provost by no means to think of staying in his own
house, for that the deponent would surely be put to death, that thereupon
the deponent determined immediately to complain to the provincial general
Washington and to beg for protection, which the deponent accordingly did,
and informed Mr. Washington how he had been treated, and begged him
to protect him from a repetition of such insults, who after enquiring who
the people were that he had thus injured the deponent and being informed
by the deponent that they were a mixture of citizens and soldiers and particularly that two provincial officers just returned from Quebec were among
the number, the said General Washington replied that they were out of the
service, that he had nothing to do with them, that he did not want to hear
any of the deponent's complaints, neither should he trouble himself with
anything of the kind, that the deponent thereupon left General Washington,
and near the General's house met Lord Sterling to whom he repeated his
complaints who among other things told the deponent it was an affair among
citizens, and that the army would not interfere in anything of that sort—that
shortly after this deponent was informed and believes that a major of the
provincials had declared that he thought the best way would be to hang up
ten or a dozen of the Tories like dogs for the rascals would not be quiet without it and that the people might do it safely enough, for that it was out in
general orders that the soldiers should not interfere let what he dare among
the inhabitants and shortly after this the deponent received a message from
the provost by no means to think of returning home, for that he could not
affect any protection, it being out in general orders that the military should
by no means interpose.[5]

Notes

1. George W. Corner, ed., *The Autobiography of Benjamin Rush: His "Travels Through Life" Together with his Commonplace Book from 1789–1813* (Princeton: American Philosophical Society, 1948), 117–19.

2. Neil Longley York, *Henry Hulton and the American Revolution: An Outsider's View*, chap. 16, "Instances of Persecutions in New England whilst the Country was in a state of Anarchy, 1774" (Boston: Colonial Society of Massachusetts, 2010), 178–81.

3. Hugh Edward Egerton, ed., *The Royal Commission on the Losses and Services of American Loyalists, 1783–1785* (New York: Arno Press and *The New York Times*, 1969), 38–40.

4. Broadside, June 9, 1776, American Antiquarian Society.

5. Affidavit by Christopher Benson, June 16, 1776, in Mackenzie Papers, June 1775–December 1779, Clements Library.

CHAPTER TWO

Early Loyalist Voices

Denouncing the Unnatural Rebellion (1775)

Introduction

Peter Oliver, chief justice of the Superior Court at Massachusetts, was connected to New England's most elite families. He addressed this excerpted lecture to the soldiers in Massachusetts who were in arms against "the laws of their country." He cautions colonists to turn away from the fatal consequences of a most wanton and unnatural rebellion.

MY FELLOW CITIZENS!

You have been addressed by the general officers of the continental army as *fellow soldiers*, and with that insinuating art which was designed to move your passions: I would not draw your attention from it, provided you will devote your cooler moments to a dispassionate consideration of its subject matter.

Suffer me on my part to address you as *fellow citizens*, for I cannot have such dishonorable thoughts of you as to suppose that when you put on the soldier that you then put off the citizen; citizens most of you were, you enjoyed the comforts of domestic life, you lately followed your different occupations and reaped the profits of a quiet and peaceable industry, and I hope in *God* that you may yet do it, without any disturbance to your innocent wives and children; but in the late courses of your lives, you must not only have given great uneasinesses to your families, but I dare to say, that all of you, were not quite free from uneasiness in your own minds. I know my dear countrymen! that many of you, have been drove to take up arms against your Sovereign, and the laws of the happiest constitution that ever human beings were blest

with; some through the necessities incident to human nature, and others by
that compulsion which the malevolent and ambitious arts of your leaders have
made necessary to deceive you with, in order to screen themselves from that
vengeance which the injured laws of society had devoted them to. Many a tear
of pity have I dropped for you and for the fate of my country, and many more
tears I fear that I shall be forced to shed for that wrath which awaits you from
an offended Heaven, and an injured government. Many of your associates have
already quitted the field of battle, to appear before that solemn tribunal where
the plea of the united force of all the colonies will be of no avail to bribe the
judgment or avert the sentence of an offended Deity. Some of them, in the ag-
onies of death, sent messages to their friends to forbear proceeding any further,
for they now found themselves in the wrong; others have repeatedly said, that
an ambition of appearing something considerable and that only, led them into
rebellion; and the unhappy leader, in the fatal action at Charlestown, (who
from ambition only, had raised himself from a bare legged milk boy to a major
general of an army) although the fatal ball gave him not a moment for reflection, yet had said in his life time, that *he was determined to mount over the heads
of his coadjutors and get to the last round of the ladder or die in the attempt*: Unhappy
man! his fate arrested him in his career, and he can now tell whether pride and
ambition are pillars strong enough to support the tottering fabric of rebellion.

But not to divert you from an attention to the *address of your officers*; I would
rather wish you to weigh it with exactness, and after you have so done, if you
then should think that it is better to trample upon the laws of the mildest
government upon earth, and throw off your allegiance to the most humane
Sovereign that ever swayed a sceptre, and submit to a tyranny uncontrouled
either by the laws of God or man, then blame none but yourselves, if the consequences should be fatally bad to you and to your families.

. . . The patriots were determined to humble *Great Britain*; and, as a first
step, they promoted a nonimportation agreement at the same time that the
wealthy and artful among them had large quantities of goods by them by
the advanced sale of which they made fortunes and ruined the small traders: They promised to send their new imported goods back to *England*, and
instead thereof, their trunks were crowded with billets of wood shavings and
brickbats, to the eternal disgrace of this province when they were opened in
England. Some of the patriots carried about papers of subscription against
importing goods from *England*, and washing women and porters, in order to
swell the list, made their marks, for write they could not, that they would
not import coaches or chariots from home: when they were told of the impropriety of such a conduct, and that the scheme would have no effect, they
replied, that they were sensible of it, but *Great Britain* would be scared by it:
they hired mercenaries in *England* to cabal and write for them and raise an
insurrection: when they were told that *Great Britain* would be roused, they
said that she was not to be dreaded; that she had neither men nor money;

that there was more money in the Colonies than in England; that if she should resent it, that the Colonies would not pay them the millions that were due to her. Not content with this insult, the General Assembly disavowed any observance of Acts of Parliament. *Great Britain*, with her usual lenity, pitied our infatuation, tho' she was at last forced to send troops to support civil government; those troops we were then to destroy, and we did our best to destroy them; but felt the fatal consequence of the attempt: our violences at last rose to such an height, that injured sovereignty and an insulted government have been roused to assert their authority, in order to curb as wanton and wicked a rebellion as ever raged in any government upon earth.

. . . I am loth to detain you any longer, my countrymen! from sober reflection: for *God's* sake, for your own sakes, for your wives and childrens sake, pause a moment and weigh the event of this unnatural civil war. You have roused the British Lion; you have incensed that power which hath crushed much greater powers than you can boast of, and hath done it without your aid too. Great Britain is not so distressed for men, or money as some would make you believe: Your conduct hath raised the resentment of the greatest powers in *Europe*, and she may, if she pleases, accept of their proffered aid. But your priests and your leaders tell you otherwise; and I will just put the case, that supposing Heaven, in righteous judgment should suffer you to conquer: look forward then to the fatal consequences of your conquest: you will be conquered by an army of your own raising, and then your dreaded slavery is fixed; the ambition and desperation of your leaders will then demand the fruit of all their toils . . .[1]

Inflamed Rebels and Scattered Friends (1775)

Introduction
In the first excerpted letter, written on May 6, 1775, after the battles of Lexington and Concord, Governor William Franklin of New Jersey laments the collapse of royal authority in the colonies. The tensions between the colonial assemblies and the empire had continued too long, and an accommodation was no longer likely. In the second letter, written just three months later, Franklin mourns that many friends of government were scattered and had no place of refuge.

To the Right Honble the Earl of Dartmouth

Perth Amboy, May 6th 1775

My Lord,

A few Days ago I was honoured with your Lordship's several Dispatches of the 22d of February and 3d of March.

The Resolution of the House of Commons on the 20 of February, declaratory of the Sense of Parliament upon the Subject of Taxation, especially as explained by your Lordship's Circular Dispatch, afforded me very particular Pleasure, as it gave me Strong Hopes that it would be productive of a thorough Reconciliation between the two Countries. This likewise was the Sentiment of such of His Majesty's Council in this Province as I had an Opportunity of communicating it to, who immediately advised the Calling of the General Assembly, that no Time might be lost in accomplishing so desirable a Purpose. But an Event has since occurred which has, in some Degree, checked those flattering Hopes, and given me Reason to apprehend that an amicable Accommodation will be with Difficulty, if at all, effected at this Time. The Accounts we have from Massachusetts Bay respecting the Proceedings of the King's Troops, and the late Engagement between them and the Inhabitants of that Province, have occasioned such an Alarm and excited so much Uneasiness among the People throughout this and the other Colonies, that there is Danger of their committing some outrageous Violences before the present Heats can subside. They are arming themselves, forming into Companies, and taking uncommon Pains to perfect themselves in Military Discipline. Every Day new Alarms are spread, which have a Tendency to keep the Minds of the People in a continual Ferment, make them suspicious, and prevent their paying any Attention to the Dictates of sober Reason and common Sense. A great Number of the Inhabitants of Freehold in Monmouth County were persuaded to believe that Hostilities were ordered to be commenced against all the Colonies, and that a Man of War was lying in the Bay near Sandy-hook with a Design to send up a Boat in the Night to carry off the Money in the Treasury, and the Records in the Secretary's Office at Amboy. In Consequence of this Report, some of the Committee of Freehold with upwards of 30 of the Militia, arm'd with Firelocks, set out on Wednesday Afternoon last, and travelled through Brunswick to Woodbridge within 3 Miles of this place, where they got about Midnight, and would have come down immediately here, in order to carry off the Treasury & Records, had they not been persuaded by some of the Woodbridge Committee to desist from their Enterprize till they could call a Meeting of the neighbouring Committees in the Morning. These Committees when they met disapproved of the Measure, & prevailed on those inconsiderate People to return Home, which they did, marching through Amboy by my Door, with Colours Drum & Fife.

All legal Authority and Government seems to be drawing to an End here, and that of Congresses, Conventions, and Committees establishing in their Place. The People are everywhere entering into Associations similar to that of New York, whereby they engage to "adopt and endeavour carry into Execution *whatever Measures* may be recommended by the *Continental Congress*, or resolved upon by the *Provincial Convention*, and that they *will in all Things follow* the Advice of their *General Committees*," &c. This Association has been entered into by many of what are here called Tories, and Friends to Government, as well as by the other Party; they being in a Manner compelled thereto through Apprehensions for their personal Safety, and as it seemed the only Expedient, in such an Exigency, for the preservation of Peace & good Order and the Security of private Property.

It is highly probable that General Gage must have had very strong Reasons, or he would not have sent out the Party to Concord, and risk'd the commencing Hostilities, at a Time when all His Majesty's Governors on the Continent had Directions, and were consequently taking Measures to promote an amicable Settlement of the present unhappy Difference. It was, however, expected that previous to the Commencement of any military Operations, the Assembly of Massachuset's Bay would have been called, and that the Governor would have laid before them the Resolution of the House of Commons, declarative of their Sentiments respecting the future Taxation of the Colonies, and explained them in the manner mentioned in your lordship's Circular Dispatch of the 3 of March: And that no hostile Measure of any kind would have been taken that could have had a Chance of bringing on an Engagement with the Troops, until after their Refusal to acquiesce with the Propositions held out in that Resolution, or that they had been warned, by a Proclamation, of the ill Consequences that would infallibly attend their Contumacy. The General's Motives for not pursuing such a Plan of Conduct will, I doubt not, from his distinguished Character, and well-known Prudence, be found strictly justifiable and proper; yet it is greatly to be regretted that the late Skirmish happened at the Time it did, as it has, in its Consequences, proved one of the most unlucky Incidents that could have occurred in the present Situation of Affairs. It will not only be a Means of retarding, if not entirely defeating the Wishes & Measures of His Majesty for a happy Reconciliation; but will endanger the Lives & properties of every Officer of Government in the King's Colonies to the Southward of New England who may refuse to acquiesce in their Proceedings. It has, indeed, been repeatedly declared that they were determined to make Reprisals, and that in case Genl. Gage should seize upon or punish any of the people of that Country, they would seize upon the King's Officers & Friends of Government, throughout the Colonies, and treat them in the same Manner. Nor have I the least Doubt but such would be the Consequence, if military Operations were carried on, and a Number of the Inhabitants are killed or taken Prisoners: For in none of the Capitals of those Southern Colonies have they, as yet, either Troops, Forts or Men of War, that can afford them any Protection. A matter which surely ought to be particularly attended to, and provided for, before any Hostilities are commenced.

Altho' there seems at present but little Hopes that the Terms proposed by the House of Commons, & approved of by His Majesty will be immediately agreed to by the several Assemblies, yet I cannot but think that when they come to be explained and rightly understood by the People, there will be a Disposition to comply with them, or some others of a similar Nature. The Assemblies will probably avoid coming singly to any Determination before they know the Sentiments of the general Congress to be held this Month at Philadelphia. I have just heard that the Lieut Governor & Council of New York have determined not to lay the propositions before the Assembly of that Province, thinking Men's Minds are at present too much heated & inflamed to consider the Matter with that Calmness & Attention which the Importance of it requires. And I am likewise informed that the Govr of Pensylvania has communicated them to the Assembly of that Province, who have declined acceding to them, & have declared that they "cannot think the Terms pointed out afford a just and reasonable Ground for a final Accommodation between G. Britain & the Colonies;" intimating besides, "that all Aids from them should be their own free & voluntary Gifts, not taken by Force, nor extorted by Fears,—that the Plan held forth may be classed under one of these Descriptions—and that if they had no *other* Objection to it they could not honorably adopt it without the Advice & Consent of the other Colonies."

It is not unlikely that I shall receive a somewhat similar Answer from the Assembly of this Province; and, indeed, I am inclined to think that every other Assembly will wait to take their Tone from the general Congress; and that therefore, unless the Plan is satisfactorily explained to them, we shall be as wide from the final Settlement of the Disputes as ever. But as they are not a legally authorised Body, and the Governors cannot take any direct Notice of them, there seems no other Method so proper for obtaining their Sentiments on the Plan, and thereby bringing the Matter to a Speedy Decision, as to communicate it as soon as possible to the several Assemblies, and give them an Opportunity of informing the Congress of the Nature of it, and of consulting them on the Occasion.—I formerly (in my Dispatch No.-) Suggested the Expediency of having a duely authorized Congress of Persons to be chosen by the several Assemblies, which should be impowered to meet and consult with such Persons as His Majesty should commission for the Purpose, and it still appears to me to be a Measure necessary to expedite the final Settlement of this troublesome & destructive Contest. For, I am convinced that Matters are now carried so far that the Americans in general are disposed to run the Risk of a total Ruin rather than suffer a Taxation by any but their own immediate Representatives and that there is not the least Reason to expect they will ever, in this Instance, consent to acknowledge the Right, even if they should be obliged to submit to the Power of Parliament. The Plan now offered to them is happily a Waving of the Exercise of that Right on Conditions corresponding with their own former Declarations, and which I cannot therefore but hope the reasonable Part of them will think it the Duty of this Country to adopt . . .[2]

My Lord, Your Lordship's most obedient & most humble Servant
William Franklin

To the Right Honble the Earl of Dartmouth

Perth Amboy, August 2, 1775

My Lord,

The same disposition and the same measures continue as mentioned in my last . . . A formal declaration has been published by the Congress and every preparation made for carrying on a war which is in their power, the particulars of which I need not mention as they are printed in all the newspapers . . . It is true that there are many friends of government still remaining in the several provinces but they are too scattered to venture forming themselves into a body especially as they have no places of strength or security to resort to. Not that I believe there are any of the gentlemen of the country who would draw their swords in support of taxation by Parliament, but there are many who would fight to preserve the supremacy of Parliament in other respects and their connexion with Great Britain, until some constitution should be formed for America consistent with that idea on just and equitable principles. There is indeed a dread in the minds of many here that some of the leaders of the people are aiming to establish a republic, rather than submit to which we have thousands who would risk the loss of their lives in defence of the old constitution and are ready to declare themselves whenever they see a chance of its being of any avail.[3]

My Lord, Your Lordship's most obedient & most humble Servant

William Franklin

Hunting of the Tories (1775)

Introduction

In this excerpted letter to the American secretary of state, Lord Dartmouth, written on August 18, 1775, Governor John Wentworth describes the explosive loss of royal authority in New Hampshire. Wentworth emphasizes that the lower class of people created the confusion that led to the "hunting of the Tories." He laments that he no longer carries the authority to bring the offenders to justice through legal process.

18 August, Fort William and Mary, N.H.

May it please your Lordship, I am very sorry to acquaint your lordship that our difficulties increase here every day, more especially since the restraining bill took place, occasioned in part by various altercations between Captain Barkley, commander of His Majesty's ship *Scarborough* in this harbour, and the people respecting the execution of said bill and the trade and commerce of the river.

On the bill's taking place Captain Barkley made an agreement with the inhabitants of the neighbouring towns on the river that he would allow them to go out in open boats and canoes unmolested to catch and bring home fresh fish on their taking permits from him and supplying the ship with a quantity of fresh beef weekly which it was agreed he should have. The people took permits from Captain Barkley to go fishing and matters went on tolerably quiet for eight or ten days till one of the man-of-war's men had deserted from the ship's boat one evening it was sent to Portsmouth. The next morning Captain Barkley took one Mead, a man belonging to Portsmouth, out of a canoe passing by the ship and sent word to town he would not let him go until the man that had deserted from the boat should be returned. This occasioned murmurs and jealousies among the lower class of people in the town who are in general glad of a pretence to create uneasiness. It was said Captain Barkley had infringed on his agreement, that they did not encourage his men to run away, and threatened if the boat came to town again they would seize upon her. Captain Barkley in a few days thought proper to release the man. Nevertheless the spirit the populace got into did not immediately subside, and on the morning of the 10th instant Captain Barkley was informed in my presence that there was an uneasiness among the people in the town and that if he sent his boat there before things grew more calm it was very likely some attack would be made upon her and that it would be better to avoid than bring on disturbances. However, between three and four o'clock in the afternoon of the same day, Captain Barkley sent one of his boats to town. Soon after she got to the wharf and the coxswain landed, he was seized upon and a number of armed men came to the wharf and called out to the boat's crew to come on shore, and upon refusal they began to fire on the boat. The men in the boat returned the fire and immediately departed; several fires were exchanged but no person was hurt. This threw the town suddenly into great confusion and a boat which I have kept at this fort that went to town in the forenoon, and at that time at a wharf just ready to come away, was taken out of the water and carried in triumph through the streets by some of the persons who fired on the man-of-war's boat joined by others. But as they were proceeding out of town to burn the boat, they were with difficulty prevented from doing it by some of the principal inhabitants, and thereupon they put it into a creek behind the town where it still remains without my being able to get it back again. While some paraded about in this manner with the boat, others employed themselves in hunting the Tories, as they term it, and went in pursuit of many persons in order to collect them together and bring them before their committee for examination and trial. These proceedings were doubtless carried on by the lower class of people, but in order to put a stop to them and quiet the town a town-meeting was called immediately and one or two persons appeared in the town-meeting who gave full evidence that the firing was first begun by the persons on the wharf at the boat's crew. A vote was then passed by them, copy of which is enclosed, expressing their disapprobation of the crime and a copy of the vote sent directly the same evening to Captain Barkley with the coxswain that had been seized upon on his coming out of the boat.

Captain Barkley in the meantime wrote a letter to me acquainting me that the boat had been fired upon and desiring that I would 'cause inquiry to be made why that act of outrage had been committed or whether the town of Portsmouth meant it as a declaration of war against the King, and if so that immediate satisfaction would be demanded and the consequence most likely would be fatal to that town.' I immediately caused the Council to be summoned to make inquiry into the matter, whose proceedings are contained in the enclosed copy of their minute on the occasion. On the 12th I enclosed to Captain Barkley copies of these proceedings expressing the fullest disapprobation of the outrage on his boat's crew and at the same time acquainted him that I was sorry the powers of government were at present so weakened as not to admit of bringing the offenders to justice by due course of law but trusted the period was not very distant when they would meet with the punishment due to their crimes. No more could possibly be done in the case, and as it was all Captain Barkley required in his letter it was thought he would be satisfied, especially as no person was hurt. But, however, instead of that he wrote a letter to me on the 14th inveighing against the people of Portsmouth and threatening them with punishment and that he expected they would deliver up to him the persons who fired on the boat or if they did not they must expect vengeance, that he intended to go up to the town with the ship to obtain justice and offered to give me the accommodation of the ship if I should embark on board. I acquainted him in answer that I lamented the impracticability of punishing offenders at present in the only way consistent with my duty to recommend, by regular course of law, and that being interrupted I was satisfied it was altogether impossible to take up the persons who fired on the boat and that, as to his proposal of going up to town, I did not think such a step eligible unless there was a second ship in the harbour but rather pregnant with consequences very detrimental to His Majesty's service, and that the security of this harbour and fort and the effect of the restraining bill in this district depended on the protection of a ship near the entrance of the harbour. With the utmost candour I gave Captain Barkley my sentiments which appeared to me to be and am satisfied were well-founded to serve His Majesty's interest; but that gentleman still urges his notions with no small share of vehemence.

Exclusive of these difficulties the communication between this fort and Portsmouth is now interrupted, nobody being suffered to come from town since Sunday last without a pass and even in that way only some persons. My particular friends are not allowed to visit me and I am entirely cut off from every supply of provision.

I hope your lordship will pardon my troubling you with so minute a detail of these circumstances but as they have a tendency to lead to consequences of a very serious nature I thought it my duty to state them thus particularly. It is much to be lamented that we should be involved in those difficulties and distresses here, as there is no doubt but the more quiet things were kept in other parts till the insurgents were dispersed the more it would conduce to His Majesty's interest.[4]

Loyalists Left Unprotected (1775)

Introduction

On August 28, 1775, Governor Josiah Martin of North Carolina sent this excerpted letter from his refuge on a British ship. Martin describes the rebel committees, which intercepted dispatches to the government, and laments the lack of military reinforcements, which abandoned the loyal to rebel factions and committees, and left him a "tame spectator."

I have taken every measure in my power to communicate to proper persons; but unfortunately before it reached my hands the Committees had so effectually possessed themselves of every avenue into the country by their spies and emissaries, who keep the most strict and vigilant watch upon every road and communication which leads towards me, that I have found myself defeated in almost every attempt I have made to correspond with the well-affected people in the upper country. All of them who have come down here to consult me about their safety have been intercepted coming or going, and searched, detained, abused, and stripped of any papers they have had about them, except a messenger from a considerable body of Germans settled in the County of Mecklenburg who brought me a loyal declaration against the very extraordinary and traitorous resolves of the Committee of that county, of which I had the honour to transmit a copy to your lordship with my last dispatches.

Thus, my lord, I am reduced to the deplorable and disgraceful state of being a tame spectator of rebellion spreading over this country, which might have been surely and effectually maintained for the King by the strength I could have collected within itself if I had been provided but six weeks ago with arms, ammunition and money. With those aids, my lord, I am confident I could have entered the country and made myself entirely master of it by this day, but without them I considered an attempt to draw the King's loyal subjects together, ill-armed or wholly unarmed as they are, destitute of ammunition and without both the means of defence and support to act against an increasing and spreading revolt that had actually enlisted half the country on its side by terror or persuasion, and which according to my information is well supplied with warlike stores that have been secretly from time to time imported into this province, would have been only to sacrifice the friends of government and to disgrace myself . . .

. . . The result of the Convention now sitting at Hillsborough will show the state of this country clearly, and I fear will manifest the fatality of suffering faction to get to such a head here which it has been impossible to prevent without drawing together and arming the friends of government, which I have not had the necessary means to effect. The few people who steal down to me in spite of the Committees' interdicts represent the inhabitants of the lower parts of this country so generally disaffected and infatuated to such a degree of madness by the influence of the seditious demagogues that the loyal subjects among them are in fear of their lives if they utter a word against their proceedings or even contrary to their liking.

The Scotch merchants at Wilmington, who so long maintained their loyalty, have lately been compelled ostensibly to join in sedition by appearing under arms at the musters appointed by the Committees, although they are still at heart as well affected as ever. In short, my lord, everything now convinces me that the time for restoring lawful government in this province by its own internal strength is past and gone. I hoped, if my proclamation of the 8th instant had circulated, it might at least have had the effect to suspend for a time the progress of revolt among the inhabitants of the interior country, whom I much fear will be seduced and alienated by the influence and artifices of the Convention now held in the heart of their country; and I know not another act of government I can do with the least prospect of advantaging His Majesty's service until I am supported by troops . . .[5]

Requesting Imperial Intervention (1775)

Introduction

As Governor William Tryon of New York observed the rising tensions in New York City, he worried that parliamentary taxes had united the American colonists and hoped that British ministers would retreat from their hardline stance. In this letter from September 5, 1775, Tryon suggests that the colonial expansion—in population and commerce—mandated an increase in the authority of the royal governors.

My Lord, in the present stage of the American controversy, advanced as it is to an open opposition to the measures of government, I shall not trouble your lordship with a minute detail of the public occurrences in this country. Every day produces fresh proof of a determined spirit of resistance in the confederate colonies. The Americans from politicians are now becoming soldiers, and however problematical it once was there can be now no doubt of their intention to persevere in their determinations to great extremity, unless they are called back by some liberal and conciliatory assurances.

Their dread of being taxed by Parliament is the grand sinew of the league. No arguments or address can persuade them that the British nation does not mean to exercise that principle, and deeply impressed with that consideration they look upon themselves as mere tenants at will of all they possess. I could wish for some explicit declaration from Great Britain to refrain from what it would never be expedient to make them again feel, because I flatter myself it would lower the present alarming irritation and end in a restoration of the common tranquillity. Would it, my lord, put anything to risk to disclaim an intention, if never meant to be carried into execution? Besides, I find on the spot such a temper as leads me to believe that, the terror of being taxed without their own cooperation once removed, and the Acts in support of that principle which alarmed them done away, the contest would either cease or such dissensions be produced among themselves as would reduce the opposition now so inauspicious to a very manageable state, when seconded by the powerful aid of government. I indulge therefore the hope that this great obstacle will be removed.

I must next remind your lordship of several particulars which, though of subordinate importance, will nevertheless require immediate attention as soon as the languid arm of authority begins again to be raised in this country.

The colonies have outgrown the government anciently set over them, which ought to rise in strength and dignity as they increase in wealth and population. It will therefore be of great utility to extend the confidence of the executive authority to the governors of the provinces as far as His Majesty can safely rely upon those he thinks fit to honour with that trust. They want more particularly ampler scope for the exercise of that liberality which is of the greatest use in every species of government, always expected by the multitude, and absolutely necessary to place the power of the King's representative above their contempt. I must therefore intercede with your lordship for an establishment that no patent in future for any office or place in the colony issue independent of the governor, and also for a settlement respecting rank and precedency: that the governor in his province take the preeminence of all others except the blood royal on every occasion not merely military, that the King's Council in their order follow the commander-in-chief of the army, and after them the Speaker of the Assembly etc . . .

The Crown is also doubly concerned in a reconsideration of the general restraints the governor lies under by the new arrangement which prevents the further granting of lands. Under that arrangement it is impossible, my lord, in a country like this where population proceeds with such large and rapid strides, to prevent intrusions upon the ungranted territory on the inland frontiers, and when these are multiplied the strength of the occupants will deter others from suing patents for their possessions who themselves are generally either too indolent or too confident in their own force to solicit grants to secure their settlements.

As the hostile preparations and appearances that surround me make it very doubtful if I may have an opportunity of sending any more public dispatches to your lordship from this country, I think it my duty to be at this time, as I have been at all others, very explicit in my sentiments on the public affairs of this colony, which are with all possible duty and fidelity most humbly submitted to His Majesty's wisdom.[6]

Criticizing *Common Sense* (1776)

Introduction

James Chalmers wrote *Plain Truth* as a direct answer to Thomas Paine's *Common Sense*. In this excerpted passage, Chalmers dismisses the optimistic portrait of a new republic portrayed in *Common Sense*. He emphasizes British military might, rejects the possibility of foreign assistance, and conjures a vision of social disorder without the glue of empire. Independence, he argues, would deprive the colonies of the moderating influence of Britain, and lead to "anarchy and intestine war." In 1777, Chalmers organized a battalion of Maryland loyalists; and in 1778, the battalion served in Pensacola, Florida, against the Spanish.

PLAIN TRUTH; CONTAINING REMARKS ON A LATE PAMPHLET, ENTITLED, COMMON SENSE

I HAVE now before me the Pamphlet, entitled COMMON SENSE; on which I shall remark with freedom and candour . . . I shall humbly endeavour to shew, that our author shamefully misrepresents facts, is ignorant of the true state of Great Britain and her Colonies, utterly unqualified for the arduous task, he has presumptuously assumed; and ardently intent on seducing us to that precipice on which himself stands trembling. To elucidate my strictures, I must with fidelity expose the circumstances of Great Britain and her colonies. If therefore, in the energy of description, I unfold certain bold and honest truths with simplicity, the judicious reader will remember, that true knowledge of our situation, is essential to our safety; as ignorance thereof may endanger it. In the English provinces, exclusive of negroe and other slaves, we have one hundred and sixty thousand; or one hundred and seventy thousand men capable of bearing arms. If we deduct the people called Quakers, Anabaptists, and other religionists averse to arms; a considerable part of the emigrants, and those having a grateful predilection for the ancient constitution and parent state, we shall certainly reduce the first number to sixty or seventy thousand men. Now admitting those equal to the Roman legions, can we suppose them capable of defending against the power of Britain, a country nearly twelve hundred miles extending on the ocean. Suppose, our troops assembled in New-England, if the Britons see not fit to assail them, they haste to and desolate our other provinces, which eventually would reduce New England. If by dividing our forces, we pretend to defend our provinces, we also are infallibly undone. Our most fertile provinces, filled with unnumbered domestic enemies, slaves; intersected by navigable rivers, everywhere accessible to the fleets and armies

of Britain, can make no defence. If without the medium of passion and prejudice, we view our other provinces, half armed, destitute of money and a navy:
We must confess, that no power ever engaged such POTENT ANTAGO-
NISTS, under such peculiar circumstances of infelicity. In the better days of
Rome, she permitted no regular troops to defend her. Men destitute of property
she admitted not into her militia, (her only army.) I have been extremely concerned at the separation of the Connecticut men from our army. It augur'd not
an ardent enthusiasm for liberty and glory. We still have an army before Boston, and I should be extremely happy to hear substantial proofs of their glory.
I am still hopeful of great things from our army before Boston, when joined
by the regiments now forming, which WANT OF BREAD will probably soon
fill. Notwithstanding the predilection I have for my countrymen, I remark
with grief, that hitherto our troops have displayed but few marks of Spartan or
Roman enthusiasm. In the sincerity of my heart, I adjure the reader to believe,
that no person is more sensibly afflicted by hearing the enemies of America
remark, that no General ever fell singly and so ingloriously unrevenged before
the inauspicious affair of Quebec. I am under no doubt, however, that we shall
become as famed for martial courage, as any nation ever the sun beheld. Sanguine as I am, respecting the virtue and courage of my countrymen, depending on the history of mankind, since the Christian Æra, I cannot however
imagine, the zeal for liberty will to such glorious efforts of heroism, as religious
enthusiasm hath often impelled its votaries to perform . . .

. . . With the utmost deference to the honorable Congress; I do not view
the most distant gleam of aid from foreign powers. The princes alone, capable
of succouring us, are the Sovereigns of France and Spain. If according to our
Author, we possess an eighth part of the habitable globe, and actually have
a check on the West India commerce of England. The French indigo, and
other valuable West India commodities, and the Spanish galeons, are in great
jeopardy from our power. The French and Spaniards are therefore wretched
politicians, if they do not assist England, in reducing her colonies to obedience.—Pleasantry apart! Can we be so deluded, to expect aid from those
princes, which inspiring their subjects with a relish for liberty, might eventually shake their arbitrary thrones.—Natural avowed enemies to our sacred
cause: Will they cherish, will they support the flame of liberty in America?
Ardently intent, on extinguishing its latent dying sparks in their respective
dominions. Can we believe that those princes will offer an example so dangerous to their subjects and colonies, by aiding those provinces to independence?
If independent, aggrandized by infinite numbers from every part of Europe, this
Continent would rapidly attain power astonishing to imagination. Soon, very
soon would we be conditioned to conquer Mexico, and all their West India
settlements, which to annoy, or possess, we indeed are most happily situated.
Simple and obvious as these truths are, can they be unknown to the people
and princes of Europe?

. . . I shall no longer detain my reader, but conclude with a few remarks on
our Author's scheme. The people of those Colonies would do well to consider

the character, fortune, and designs of our Author, and his independents; and compare them with those of the most amiable and venerable personages in, and out of the Congress, who abominate such nefarious measures. I would humbly observe, that the specious science of politics, is of all others, the most delusive. Soon after the Revolution; the ablest states-men in England, and other parts of Europe; confidently predicted National ruin, infallible ruin, soon as the Public debt exceeded fifty millions sterling. The Nation now indebted nearly thrice that sum; is not arrived at the zenith of her credit and power. It is perhaps possible to form a specious system of government on paper which may seem practicable, and to have the consent of the people; yet it will not answer in practice nor retain their approbation upon trial. "All plans of government (says HUME) which suppose great reformation in the manners of mankind, are merely imaginary."

The fabricators of Independency have too much influence; to be entrusted in such arduous and important concerns. This reason alone, were sufficient at present, to deter us from altering the Constitution. It would be as inconsistent in our leaders in this hour of danger to form a government; as it were for a Colonel forming his battalion in the face of an enemy, to stop to write an essay on war . . .

. . . Notwithstanding our Author's fine words about toleration: Ye sons of peace and true christianity; believe me, it were folly supreme, madness, to expect angelic toleration from New-England, where she has constantly been detested, persecuted and execrated. Even in vain would our Author: or our CROMWELL cherish toleration; for the people of New-England, not yet arrived in the seventeenth or eighteenth century, would reprobate her.—It is more than probable to suppose, that the New-England governments would have no objection to an Agrarian law; nor is it unreasonable to suppose, that such division of property would be very agreeable to the soldiers. Indeed their General could not perhaps with safety to his existence as a General, refuse them so reasonable a gratification, particularly, as he will have more than one occasion for their services. Let us however admit that our General and troops, contradicting the experience of ages; do not assume the sovereignty. Released from foreign war; we would probably be plunged into all the misery of anarchy and intestine war. Can we suppose that the people of the south, would submit to have the seat of Empire at Philadelphia, or in New England; or that the people oppressed by a change of government, contrasting their misery with their former happy state, would not invite Britain to reassume the sovereignty. . . . INDEPENDENCE AND SLAVERY ARE SYNONYMOUS TERMS.[7]

Rejecting Violence (1776)

Introduction

Despite the large number of New Englanders in Nova Scotia, the colony remained loyal to Britain. In this excerpted letter from the September 10,

1776, issue of the *Nova Scotia Gazette and Weekly Chronicle*, some Nova Scotians describe their considerations for rejecting rebellion.

The Demagogues, which raised this disturbance, are a motely crew of hungry lawyers, men of broken fortunes, young persons eager to push themselves in the world, others, gentlemen of opulence, vain & blustering—Amongst this medley there are several of good party, and great reading, but withal little versed in the complicated interests, and springs, which move the great political world, because untutored in the Courts of Europe, where alone that science is to be acquired—These could not miss perceiving the growing importance, as they call it, of America, and what she might one day arrive to: so far indeed they judged with propriety, if they would only give time, and leave her to herself; but the greatness of the object dazzled the eyes of their understanding; and they began to think Empire, without considering the infant state of their country, how much it is [in] want of every requisite for war, what a mighty nation they have to contend with, & that the united interest of every other nation in Europe likewise forbids their being anything more than dependent colonies—However, as if envying their prosperity, they hastened to bring on the great and glorious day, which would hail them masters of a quarter of the globe; and set up claims which, they thought, would either place them in that elevated station or in one more suitable to their present condition viz. to make the Mother Country drudge and slave to support, and protect them, for yet a while longer, without contributing a farthing more towards that expence that they should think proper; afterwards how soon they could no longer bear the thoughts of dependence, and that they could emancipate themselves (which indeed this mode would soon enable them to do) to dispute the expediency of the purposes for which their aids were to be applied, offer only a triffling sum, taking that opportunity of declaring for independence and maintain it too. . . .

The menaces of the Americans to run to arms, their violent proceedings in the first stage of the insurrection, their levying troops, which every where belongs to the executive branch, so notoriously . . . their collecting warlike weapons . . . were all such strong acts of rebellion as no government could put up with, it destroyed the merits of their cause, were it otherwise good: for resisting legal authority in that manner, however warrantable when oppression is intollerable, is yet a nice affair, and can only be justified, when tyranny is well ascertained, generally felt, and after the milder methods of redress have been ineffectually tried; which the impartial world is satisfied was by no means their case.

Had they acted in a moderate, dutiful, and justifiable manner, like subjects averse to break with their Sovereign, like men, who even in their own cause wished only for material justice, and not actuated by any indirect views but by the force of the principles, they protested; there is no doubt but whatever appeared to them harsh and dangerous, in the claims of Great Britain, would have been departed from, and matters settled on the basis of indulgence to the Colonies, and justice to the Mother country. But his Majesty's Paternal voice was bar'd access to his beloved subject; He could not treat with them, but thro' the false, and villainous medium of the proud demonogues, who paid no regard to truth, to loyalty, to peace or justice.[8]

Notes

1. Douglass Adair and John A. Shutz, eds., *Origin and Progress of the American Revolution: A Tory View* (San Marino: Huntington, 1961), 158–61.

2. Sheila Skemp, ed., *Benjamin and William Franklin: Father and Son, Patriot and Loyalist* (Boston: St. Martin's Press, 1994), 178–82.

3. K. G. Davies, *Documents of the American Revolution*, vol. 11 (Shannon: Irish University Press, ca. 1972–ca. 1981), 65–66.

4. Davies, *Documents of the American Revolution*, vol. 11, 76–78.

5. Davies, *Documents of the American Revolution*, vol. 11, 88–92.

6. Davies, *Documents of the American Revolution*, vol. 11, 100–102.

7. From Appendix B of *Common Sense*, edited by Thomas Larkin, excerpts taken from 2nd ed.; originally from *Plain Truth; Addressed to the Inhabitants of America, Containing, Remarks on a Late Pamphlet, Entitled Common Sense* (Philadelphia: Humphreys, 1776), 158–70.

8. George A. Rawlyk, ed., *Revolution Rejected, 1775–1776* (Scarborough: Prentice-Hall, 1968), 25–27.

CHAPTER THREE

Plans for Union

Albany Plan of Union (1754)

Introduction

During the summer of 1754, seven northern colonies met in Albany, New York, to create a plan that would protect local colonial interests within the British empire. Inspired by the necessity of common defense against the French and the Indians, the Albany Plan proposed a union of contiguous colonies in a local confederation. The Albany Plan imagined the creation of an in-between authority that would mediate between the Crown and the colonies for the purpose of protecting the colonists against the Natives and the British against the French. William Smith's father, the elder William Smith, participated in the Albany Conference. Also see William Smith's 1767 Plan of Union.

> PLAN of a Proposed UNION of the several Colonies of Massachussetts Bay, New Hampshire, Connecticut, Rhode Island, New York, New Jerseys, Pennsylvania, Maryland, Virginia, North Carolina, and South Carolina, for their mutual defence and security, and for extending the British Settlements in North America.
>
> That humble application be made for an Act of the Parliament of Great Britain, by virtue of which, one General Government may be formed in America, including all the said Colonies, within, and under which Government, each Colony may retain each present constitution, except in the particulars wherein a change may be directed by the said Act, as hereafter follows.

That the said General Government be administered by a president General, to be appointed and supported by the Crown, and a grand Council to be chosen by the representatives of the people of the several Colonies, meet in their respective assemblies.

That within Months after the passing of such Act, The house of representatives in the several Assemblies, that Happen to be sitting within that time or that shall be specially for that purpose convened, may and shall chose, Members for the Grand Council in the following proportions, that is to say:

Masachusets Bay 7
New Hampshire 2
Connecticut 5
Rhode Island 2
New-York 4
New Jerseys 3
Pensylvania 6
Maryland 4
Virginia 7
North Carolina 4
South Carolina 4
48

Who shall meet for the present time at the City of Philadelphia, in Pennsylvania, being called by the President General as soon as conveniently may be after his appointment.

That there shall be a New Election of Members for the Grand Council every three years, and on the death or resignation of any Member, his place shall be supplyed by a new choice at the next sitting of the Assembly of the Colony he represented.

That after the first three years, when the proportion of money arising out of each Colony to the General Treasury can be known, The number of Members to be chosen, for each Colony shall from time to time in all ensuing Elections be regulated by that proportion (yet so as that the Number to be chosen by any one province be not more than seven nor less than two).

That the Grand Council shall meet once in every year, and oftener if occasion require, at such time and place as they shall adjourn to at the last preeceding meeting, or as they shall be called to meet at by the President General, on any emergency, he having first obtained in writing the consent of seven of the Members to such call, and sent due and timely notice to the whole.

That the Grand Council have power to chuse their speaker, and shall neither be dissolved, prorogued, nor continue sitting longer than six weeks at one time without their own consent, or the special command of the Crown.

That the Members of the Grand Council shall be allowed for their service ten shillings sterling per diem, during their Sessions or Journey to and from the place of Meeting; twenty miles to be reckoned a days Journey.

That the Assent of the President General be requisite, to all Acts of the Grand Council, and that it be his Office, and duty to cause them to be carried into execution.

That the President General with the advice of the Grand Council, hold or direct all Indian Treaties in which the general interest or welfare of the Colonys may be concerned; and make peace or declare War with the Indian Nations. That they make such Laws as they judge necessary for the regulating all Indian Trade. That they make all purchases from Indians for the Crown, of lands [now] not within the bounds of particular Colonies, or that shall not be within their bounds when some of them are reduced to more convenient dimensions. That they make new settlements on such purchases by granting Lands, [in the King's Name] reserving a Quit rent to the Crown, for the use of the General Treasury.

That they make Laws for regulating and governing such new settlements, till the Crown shall think fit to form them into particular Governments.

That they raise and pay Soldiers, and build Forts for the defence of any of the Colonies, and equip vessels of Force to guard the Coasts and protect the Trade on the Ocean, Lakes, or great Rivers; but they shall not impress men in any Colonies without the consent of its Legislature. That for these purposes they have power to make Laws And lay and Levy such general duties, imposts or taxes, as to them shall appear most equal and just, considering the ability and other circumstances of the Inhabitants in the several Colonies, and such as may be collected with the least inconvenience to the people, rather discouraging luxury, than loading industry with unnecessary burthens. That they might appoint a General Treasurer and a particular Treasurer in each Government when necessary, and from time to time may order the sums in the Treasuries of each Government, into the General Treasury, or draw on them for special payments as they find most convenient; yet no money to issue but by joint orders of the President General and Grand Council, except where sums have been appropriated to particular purposes, and the President General is previously impowered by an Act to draw for such sums.

That the General accounts shall be yearly settled and reported to the several Assemblies.

That a Quorum of the Grand Council impowered to act with the President General, do consists of twenty five Members, among whom there shall be one or more from a majority of the Colonies. That the Laws made by them for the purposes aforesaid, shall not be repugnant but as near as may be agreable to the Laws of England, and shall be transmitted to the King in Council for approbation, as soon as may be after their passing, and if not disapproved within three years after presentation to remain in Force.

That in case of the death of the President General, the Speaker of the Grand Council for the time being shall succeed, and be vested with the same powers and authority, to continue until the King's pleasure be known.

That all Military Commission Officers, whether for land or sea service, to act under this General constitution, shall be nominated by the President

General, but the aprobation of the Grand Council is to be obtained before they receive their Commissions; and all Civil Officers are to be nominated by the grand Council, and to receive the President General's approbation before they officiate; but in case of vacancy by death or removal of any Officer Civil or Military under this consititution, The Governor of the Province in which such vacancy happens, may appoint till the pleasure of the President General and grand Council can be known. That the particular Military as well as Civil establishments in each Colony remain in their present State this General constitution notwithstanding. And that on sudden emergencies any Colony may defend itself, and lay the accounts of expence thence arisen, before the President General and Grand Council, who may allow and order payment of the same as far as they judge such accounts just and reasonable.[1]

William Smith Jr. Plan (1767)

Introduction

William Smith Jr. was the son of William Smith, one of the originators of the Albany Plan of 1754. As early as 1767, the articulate and cosmopolitan New York councilor William Smith Jr. urged the British Parliament to "bend" to negotiate with colonial demands. During the last years of the war, Smith became a trusted loyalist within the inner circles of British administration and was appointed as New York's chief justice. After the war, Smith became chief justice of Quebec.

> It is of Necessity then, that a Constitution be devised, friendly to every Branch of the great Whole, and linking Great Britain and her Colonies together, by the most indesoluble Ties.
>
> As the Contest arose, from a Foresight of the Inconveniences, attending a Resort to so many *seperate* Assemblies, the most obvious Remedy seems to be, a Consolidation of all these little, continental Parliaments into *one*.
>
> It is not proposed to annihilate the Assemblies, but that there be a Lord Lieutenant as in Ireland, and a Council of at least Twenty four Members, appointed by the Crown, with a House of Commons, consisting of Deputies chosen by their respective *Assemblies*, to meet at the central Province of New York, as the Parliament of North America.
>
> A Parliament is no Novelty; and therefore we shall not be perplexed in settling its Powers, and the Privileges of the several Branches. Let it be in general understood, that to this Body the Royal Requisitions for Aids are to be made, and that they are to have Authority, to grant for all, and to settle the Quotas of each; leaving the Ways and Means to their seperate Consideration, unless in Cases of Default.
>
> The Number of the Council may depend upon the Royal Pleasure; but to preserve their Independency, they ought to be Men of Fortune, and hold their

Places for Life; with some honorable Distinctions to their Families, as a Lure to prevent the Office from falling into Contempt.

The Number of the Delegates, will naturally be proportioned to the comparative Weight and Abilities, of the Colonies they represent. The two Floridas, Rode Island, Nova Scotia and Georgia ought each to have five. New Hampshire, Marriland, North Carolina and Quebec seven. South Carolina and New Jersey eleven. New York, Pensilvania and Connecticut twelve and Massachusets Bay and Virginia fifteen.

The whole House will thus consist of one hundred and forty one Members. A small Number, considering the Importance of their Trust. Besides Accident, Business and Disease will Occasion the Absence of many. They may be afterwards increased, when the Colonies are become more populous and desire it. The Crown to retain its antient Negative, and the British Parliament its Legislative Supremacy, in *all Cases* relative to *Life Liberty and Property*, except in the Matter of Taxations for *general Aids*, or the immediate, internal Support of the American Government.*

This Project is manifestly free from all the Objections, that lay either against that, which subjects American Property to the British Disposition; or the other, which asks that each Colony, should participate *so largely* in the Councils of the Empire, as to have the Power of refusing Aids; tho' thought necessary for the common Safety, by the *united Voice* of Great Britain and all the Rest of her extensive Dominions.

It may be said of every one of the Colonies, that our Assemblies are unequal to the Task, of entering into the Views of so wise, and so great a Nation as Great Britain is, and from which we are so far removed. Indeed it is not to be expected from an Infant Country, many of whose Assemblymen represent little obscure Counties . . .

But in a Parliament, chosen *not by the Counties*, but by the *Representatives* of the Colonies, we shall collect the Wisdom of the whole Continent, and find the Members acting upon Principles, doubly refined from popular Lees, and with a Liberality unbiassed by the partial Prejudices, prevalent in the little Districts by which they were sent.

Unspeakable Advantages will also flow, from the Introduction of a *dignified* Government, into a Country long neglected, and where, on Account of its being little known to Great Britain, and the Diversity of their Colony Constitutions, many Disorders have crept in, in some Instances dangerous and detrimental to the Colonies, and their British Creditors, and derogative of the just Rights, and many Prerogatives of the Crown, most friendly to Peace and good Order.

But the Capital Advantages of this Scheme, will be the Recovery of the Colonies, to a firm Confidence in the *Justice* and *Affection* of the Parent State. And by opening to her the Conduits of sure, full and constant Information, enabling her so to regulate and improve this vast, dependant, growing Territory, as to unite every Branch of the Empire, by the Cords of Love and Interest, and give Peace, Health and Vigor to the whole.[2]

Joseph Galloway Plan of 1774

Introduction

Pennsylvania Assemblyman Joseph Galloway proposed a plan of union to the First Continental Congress in 1774. Convinced that Congressional leaders only pretended to seek reconciliation, Galloway hoped that a concrete plan—one that supported American autonomy within the British empire—would win support. Although Galloway did not believe that Britain should tax the colonies, he continued to uphold the supremacy of Parliament. Galloway's plan shared elements of the Albany Plan and William Smith's 1767 Plan. Galloway's plan did not pass Congress.

A plan of a proposed Union between Great Britain and the Colonies of New Hampshire, The Massachusetts Bay, Rhode Island, Connecticut, New York, New Jersey, Pennsylvania, Maryland, the three lower Counties on Delaware, Virginia, North Carolina, South Carolina and Georgia.

THAT a British and American Government for regulating the Administration of the general Affairs of America be proposed and established in America, including all the said Colonies; within and under which Government each Colony shall retain its present Constitution and powers of regulating and governing its own internal Police in all Cases whatsoever.

That the said Government be administer'd by a president General to be appointed by the King and a Grand Council to be chosen by the Representatives of the people of the several Colonies in their respective Assemblies, once in every three years.

That the several Assemblies shall choose Members for the Grand Council in the following Proportions—viz.

New Hampshire
Massachusets Bay
Rhode Island
Connecticut
New York
New Jersey Pensylvania
Delaware Counties
Maryland
Virginia
North Carolina
South Carolina
Georgia

Who shall meet at the City of _____ for the first Time being called by the President General as soon as conveniently may be after his Appointment.

That there shall be a new Election of Members for the Grand Council every three years, and on the Death Removal or Resignation of any Member his place shall be supplied by a new Choice at the next sitting of the Assembly of the Colony he represented.

That the Grand Council shall meet once in every year if they shall think it necessary, and oftener if occasion shall require, at such Time and place as they shall adjourn to at the last preceeding Meeting, or as they shall be called to meet at by the president General in any Emergency.

That the grand Council shall have power to choose their Speaker and shall hold and exercise all the like Rights Liberties and privileges as are held and exercised by and in the House of Commons of Great Britain.

That the president General shall hold his office during the pleasure of the King, and his Assent shall be requisite to all Acts of the Grand Council and it shall be his Office and duty to cause them to be carried into Execution.

That the president General by and with the Advice and Consent of the Grand Council hold & exercise all the Legislative Rights, Powers and Authorities necessary for regulating and administering all the general Police & Affairs of the Colonies in which Great Britain and the Colonies of any of them, the Colonies in general or more than one Colony are in any Manner concerned as well civil and criminal as commercial.

That the said president General and Grand Council be an inferior and distinct Branch of the British Legislature united and incorporated with it for the aforesaid general purposes; and that any of the said general Regulations may originate and be formed and digested either in the Parliament of Great Britain or in the said Grand Council, and being prepared transmitted to the other for their Approbation or Dissent and that the Assent of both shall be requisite to the validity of all such general Acts or Statutes.

That in Time of War all Bills for granting Aids to the Crown prepared by the Grand Council and approved by the president General shall be valid and passed into a Law without the Assent of the British parliament.[3]

John Randolph Plan of 1780

Introduction

John Randolph served as an attorney general in Virginia for nine years. In 1775, when the outbreak of hostilities forced him to choose between the empire and his birthplace, he left for the British Isles. His excerpted proposal came from a mood of heady optimism after the summer of 1780 when the British victoriously captured Charleston, South Carolina. His hard-line stance stands distinct from previous loyalist proposals.

I must add my opinion, that the Colonies are of too great an Extent, to admit of one Government; and that to divide them into two or more Districts, wou'd only encrease the Difficulties, which must attend so complex a Regulation. Wherefore, I must take the Liberty, humbly to offer, as my Sentiments, that the future Government of America, ought to be as little compounded as possible; and, that each Colony be left to its antient Institutions, retrenching only, the Luxuriance of some Parts, and strengthening others, which are too weak, to become Effectual.

. . . Some Line therefore must be drawn, by which the important Subject of legislative authority may be settled, that no occasion of national Uneasiness, may be given on either Side.

As in every Dispute, which has been carried on with Violence, some Points must be given up, on both Sides in order to establish a perfect Reconciliation; and as it is my Wish, that the utmost Cordiality and affection may forever cement the two great Countries, which are now engaged in an unnatural Contest
. . .

That a People rais'd and supported by the Exertions and Treasure of G. Britain, shou'd contribute a Quota towards defraying the great and unavoidable Expences of Government; the Americans themselves in their cooler Moments of Reflection, must, I am persuaded, think very becoming and reasonable; but how to settle this Contribution, upon Principles satisfactory to each Party, is the great difficulty which will attend, the Completion of an accommodation.

As the principal advantages to be derived from America, must arise from its Trade, that Branch ought to be attended to, with the utmost Minuteness. The acts of Navigation ought to be preserv'd, as sacred. It is absurd in the Americans to complain of them . . . Had they not flourish'd under the Wisdom of these Laws, tho' not to the Degree, which they vainly imagin'd they had, they cou'd not have entertain'd such an Idea of their Power, and with so much Insolence, have denied the authority of this Kingdom.

. . . To grant a Freedom of Trade, to the Colonies, wou'd be a Measure, very injurious to this Country. There are some Commodities which the Americans must be supplied with from G. Britain; but there are others, and perhaps in a greater Number, which, was it not for these acts, wou'd be drawn from foreign Markets.

. . . Appeals from the Colonies ought to be free. They are the Birthright of the Subject, and constitute one of the most valuable Priviledges, he enjoys. They rectify improper Judgments, and protect the Rights of Absentees, who maintain but an unequal Contest with the Natives, who are present, and have an opportunity of availing themselves of their Influence, at their Trials. They lay open the Circumstances of the People, and cause in the Prosecution of them, large Sums of money to be expended in this Kingdom.

The Situation of the Clergy in America, is by no means on a proper Footing. Their Duty is laborious, and their Stipends, parsimonious. Except in the proprietary Governments, where they are appointed by the Governors, (and for the greater Part have ample Incomes,) they are chosen by the Vestries of the different Parishes, with a Lapse to the Crown, if kept vacant a limited Time. The Governors have little to do with them, but in this Instance, and they consider themselves as totally independent of the Crown. When they are guilty of an ecclesiastical offence, they deny the authority of the civil Power to try them: and the Bishops of London have never of late Years establish'd a proper Judicature to punish them. This gives them an Impunity in their sacerdotal Transgressions, to the Disgrace to Justice, and the Reproach of their Diocesans . . .

The Want of Consequence and authority in the Kings Representatives, has been a capital Defect in the Government of the Colonies. It has strengthen'd Democracy, and produced neglect in the People. The Prospect of Favour and the Motives of Fear, had but little operation amongst them. They knew that the Governors had few Things in their Gift; and that Punishment de- pended on the Law, which was in a great Degree, subject to their Construction of it. This led them to consider their Chief, as no more than a Cypher, and to rely on their own Strength and Unanimity, for Support. This was not the Case, in the proprietary Colonies; for there, the Governors had Powers sufficient to make them great, and of Course respected by the People . . .

. . . Upon the fullest Consideration of this Subject, my opinion shortly is, that the Americans ought not to be united under one Form of Government; because, if they concur in this Measure, they will become too powerful; if not, they will be perpetually dissatisfied.

That if any Reformation is made, it ought not to be too complicated, for if it is, like a great Machine, it will frequently be out of order; and to a plain People, the simplest will be the most suitable, as it will be the best understood, and most easy to be observed.

That no Representation of the Colonies, be admitted in Parliament, because it will create Difficulties, form Parties, and grieviously multiply the Business of every Session.

That since the Colonies have manifested such a Disposition to rebel, they ought to be divided and kept asunder as much as possible; for this Purpose, all Congresses Conventions and Committees should be prevented, and the hated Words expung'd from their Vocabularies, if that could be effected.

That to pacify them, that Bugbear of Taxation ought to be renounc'd; but full Compensation for it, be made, by the annual allowance, which they shou'd be obliged to pay.

That their Trade, except as to the Spanish Main, be absolutely confin'd to the british Dominions, and that all the Regulations in the Acts of Navigation be preserv'd and most strictly adhered to.

That the proprietary Governments be abolish'd, that no such Powers as the Proprietors Possess'd, be hereafter lodg'd in the Hands of Subjects.

That the executive Power be strengthen'd, in order to curb the Insolence and Encroachments of the People.

That their Courts be left on their old Footing, abolishing the new Courts of Admiralty and with them the Board of Commissioners of the Customs.

In short that when they have given sufficient Proofs that they have recover'd their Senses, and feel the Value of a Connection with G. Britain, in Preference to all others, they be reciev'd into the Bosom of this Country, and cherish'd with that parental Kindness, which is due to a Son, who with filial Respect, submits himself to the authority of his Father.

A Steady Perseverance in these Principles will I am fully persuaded, re-establish his Majesty in the happy Government of the Colonies and make him the greatest, as he must be acknowledged to be, the best Prince upon Earth.[4]

Jonathan Sewell's Plan (1785)

Introduction
The idea of a colonial union under the British Crown remained credible after the rebellion. New England's loyalist judge Jonathan Sewell set forth his proposal for the governance of Britain's remaining North American colonies. Sewell's clash with rebel mobs in New England and his exile in England since 1775 may have created the bitterness that marks this document. Witnessing the revolution at its center, Sewell diagnosed the loss of centralized authority as the primary cause. Sewell later served in the Vice Admiralty Court in Nova Scotia.

FEW MEN, I fear, propose anything in favour of government with a view entirely abstracted, from private interest. And certainly, when such a suspicion prevails, it must throw a disagreeable shade over the offered plan. To prevent therefore all imputations of that kind, I, on honor, do solemnly declare, that I have not a desire for any employment under government. Because, for several reasons, I am persuaded, that it is not in my power, to fill any office with a degree of ardour and reputation at all proportionate to my wishes. My only request now is that His Majesty may suffer an old and faithfull officer, tho nearly ruined by his uniform and constant attachment to his Majesty's government to retire on what, considering his former style of life & services can not be deemed extravagant.

In order to found a permanent and happy constitution in his Majesty's colonies on the Continent of America, I conceive it necessary to give one general form of government to all such as are or may be settled by natural born British subjects. Such an establishment will prevent that confusion, which must result from different systems; especially in places contiguous to each other, and inhabited by such subjects. The people now in contemplation are such, and by birth entitled to all the rights and privileges of Englishmen. Therefore the form of government in such British colonies ought to be as similar to the constitution of Great Britain as the distance of the countries, and the difference between a parent State and colonies will admit.

This grand and important object justly merits the most accurate attention, as well as the most serious exertions of men of the first abilities and purest principles. Radical errors, in all cases, must prove destructive. And particularly so in rules formed for the regular and proper government of societies. If error is originally admitted into the plan, it will be found more difficult to remedy, and will produce a greater variety of evils than anyone can readily point out. And as it is scarce possible materially to alter the public constitutions of any people; especially an informed and free one, without imminently endangering the safety and happiness of the whole community, the greatest care ought to be used in the original formation of a government or constitution for subjects of that description.

I am very conscious, that it is far beyond my present abilities to give a complete draft of the desirable and necessary plan. So complex is the nature, and so extensive and interesting are the consequences of it, that none should attempt it but such as have their heads and hearts more entire and more at ease than I can boast of. Therefore my only attempt will be to give some general hints on the subject, in the order they occur to my mind, and leave such to be properly arranged and corrected by some masterly hand. In doing even this, my want of every book necessary to assist my memory, and inform my judgment, will abridge my observations.

In governmental concerns many difficulties have arose in America. But nothing contributed to their existence so much as the distance of that country from Great Britain. Too often, before proper information could be given to, and instructions received from the latter, such have swelled into real evils. Sometimes local circumstances shifted so suddenly and violently between the giving information, and receiving instructions how to act, as entirely to change the immediate and proper objects of attention. So that Government could not avoid proceeding on erroneous principles in the application of a remedy. And too frequently an immediate one, which could not constitutionally be procured till government afforded it, was indispensibly necessary to stop disorders in the body politic. The great lapse of time before it could be obtained gave full scope for such disorders to encrease and rage so universally; as to render the intended remedy ineffective. The late rebellion affords many melancholly instances in support of the above remarks.

To guard against, as much as possible, such dangers in future, no better method, probably, can be suggested than the appointment of a Lord Lieut or Govr Genl over the whole of such colonies, with a Council of persons, duly qualified for the trust, on which everything depends, under the style of privy counsellors, or any other which may be thought proper. His Lordship to be president. And a certain number, which must be proportioned according to the whole, to make a board. This president and Council to be invested not only with ample general powers in America, but expressly with the following:

First, to convene before them all or any of the provincial Governors, either to procure information of the general or particular state of all or any one of the colonies.

Secondly, on any sudden emergency, officially to advise, or order such Govr how to act. And to render that power effectual, express instructions should be given to such Governors, in all such cases, immediately to inform the said President and Council thereof, and to obey their advice or peremptory orders thereon.

Thirdly, on the mal-conduct of any such Governor, the sd Govr Genl to be impowered either to reprimand or suspend him from his office; as the case may require. And if the latter, only until his Majesty's pleasure can be known. And to appoint some proper person to succeed him in the interim. In all instances of suspension, the person deprived of his office to have, in writing, and under the hand and seal of the said President, the reasons for it, within from the day of the suspension.

Fourthly, the President and Council, and in case of the nonconcurrence of the latter with the former, the President alone, to have the power of commanding the assistance, and directing the actual service of the military, within such colonies, both by land and by sea, in cases of imminent danger and popular insurrections. For which purpose they should be clothed expressly with sufficient civil authority. And at all times of fortifying where, and in such manner as they shall think fit, subject only to his Majesty's controul, and making full recompence for any private property that may be damaged thereby.

Fifthly, to reduce the medium of all such british colonies to one general standard.

And lastly, to have a superintending power over all laws, both temporary and perpetual, to be made in and by any of the legislative courts in the colonies aforesaid. And before any such law shall be in force to approbate the same. For which end each colony should be obliged to cause such laws to be laid before the said President and Council, who, within a given time, should also be obliged, under their or a majority of their hands and seal of their board, either to approve or negative the same and to give due notice thereof to the Governor and Council of such Colony. But in case of the latter, such colony to have the right of sending the same to his Majesty for his inspection and royal approbation, which if granted, such law should be in full force notwithstanding the negative of the Ld Lieut and his Council.

. . . The appearance of any jealousy in the parent state over her colonies, if without foundation, will be too much for the spirit of virtuous and valuable English subjects long to bear. And if such jealousy, in some degree, should be justifiable, it will serve the factious as a most dangerous weapon against government, and to lessen the ardor of the more cool and better disposed, in favour of it. Reason certainly dictates that in all free governments, whenever trustees are appointed for the reciprocal happiness of the Sovereign and the subjects, such should be placed on the surest and most liberal footing, which the subordination necessary in all States will admit. A deference for, and obedience to the Ministers of government, and their acts, are the only true and durable cements of society; therefore, whatever best cultivates and ensures those indispensible requisites, must ultimately prove the best calculated and most effectual for the interest of all parties. Many other observations naturally offer on this subject. But to proceed further into it would be exceeding the limits I have set myself. And I hope a misappropriation of time . . .

Instead of his Majesty granting each government, consisting of natural born subjects, a charter. Quaere, if it would not be more safe to enact one general Act of Parliament, to be called and to operate as the Magna Charta of such subjects, comprehending all, which might be contained in such charters relative to the mere rights and privileges of the people? As this may be thought an infringement on the royal prerogatives, I will not venture an opinion on it. However, if such charters shall originally proceed from his Majesty, may not an Act confirming certain essential parts thereof pass? I apprehend that valuable consequences will flow from it. On the one hand, the Americans have held, and possibly may again hold, that charters are compacts between the King and them. And that Parliament, not being a party, have not any cognizance of, or jurisdiction over those compacts, consequently can neither abridge, or enlarge the same. On the other, Parliament have claimed and exercised the right of doing the first, which includes a like power as to the last. The above method will settle that most dangerous dispute, by connecting the American constitutions expressly with the authority of Parliament. I do not mean that such an Act shall be any legal bar to proceeding, if necessary, in the ordinary course of the law to vacate such charters for the non-user or mis-user thereof.

The Counsellors in each province to be appointed by his Majesty agreeable to the late institution in the Massachusetts. The neglect of this measure in the founding of that province, and the public evils resulting therefrom, sufficiently evince the necessity of it; as well for the interest of the people as of the King. Such should be under the power of the Coy' so far as relates to suspension, which should remain in force till his Majesty's will thereon can be known: unless such suspension should be revoked by the Lord Lieu' by the advice of a majority of his Council, to whom the party suspended should have a right to apply for redress. But the Governor should be obliged, in writing under his hand, and the seal of the province, to give his reasons therefor to the suspended person within days from such suspension. Nor should any charges, but such as may be contained in the said writing be admissible either before the King in Council or the Lord Lieu' and Council, to criminate the accused party. No pay from the Crown shd be allowed Councellors . . .

As town meetings have been the sources of much evil, and as such meetings must be, it is necessary, that the same should be expressly confined within the proper limits. I know of no method more adequate to the necessity than pointing out in the most explicit and definitive terms, for what purposes such shall be called, and when and where held. The regulations to extend expressly to adjournments of such meetings, as well as to their opening. Latterly under the word "Prudentials" used in some provincial acts for the regulation of town meetings, particularly in Boston, the voters assumed legislative and other powers never intended to be vested in them. Therefore no such general term ought to be used in the institution of such assemblies—but every object within yr cognizance ought expressly to be marked ought.

In such meetings the people have knowingly exceeded their authority, though in consequence thereof they wilfully exposed themselves to a law-process for so doing; yet the remedy not being as sudden as the mischeif, the latter was effected. Therefore Q: whether it will be improper, in cases of necessity, to give the Governor or Commander in Chief with the advice of Council for the time being, express authority, by force if required, to disperse such assemblies when they clearly assume an excess of power, and of course become unlawfull? This point I confess to be very delicate; yet it is very interesting to government. If this method shd be thought too harsh, another offers, i.e. by Statute or by the Charter to render null & void all votes, acts & business of such meetings if in any one instance they exceed their power. This must be confessed not so effective a mode as the former.

In all colledges and other public seminaries of learning Caution ought to be used to prevent the principal trusts being lodged in the hands of gentlemen whose religious tenets point them decidedly to republicanism. The heads of all societies have a great influence over the youth belonging to the same. A slight retrospection of the late conduct in America will not only substantiate this observation, but evince the danger hereby intended to be avoided. However I would not be understood as aiming at any illiberal distinction between different opinions among protestants. For certainly I detest all degrees of persecution in all systems.

The ports for entering and clearing vessels should be as few as possible, consistent with the nature and convenience of the trade of the colony. For in such, distant from the Metropolis, it is next to impossible to prevent smuggling. Sometimes the under officers, so situated, have not force enough for that purpose. But oftener, being at a distance from their Superiours, are, for obvious reasons, inattentive or something worse.

All fortresses to be garrisoned by the King's troops, which must be under the command of the Lord Lieut. No ships of war to be built, or employed by the Colonists without his permission in writing under his hand and seal of office.

All the Acts of trade relative to the colonies ought to be very carefull revised, in some instances corrected, in others repealed, and collected into one seperate code. At present they are too much blended with Acts respecting Great Britain and Ireland. This naturally creates confusion, and consequently difficulties in the construction of the first mentioned acts.

The masts Acts in a very special manner require attention. And I am persuaded an entire alteration. Every appointmt which is to be vested in his Majy ought to be expressly reserved to him in the charter.

The vacant Crown lands in America ought to be managed with the utmost prudence both for the preservation of masts, and settlement of the same with people, I mean protestants, attached to the british constitution and government. Nor ought those lands to be granted to any person in very large quantities; for such grants are public evils.

The within mentioned general heads include a numerous variety of particulars. To collect and methodize which will prove a very arduous task and engross much time. A minute and accurate inspection of the laws and charters, especially the last, of the late colonies, and a knowledge, founded on experience, of what has occurred under the same, as well as a competent knowledge of the british constitution will, I humbly conceive, be found necessary to complete the important business. But as those particulars are not intended to be the subjects of the present enquiry, I shall leave the same to other gentlemen much better qualified for so large and interesting a business than I *ever* was. And only add *Non sum qualis eram.*

It may be objected that this plan is attended with many and great difficulties, and much labour. I own the charge to be true: but must also remark, that the only proper time for settling a regular and wise constitution for his Majesty's American colonies is the present. And that delays will not lessen but add to and encrease such difficulties. And lastly, that the vast importance of the object to be obtained, if judiciously conducted, must infinitely outweigh every other consideration.[5]

Notes

1. Timothy J. Shannon, *Indians and Colonists at the Crossroads of Empire: The Albany Congress of 1754* (Ithaca: Cornell University Press, 2000), 241–44.

2. Robert M. Calhoon, "William Smith Jr.'s Alternative to the American Revolution," *William and Mary Quarterly* 22 (1965): 105–18.

3. Julian Boyd, *Anglo-American Union: Joseph Galloway's Plans to Preserve the British Empire, 1774–1778* (Philadelphia: University of Pennsylvania Press, 1941), 112–14.

4. Miscellaneous Collection, Clements Library, 1778 (Subject: Randolph's hope for reconciliation between England and America and success of the Carlisle commission). Also see Mary Beth Norton, "John Randolph's Plan of Accommodations," *William and Mary Quarterly* 28 (1971): 106–20.

5. Boyd, 157–72.

CHAPTER FOUR

Loyalist Resilience

Loyalist Persuasions (1776 and 1777)

Introduction

The following excerpts published in the loyalist newspaper, *The New York Gazette and Weekly Mercury*, show British and loyalist attempts at building an ideological coalition to counter the rebel challenge. The essayists argued that a group of ambitious and designing rebel leaders who used mob violence and falsehoods to gain consent stood no chance against principled, experienced, and united Britons.

The Finest Britons

The King's Forces are in remarkable good health and spirits, and seem resolved to convince the world, that they not only bear the Name but Nature of Britons and while they fight with their usual ardor in the cause of the King and Constitution, they know how to treat even Ungrateful Rebels with Pity and Humanity.

The Rebels have lost the best and finest of the Province of New York: the Regulars have obtained it. The Rebel Army is dismayed, and in great Distress for proper Cloating; the King's Troops are in high Spirits, and well supplied with Necessaries of every Kind . . .

So vast a fleet was never seen together in this Part, or perhaps in all America before. The Ships are stationed up the East River or Sound as far as Turtle Bay: and, near the Town the multitude of Masts carries the appearance of a Wood. Some are moored up the North River; others in the Bay between Red and Yellow-Hook; some, again off Staten Island and several off Pawles Hook, and towards the Kills. The Men of war are moored chiefly up New York Sound and make with the other ships, a very magnificent and formidable Appearance . . .[1]

A Desperate and Malevolent Faction

There is no reason to wonder when all things are considered at the confused behaviour of the Rebels upon some late occasions. I am one of those, who do not so much impute this deficiency of conduct to a timidity of nature (for it must be owned that upon some occasions the Provincial troops have acted with gallantry) as to a secret doubt and distrust that the cause they are engaged in is fundamentally wrong or will lead to consequences they must naturally abhor.

War upon doubtful grounds is not the principle of the Hero and certainly will never make one. And when a suspicious arises, that bravery may be abused to serve a purpose it was not called forth to support, one may imagine that the keenest courage must lose its edge and the stoutest heart its energy . . . If the Rebels therefore have been found deficient in spirit and conduct, it ought to be imputed to the badness of their cause and the doubtful opinion which in general they entertain of it . . . They are fighting against their lawful Sovereign, in whose allegiance they were born; are aiming to sap the foundations of the British Empire, by which they have been generously protected and supported; they are endeavouring to establish a government in the hands of base and unworthy men; they have defrauded for this purpose their creditors in Britain of vast sums, and are extorting others from the people here; and they have overwhelmed this Continent in confusion and bloodshed in order to accomplish these and other purposes of a desperate and malevolent faction. Can such men hope to prosper? Can that cause make any man brave, which would render an honest man a coward?[2]

Rebel Falsehoods

The following infamous Falsehood published in one of the Philadelphia newspapers of the last Month, afford a Specimen of the Arts, which an abandoned set of traitors to their King and Country are using, to delude and inflame the Minds of their Fellow-Subjects to support their rebellion. This injured and insulted Country, when once the Truth (now industriously with-held) is laid upon, will no doubt be foremost to avenge the Miseries it feels, upon the Heads of the Miscreants who occasioned them. Nothing more plainly shews the Intention of these Political Imposters than their Care to prevent the Circulation of Truth, and their Rage in punishing those within their Power who have dared to speak it.[3]

Violence or Liberty?

Newport: The Spirit of Jealousy which the Leaders in the American Rebellion endeavored by every Artifice to create, hath now happily begun to change its Objects; and as the Distemper evidently grows more violent as they arrive at the last Stage of their political insanity, the most happy Consequences may soon be expected. In Boston, they have repeatedly assembled and like true Sons of LIBERTY, broke open a number of Stores, took out their Contents, and with a GENEROSITY peculiar to FREEMEN, liberally distributed to those who begin to find that Liberty, though a charming Word, will afford but little solid satisfaction to a starving Family. . . . It is likewise Matter of Pleasure, that the Stores which they have opened, belonged to Men who have been foremost in promoting the present Rebellion. Thomas Boyleston, has had his store opened by a Body of Women, and poor Man, very narrowly escaped a more dangerous Operations.[4]

British Defeat Impossible

What then can be the consequence of this rash and violent measure and degeneracy of representation, confusion of councils, blunders without number? The most respectable characters have withdrawn themselves and are succeeded by a great majority of illiberal and violent men.

Can you, have you the least confidence in a set of undisciplined men and officers, many of them have been taken from the lowest of the people, without principle, without courage; take away them who surround your pardon. How very few are there you can ask to sit at your table? As to your little navy, of that little, what is left?

Oh my dear Sir, how sadly have you been abused by a faction void of truth, and void of tenderness to you and your country? They have amused you with hopes of a declaration of war on the part of France. Believe me, from the best of authority, it was a fiction from the first. Early in the year 1776, a French Gentleman was introduced to me, with whom I became intimately acquainted. His business, to all appearance, was to speculate in the mercantile way . . . He frequently told me that he hoped the Americans would never think of independency; he gave me his reasons—Independency can never be supported unless France should declare war against England. I well know the state of her finances, years to come will not put them in a situation to enter upon a breach with England.

From your friends in England you have nothing to expect, their numbers have diminished to a cipher; the spirit of the whole nation is in activity, a few foundling names among the Nobility, though perpetually ringing in your ears and without character, without influence.

All orders and ranks of men in Great-Britain are now unanimous and determined to risk their all with content.

Trade and manufactures are found to flourish and new channels are continually offering, that will perhaps more than supply the loss of the old. In America, your harbours are blocked up, your cities fall one after another; fortress after fortress, battle after battle is lost.

A British army, after having passed unmolested through a vast extent of country, have possessed themselves of the capital of America. How unequal the contest! How fruitless the expence of blood? Under so many discouraging circumstances, can Virtue, can Honour, can the Love of your Country, prompt you to proceed? Humanity itself, and sure humanity is no stranger to your breast, calls upon you to desist. Your army must perish for want of common necessaries or thousands of innocent families must perish to support them; wherever they encamp, the country must be impoverished; wherever they march the troops of Britain will pursue and must complete the destruction which America herself has begun; perhaps it may be said, it is better to die than to be made slaves. This indeed is a splendid maxim in theory, and perhaps in some instances may be found experimentally true; but when there is the least possibility of an happy accommodation, surely wisdom and humanity call for some sacrifices to be made, to prevent inevitable destruction. You will know there is but one invincible bar to such an accommodation, could this be removed, other obstacles might readily be removed.

Let them, if they please, prepare some well-digested constitutional plan, to lay before them at the commencement of the negotiation; when they have gone this far, I am confident the usual happy consequences will ensue; unanimity will immediately take place through the different provinces; thousands who are not ardently wishing and praying for such a measure, will step forth and declare themselves zealous advocates for constitutional liberty, and millions will bless the hero that left the fist of war, to decide this most important contest with the weapons of wisdom and humanity.

Sir, let no false ideas of worldly honour deter you from engaging in so glorious a talk, whatever censures may be thrown out, by mean illiberal minds, your character will rise in the estimation of the virtuous and noble; it will appear with luster in the annals of history, and form a glorious contrast, to that of those, who have fought to obtain conquest, and gratify their own ambition by the destruction of their species, and the ruin of their country.

Be assured, Sir, that I write not this under the eye of any British officer, or person connected with the British army, or ministry. The sentiments I express are the real sentiments of my own heart, such as I have long held, and which I should have made known to you by letter before, had I not fully expected an opportunity of a private conference.

I love my country, I love you; but the love of truth, the love of peace, and the love of God, I hope I should be enabled if called upon to trial to sacrifice every other inferior love.

Your interpretation and advice, I am confident, would meet with a favourable reception from the authority under which you act, if it should not, you have an infallible recourse still left, negotiate for your country as the head of your army.[5]

Expressing Optimism (1778)

Introduction

In a letter of November 22, 1778, written to Pennsylvania loyalist Joseph Galloway (then in England), New Jersey loyalist Isaac Ogden expresses his confidence in widespread loyalist support, his belief that the rebel cause neared collapse, and his hope that the British would take stronger measures to suppress the rebellion. Ogden also observes that the French alliance did not automatically strengthen the rebel cause. Finally, he expresses hope that William Franklin, son of Benjamin Franklin, would unify the loyalist cause.

Among the common ranks of life [in New Jersey], a great majority would eagerly seize the terms offered by the Commissioners, if they dared. They are heartily tired of the war, and groan under the yoke of tyranny, and the heavy taxes that are imposed on them. Add to this, the scarcity of provisions and necessaries of life, which has enhanced the price almost beyond the bounds of toleration.

. . . The French alliance, although it has afforded a temporary relief even amongst the most violent (the thinking part I mean) is detested, much more so by those who are only lukewarm or friends to Government. From New Jersey there have taken up arms and joined the King's Troops since they came into the country, upwards of two thousand five hundred and at least five hundred more refugees are now within the lines of the King's Army.

. . . The commissioners have had an opportunity of gaining such knowledge in this country that they will be enabled to inform his majesty that great number of his American subjects, through all trials and perils, steadfastly and faithfully preserve their attachment to him: that they have sacrificed their fortunes, and are willing to devote their lives to his service, and any interested and malevolent reports to the contrary, the commissioners will no doubt contradict.

Their last manifesto, which I believe you saw in this country was suppressed among the Rebels and not allowed to circulate. Great numbers of pamphlets, containing all their proceedings, have lately been published—and endeavors are made to disperse them in the country.

. . . I heartily congratulate you on the release of Governor Franklin. Great part of his time since he came in has been taken up in getting redress for suffering Friends to Government—he has happily succeeded (after much doubt fear and difficulty) with the commander in chief in one instance which I will give you. Some time since a number of refugees from Connecticut employed by Gen. Tryon to cut wood on LI were taken off by a party from New England and sent to their different counties for Tryal who of course must without the interposition of the general suffer death, or a worse situation—Gov. Franklin proposed and insisted that an equal number of Connecticut prisoners should be selected and retained as hostages for these unfortunate persons. He succeeded as to have these eight men delivered up to him. (exchange prisoners—Franklin proposed). If it succeeds, it will have many good effects; first in saving the lives of the prisoners—secondly, in evincing a certain spirit that has long been wanting—thirdly, in convincing the friends of Government, throughout the continent, that some attention is paid to them, and that Government will no longer tamely see, some of the King's best subjects sacrificed with impunity. Governor Franklin has, with success, been the advocate for many ill-treated Refugees, I could wish he had the appointment of Super Intendent General of Refugees.

. . . The Idea prevails here that this Country will be abandoned by the King's Troops the next Spring but I cannot entertain one so disgraceful & destructive to the British Empire. To abandon this country is to give up the West Indies, for whoever have this Country will have the West India Islands.

. . . The rebellion hangs by a slender thread. The majority of the Inhabitants dissatisfied with their present Tyrannical Government—Their Money depreciating—The French Alliance in general detested—Provisions scarce & that scarcity increasing. . . .

In this situation what is necessary to crush the Rebellion—it is easily answered—only one vigorous campaign, properly conducted—I mean by this, that the Person commanding should be a man of Judgment, of Spirit, & Enterprise, and one who would made himself acquainted with the Geography of the Country and a few more Troops to supply the place of those gone to the West Indies.

In this case, one Province would soon be conquered, when only by disarming the Rebels and putting Arms into the hands of the King's Friends it would be kept & thousands of oppressed and persecuted Friends of Government would take Refuge there and very soon form such a body of men that Washington with his whole Force would be afraid to approach.

There has lately been made a Calculation of the Refugees within the lines of New York, & including those who have joined the Provincial Corps, they amount to upwards of ten thousand. The most of these persons have from their attachment to their Sovereign abandoned their Fortunes and from Affluence are reduced to Indigence which they bear with Patience, in full confidence that the Faith of Government, and the Promises of Protection, repeatedly given them, would be sacredly observed.[6]

Confronting Confiscation Laws (1779)

Introduction

This excerpt, from October 22, 1779, is taken from the "Act for the Forfeiture and Sale of the Estates of Persons who have adhered to the Enemies of this State, and for declaring the Sovereignty of the People of this State, in respect to all Property within the same." This law listed New Yorkers who were considered to be enemies of the rebel cause. The named were banished from the state, and the rebel government confiscated their property. Like New York, most of the other colonies had similar confiscation laws.

Whereas, during the present unjust and cruel war, waged by the King of Great Britain, against this State and the other United States of America, divers persons holding or claiming property within this state, have voluntarily been adherent to the said King, his fleets and armies, enemies to this State and the said other United States, with intent to subvert the government and liberties of this state and the said other United States, and to bring the same into subjection to the crown of Great Britain; by reason whereof, the said persons have severally justly forfeited all rights to the protection of this state, and to the benefit of the laws under which such property is held or claimed: And whereas, the public justice and safety of this state absolutely require that the most notorious offenders should be immediately hereby convicted and attainted of the offence aforesaid, in order to work a forfeiture of their respective estates, and vest the same in the people of this state; And whereas, the constitution of this state hath authorized the legislature to pass Acts of attainder for crimes committed before the termination of the present war.

. . . The said persons banished from this State and declared Felons, without benefit of clergy, if found within it. And it be it further enacted by the authority aforesaid, That the said several persons herein before particularly named, shall be and hereby are declared to be for ever banished from this State; and each and every of them, who shall at any time hereafter be found in any part of this State, shall be, and are hereby adjudged and declared guilty of felony, and shall suffer death as in cases of felony, without benefit of clergy.

. . . Be it further enacted by the authority aforesaid, That it shall and may be lawful for the grand jurors at any supreme court of judicature to be held for this state, or any court of oyer and terminer and general goal delivery, or general and quarter sessions of the peace, to be held and for any county within this state, whenever it shall appear to such grand jurors by the oath of one or more credible witness or witnesses, that any person or persons, whether in full life or deceased, generally reputed, if in full life, to hold or claim, or if deceased to have held or claimed, at the time of their death respectively, real or personal estate within this state, hath or have been guilty of the offence aforesaid, to prefer bills of indictment against such persons as shall then be in full life, for such offence, and in relation to the offence committed by such persons in their lives time, as shall then be deceased, severally and respectively, notwithstanding that such offence many have been committed elsewhere than in the county for which such grand jurors shall be summoned. That in every indictment to be taken in pursuance of this act, the offence or offences shall be charged to have been committed in the county where the indictment shall be taken, not-withstanding such offence or offences may have been committed elsewhere; and it shall not be necessary to set forth specially, whether the several persons charged in such indictment were respectively deceased or in full life, or were reputed to hold or claim real or personal estate within this state. And on every such indictment shall be indorsed that the same was taken in pursuance of this act, and the day when the same was preferred into court . . .[7]

Documenting Rebel Weakness (1780)

Introduction

John Cunningham collected the excerpted information on February 26, 1780. Originally from Edinburgh, Cunningham lived in New Jersey for four years before the rebellion began. During the war, he joined the loyalist militia in New Jersey and provided intelligence to British headquarters. The problem of gathering information from unknown informants plagued the British effort, especially during the first two years of the war.

> The [Continental] army is very discontented and dwindles very fast. Many desert homewards and elsewhere. None whose times are out can be prevailed on to enlist at any rate. The causes of disgust many. They despise the pay—they hate the French—they are enraged at the retention of men whose times are out.
>
> The people of the country are loud in their complaints both in Pennsylvania and Jersey. He has heard hundreds declare a design to remove from the continent. The desertions in the army greatly discourage those who are left. a little more activity and some encouragements from the Britain he thinks would bring oft many of the officers who are in a general way poor as well as the men.
>
> When last at Morristown he saw many of Gen. Tryon's [Governor William Tryon from New York] late proclamations offering pardons to deserters—some women carried them out—they cannot fail being publickly known—tho' he saw none at the hands of the soldiers.[8]

Pledging Declaration of Dependence (1781)

Introduction

Published in New York City's The Royal Gazette, the loyalists' Declaration of Dependence summarized the loyalist complaints against rebel leaders. Issued as a direct response to the Declaration of Independence, it articulated the alternative loyalist vision for the future of the American colonies. The Declaration blasted the Continental Congress and sought to preserve the colonies' connection to Britain.

When in the course of human events it becomes necessary for men, in order to preserve their lives, liberties and properties, and to secure to themselves, and to their posterity, that peace, liberty and safety, to which by the laws of nature and of nature's God they are entitled, to throw off and renounce all allegiance to a government, which under the insidious pretences of securing those inestimable blessings to them, has wholly deprived them of any security of either life, liberty, property, peace, or safety; a decent respect to the opinions of mankind, requires that they should declare, the injuries and oppressions, the arbitrary and dangerous proceedings, which impel them to transfer their allegiance from such their oppressors, to those who have offered to become their protectors.

We hold these truths to be self evident, that all men are created equal; that they are endowed by their Creator with certain rights, that among those, are life, liberty, and the pursuit of happiness; that to secure those rights, governments are instituted; that whenever any form of government becomes destructive to these ends, it is the right of the people to alter or to abolish it, or to renounce all allegiance to it, and to put themselves under such other government, as to them shall appear best calculated and most likely to effect their safety and happiness; it is not indeed prudent to change for light and transient causes, and experience hath ever shewn, that men are disposed to suffer much before they can bring themselves to make a change of government; but when a long train of the most licentious and despotic abuses, pursuing invariably the same objects, evinces a design to reduce them under anarchy, and the distractions of democracy, and finally to force them to submit to absolute despotism, it is their right, it becomes their duty, to disclaim and renounce all allegiance to such government, and to provide new guards for their future security.

Such have been our patient sufferings, and such is now the necessity which constrains us to renounce all allegiance to Congress, or to the governments lately established by their direction.

The history of Congress, is a history of continued weakness, inconsistency, violation of the most sacred obligations of all public faith and honour, and of usurpations, all having in direct object the producing of anarchy, civil feuds, and violent injustice, which have rendered us miserable, and must soon establish tyranny over us, and our country.

To prove this let facts be submitted to the candid world.

They have recommended and caused laws to be passed, the most destructive of the public good, and ruinous to individuals.

Availing themselves of our zeal and unanimity to oppose the claims of the British Parliament, and of our unsuspecting confidence in their solemn professions and declarations, they have forbidden us to listen to, or to accept any terms of peace, until their assent should be obtained.

They have refused to accept of, or even to receive proposals and terms of accommodation and peace, though they know the terms offered exceeded what the Colonies in America had unanimously declared would be satisfactory, unless the Crown would relinquish a right inestimable to it and to the whole empire, and formidable to Congress only.

They have excited and directed the people to alter or annull their ancient constitutions, under which, they and their ancestors, had been happy for many ages, for the sole purpose of promoting their measures.

They have by mobs and riots awed Representative Houses, repeatedly into a compliance with their resolutions, though destructive of the peace, liberty, and safety of the people.

They have by their misconduct, reduced us to all the dangers and distress of actual invasion from without, and to all the horrors of a cruel war within.

They have not only prevented the increase of the population of these states, but by fines, imprisoning, and banishments, with the losses by war, they have caused a rapid depopulation.

They have corrupted all the sources of justice and equity by their Tender Law, by which they destroyed the legal force of all civil contracts, wronged the honest creditor, and deserving salary man of his just dues, stripped the helpless orphan of his patrimony, and the disconsolate widow of her dower.

They have erected a multitude of new offices, and have filled them with men from their own body, or with their creatures and dependants, to eat out the substance of the people; they have made their officers dependant on their will for the tenure of their offices, and the payment of their salaries.

They have raised a standing army and sent it into the field, without any act of the legislature, and have actually rendered it independent of the civil power, by making it solely dependant on them.

They have combined with France, the natural and hereditary enemy of our civil constitution, and religious faith, to render us dependant on and subservient to the views, of that foreign, ambitious, and despotic monarchy.

They have suffered their troops to live repeatedly on free quarters on the inhabitants, and to strip them by force of the necessaries of life, and have protected them from either trial or punishment under the plea of necessity, which necessity if real, was caused by their treacherous views, or unpardonable negligence.

They have ruined our trade, and destroyed our credit with all parts of the world.

They have forced us to receive their paper, for goods, merchandise, and for money due to us, equal to silver and gold, and then by a breach of public faith in not redeeming the same, and by the most infamous bankruptcy, have left it on our hands, to the total ruin of multitudes, and to the injury of all.

They have driven many of our people beyond sea, into exile, and have confiscated their estates, and the estates of others who were beyond sea before the war, or the existence of Congress, on pretence of offences, and under the sanction of a mock trial, to which the person condemned was neither cited or present.

They have abolished the true system of the English constitution and laws, in thirteen of the American Provinces, and established therein a weak and factious democracy, and have attempted to use them as introducing the same misrule and disorder into all the Colonies on the continent.

They have recommended the annihilating of our charters, abolishing many of our most valuable laws, and the altering fundamentally the form of our government.

They have destroyed all good order and government, by plunging us into the factions of democracy, and the ravages of civil war.

They have left our seas unprotected, suffered our coasts to be ravaged, our towns to be burnt, some of them by their own troops, and the lives of our people to be destroyed.

They have without the consent or knowledge of the legislatures, invited over an army of foreign mercenaries to support them and their faction, and to prevent the dreadful scenes of death and desolation from being closed by an honourable peace and accommodation with our ancient friend and parent.

They have fined, imprisoned, banished, and put to death some of our fellow citizens, for no other cause but their attachment to the English laws and constitution.

They have countenanced domestic tumults and disorders in our capital cities, and have suffered the murder of a number of our fellow citizens perpetrated under their eyes in Philadelphia, to pass unnoticed.

They first attempted to gain the savage and merciless Indians to their side, but failing in making them the presents promised and expected, have occasioned an undistinguished destruction to ages, sexes, and conditions on our frontiers.

They have involved us in an immense debt, foreign as well as internal, and did put the best port and island on our continent, into the hands of the foreigners, who are their creditors.

They have wantonly violated our public faith and honor, and destroyed all grounds for private confidence, or the security of private property, have not blushed to act in direct contradiction to their most solemn declaration, and to render the people under their government, a reproach and a bye word among the nations.

In every stage of these proceedings, they have not been wanting to throw out before us, specious excuses for their conduct, as being the result of necessity and tending to the public good.—In every stage since their public conduct, began to contradict their public declarations, our minds have been overwhelmed with apprehensions; and as our sufferings have increased, our tears have flowed in secret. It has been dangerous and even criminal to lament our situation in public. The unsuspecting confidence which we with our fellow citizens reposed in the Congress of 1774, the unanimous applause, with which their patriotism and firmness were crowned, for having stood forth, as the champions of our rights, founded on the English constitution; at the same time that it gave to Congress the unanimous support of the whole continent, inspired their successors with very different ideas, and emboldened them by degrees to pursue measures, directly the reverse of those before adopted, and were recommended, as the only just constitutional and safe.—Congress in 1774, reprobated every idea of a separation from Great-Britain, and declared that they looked on such an event as the greatest of evils.—They declared that a repeal of certain acts, complained of, would restore our ancient peace, and harmony.—That they *asked but for peace, liberty and safety.—That they wished not for a diminution of the royal prerogative, nor did they solicit the grant of any new right.* And they pledged themselves in the presence of Almighty God, that they *will ever carefully and zealously endeavour to support and maintain the royal authority of Great-Britain over us, and our connection with Great-Britain—and our councils had been influenced only by the dread of impending destruction.*

The acts complained of have been repealed, yet how have Congress given the lie, to these their most solemn professions! In '774, they declared themselves concerned for the honour of Almighty God, whose pure and holy religion, our enemies were undermining—They pointed out those enemies, and the danger in which our holy religion was by their complaints of the establishment of the Roman Catholic religion in Canada; they say, "It is a religion which has deluged the Island of Great Britain with blood, and dispersed impiety, persecution, murder, and rebellion through every part of the world." We find the present Congress not only claiming a new right, and hazarding every thing valuable in life, to the present and future generations in support of it, but we also find them, leagued with the eldest son of this bloody, impious, bigoted, and persecuting church, to ruin the nation from whose loins we sprung, and which has ever been the principal bulwark in Europe, against the encroachments and tyranny of that church, and of the kingdoms devoted to her: we think it not too severe to say, that we find them as intoxicated with ambition of Independent sovereignty, as that execrable Roman Daughter, who drove the wheels of her chariot over the mangled body of her murdered father, in her way to the capitol.

We find that all their fears and apprehensions from the Roman Catholic religion in Canada, have vanished or sunk to nothing, when put in competition with their political views, and that they have attempted to seduce the Canadians to their side, by promises of still greater religious establishments; and to shew that they were in earnest, have countenanced this impious religion by attending its ceremonies and worship in a body.—We find them at one time boasting of their patriotic and religious ancestors, who braved every danger of unknown seas, and coasts, to preserve civil and religious freedom, and who chose rather to become exiles, and suffer every misery that must await them, on a savage and unexplored coast, than submit to civil, but above all religious innovations—at another time we find them destroying the British Constitution, the pride of their ancestors, and encouraging a religion which they held in abhorrence, as idolatrous and tyrannical.—We find them contending for liberty of speech, and at the same time controlling the press, by means of a mob, and persecuting everyone who ventures to hint his disapprobation of their proceedings.

We find them declaring in September 1779, that to payoff their paper money, at less than its nominal value, would be an unpardonable sin, an execrable deed. "That a faithless bankrupt Republic would be a novelty in the political world, and appear like a common prostitute among chaste and reputable matrons," would be "a reproach and a bye-word among the nations, &c."

We find the same Congress in March following, liquidating their paper debt at 2½ per cent. or 6d. in the pound.

We should fill volumes, were we to recite at large their inconsistency, usurpations, weaknesses and violations of the most sacred obligations—We content ourselves with the above brief recital of facts known to the world and attested by their own records

We have sufficiently shewn that a government thus marked and distinguished from every other, either despotic or democratic, by the enormity of its excesses, injustice and infamy, is unfit to rule a free people.

We therefore, Natives and Citizens of America, appealing to the impartial world to judge of the justice of our cause, but above all to the supreme Judge of the World for the rectitude of our intentions, do renounce and disclaim all allegiance, duty, or submission to the Congress, or to any government under them, and declare that the United Colonies or States, so called, neither are, nor of right ought to be independent of the crown of Great-Britain, or unconnected with that empire; but that we do firmly believe and maintain "*That the Royal Authority of the Crown of Great-Britain over us, and our connection with that kingdom ought to be preserved and maintained, and that we will zealously endeavor to support and maintain the same;*" and in the support of this declaration, with a firm reliance on the protection of Divine Providence, we mutually pledge to each other, and to the crown and empire of Great-Britain, our lives, our fortunes, and our sacred honor.[9]

Notes

1. *The New York Gazette and Weekly Mercury*, October 6, 1776.
2. "Irenicus," *The New York Gazette and Weekly Mercury*, October 28, 1776.
3. *The New York Gazette and Weekly Mercury*, March 10, 1777.
4. *The New York Gazette and Weekly Mercury*, April 25, 1777.
5. *The New York Gazette and Weekly Mercury*, December 1, 1777.
6. New York Public Library, Balch Papers, Isaac Ogden to Joseph Galloway, November 22, 1778.
7. The New York Act of Attainder, or Confiscation Act; found in "Greenleaf's Laws of New York from the First to the Twentieth Session Inclusive," vol. 1, p. 26.

It is also in chap. 25 of the Laws of the Third Session of the New York Legislature, and was passed on October 22, 1779.

8. John Cunningham Intelligence, February 26, 1780, Clinton Papers, Clements Library.

9. *The Royal Gazette*, November 17, 1781.

CHAPTER FIVE

Loyalist Military Involvement

Preaching to Loyalist Soldiers (1777)

Introduction

The Reverend Charles Inglis supported a militant stance against rebel leaders who he believed fanned the flames of rebellion. In this excerpted sermon, Inglis encourages loyalist soldiers to fight for the rights protected by the British constitution. Inglis spent the war in the British headquarters of New York City. As a reward for his loyalty during the revolution, Inglis received an appointment as the first bishop of Nova Scotia.

NEVER, I will boldly & without hesitation pronounce it, never was a more just, more honourable, or necessary Cause for taking up arms than that which now calls you into the Field. It is the Cause of Truth against Falsehood, of Loyalty against Rebellion, of legal Government against Usurpation, of Constitutional Freedom against Tyranny—in short it is the cause of human happiness of millions against Outrage and Oppression. Your generous efforts are required to assert the Rights of your amiable, injured Sovereign—they are required to restore your Civil Constitution which was formed by the Wisdom of ages, and was the Admiration and Envy of Mankind—under which we and our Ancestors enjoyed Liberty, Happiness, and Security—but is now subverted to make room for a motley fabric, that is perfectly adapted to popular Tyranny. Your bleeding Country, through which Destruction and Ruin are driving in full career, from which Peace, Order, Commerce, and useful Industry are banished—Your loyal Friends and Relations groaning in Bondage under the iron scourge of Persecution and Oppression—all these now call upon you for Succour and Redress.

It is not wild, insatiable Ambition which sports with Lives and Fortunes of Mankind that leads you forth, driven from your peaceful Habitations for no other Cause than honouring your King, as God hath commanded; you have taken up the Sword to vindicate his just Authority, to support your excellent Constitution, to defend your Families, your Liberty, and Property, to secure to yourselves and your Posterity that Inheritance of constitutional Freedom to which you were born; and all this against the Violence of usurped Power, which would deny you even the right of Judgment or of Choice, which would rend you from the Protection of your parent State, and eventually place you— astonishing Infatuation and Madness—place you under the despotic Rule of our inveterate Popish Enemies, the inveterate Enemies of our Religion, our Country and Liberties . . .[1]

Volunteering Military Assistance (1780)

Introduction
By 1780, some New York refugees, originally from New England and the mid-Atlantic colonies, embodied themselves under their own leaders. The Associated Loyalists, as they called themselves, were headed by Governor William Franklin of New Jersey. These militants hoped to create an autonomous military organization and assist the British in suppressing the prolonged rebellion.

His majesty having been graciously pleased to approve of a plan for the purpose of employing the zeal of his faithful subjects in North America, in annoying the sea coasts of the revolted provinces and distressing their trade, either in co-operation with his Majesty's land and sea forces, or by making diversions in their favour, when they are carrying on operations in other parts; and for that purpose has been also pleased to nominate a number of Gentlemen as a board of directors for the conduct and management of said business.

And his excellency SHC, K.B. and commander in chief, having issued a commission constituting their excellencies William Franklin, Esq., governor of NJ, and Josiah Martin, governor of NC, and Timothy Ruggles, Daniel Coxe, George Duncan Ludlow, Edward Lutwyche, George Rome, George Leonard, Anthony Stewart, and Robert Alexander Esquires, a board of directors for the purposes aforesaid with powers to embody and associate all such persons as may be willing to act under their orders, and with his approbation, to plan and direct any Enterprise they may think expedient.

We the subscribers do hereby agree to be subject to the following rules and regulations and bind ourselves for the true observance of the same to the board of directors.

First: Subject to and strictly obey all such rules and orders as shall, from time to time, be established and ordained by the Board of Directors for the regulation and good government of this Association; we will at all times yield a chearful and ready obedience to all Officers who shall, on the recommendation of the Board, be commissioned by the commander in chief, and conform ourselves, in every respect, to that orderly conduct and good discipline so essentially necessary for our personal security and success of every enterprise.

While it not our intention, while we become Adventurers in this undertaking, and by our exertions provide for ourselves and Families, as well as aid his Majesty's arms, to be bound for an unlimited time, or viewed in the light of enlisted soldiers, it is hereby provided, that if any of us should in future chuse to withdraw from this Association, we shall be at full liberty to do so: previous, however, to a dismission, the person desiring the same, shall give at least three months notice in writing of his intentions to the board of directors or his commanding officer, to be reported to the Board . . .

Second: for equitable distribution of captures that may be made by the associators, and as an inducement to behave with courage and perseverance on all occasions of duty, and as it is our wish, that no quiet inoffensive inhabitant or other innocent person without the lines shall suffer by this establishment, and our determination that all excesses, barbarities or irregularities . . . shall be avoided . . . 10% of proceeds of all captures shall first be appropriated as retribution fund for satisfying such claimants who may, on a full Enquiry, be entitled to compensation . . .

[A] further sum of 10% [be] set apart as charity fund for relief and support of any who may be sick, wounded, maimed, or otherwise disabled in the service, and for the maintenance of widows and orphans belonging to the association.

[A] reservation of 5% shall be assigned to a reward of such officers, who by their judicious or spirited conduct, shall merit particular distinction.

last two are submitted entirely to the judgment and direction of the Board.

remainder equally divided amongst all the associators concerned in the enterprise without regard to rank or station.

Third: if effects taken from loyal, quiet, or inoffensive inhabitant, and distributed the amount of the same shall when ordered by the commander in chief of his Majesty's land forces, be repaid from future campaigns.

Fourth: if taken prisoner or killed: in the first case the person so taken and in the latter his legal representative, shall nevertheless receive as full a share as the other Associators concerned in the enterprise.

Fifth: consent and agree that such courts, composed of our own officers, as may be appointed for the purpose by the Board, shall be held whenever the irregular, disobedient, or disorderly behavior of any individual may render them necessary.

The proceedings to be conducted according to justice and equity; and in case of guilt, the punishment directed (not extending beyond fine or expulsion according to the nature of the offense) to be subject to the revision and mitigation of the board, on appeal by the person deeming himself aggrieved.[2]

Organizing Loyalist Militia (1781)

Introduction

This excerpted regiment list of rules from North Carolina's David Fanning, written on September 25, 1781, shows local attempts to organize a well-ordered and disciplined military force of loyal militias to compete with rebel units. During 1781–1782, Fanning's men presented formidable opposition to rebel forces.

> I then Represented to Major Craigg that with his approbation I would establish certain Regulations for the conduct of the militia which he approved off and was obliging Enough on my giving them to him to convict and confirm the following Rules which where in a short time after that had printed and distributed in the country—
>
> Rules and Regulations for the well Governing the Loyal Militia of the province of North Carolina—
>
> 1st No person for to be admitted a militia man untill he takes the oath of allegiance to his Majesty which is allways to be done before three Senior Officers of the Regiment on the spot.
>
> 2d all persons once Enrolled in a militia Company and having taken the Oath abovementioned will be Considered as Entitled to every priviledge and protection of a British Subject, and will on being detected joining the Rebels will be treated as a Deserter and Traitor—
>
> 3d Every militia man is to Repair without fail or Excuse Except Sickness at the time appointed to the place assigned by his Coln or Capt with his arms and accoutrements and is not to quit his Company on any pretence whatever, without the Knowledge and permission of his Captain Or Commanding Officer—
>
> 4th The Colonel of every County has full power to Call his Regiment together and march them when necessary for his Majesties service, the Capt of Each Company has also power to assemble his Company when any Sudden Emergency Renders it necessary and which he is to Report as soon after as possible to his Colonel.
>
> 5th Mutual assistance is to be given on all occasions But as it is impossible to give positive Directions on this subject, it is left to the discretion of Colonels of Regiments who must be answerable that their Reasons for not affording assistance when Required are sufficient.
>
> 6th when the militia of different Counties are Embodied the senior officer is to Command Colonels of Regiments are Immediately to determine the present

Rank of their Caps in which Regard is to be had to Seniority of Commission or Service—in Cases of Vacancies Colonels may Grant temporary Commissions till Recourse can be had to the commanding officer of the Kings Troops.—

7th the men are to understand that in what Relates to the service they are bound to Obey all officers tho' not immediately belonging to their own Companies—

8th Courts Martial may Sit by the Appointment of the Colonel or Commanding Officer and must Consist for the trial of an officer of all the officers of the Regiment he belongs to Except the Colonel or Commanding Officer and for the trial of a non Commissioned officer or private man of 2 Captains 2 Subalterns and 3 private men, the latter to belong to the same Company as the person to be tried: the oldest Capt to preside and the sentence of the Court to be determined by plurality of Votes and approved of by the Commanding Officer—

9th No Colonel is to supercede an officer without trial but he may suspend him till he can be tried—

10th Quitting Camp without permission, Disobedience of Orders neglect of duty plundering and all Irregalarities and disorders subversive of Good order and discipline are to be punished at the discretion of a Court martial—Constituted as above mentioned and by the approbation of the Colonel or Commanding Officer, who has power to pardon or Remit any part of a punishment but not to Encrease or alter it—

11th Every man must take the Greatest care of his arms and ammunition and have them always Ready for service—

12th when the militia is not Embodied they are at all times to be attentive to the motions of the Rebels and Emediately to acquaint the nearest officer of any thing may Discover who is to communicate it to his Colonel or other. Officers as may be Requisite—

13th It is the duty of every person professing allegiance to his Majesty to communicate to the commanding officer of the nearest British post every, intiligence he can procure of the assembling or moveing of any bodies of Rebels, persons employed on this occation shall always be paid.

14th Colonels of Regiments may assemble any number of their men which they may think necessary to be posted in particular spots of their Districts their time of service on these occations is to be limited and they are at the Expiration of it to be Relieved by others.—Great Care is to be taken that no partiality is shown but that each take an equal proportion of duty, for which purpose Alphebatical Rolls are to be Kept by which the men are to be warned.—Every Captain is to Keep an account of the number of days each man of his Company serves.

The strict observeance of the Above Regulations is Strongly Recommended as the best means of the Kings faithful subjects a manifest superiority over the Rebel militia and ensure them that success their Zeal and Spirit in the cause of their Country entitles them to Expect.—

Head Quarters Wilmington. 25th Sepm 1781.

I then thought it prudent to administer the following Oath of Allegiance unto those people I was dubious of—

I A. B. do Swear on the holy evangelists of almighty God to bear true allegiance to our sovereign Lord King George the third and to uphold the same. I do voluntarily promise for to serve as militia under any of the officers appointed over me and that I will when Lawfully warned by our said officers assemble at any place by them Directed in case of danger, in the space of 8 hours, I will Go with my arms and accoutrements in Good order to Suppress any Rebels or others the Kings enemies, that I will not at any time Do or cause to be done any thing prejudicial to his majesties Government or suffer any Intercourse or Correspondence with the Enemies thereof, that I will make Known any plot or plots any wise Inimical to his Majestyes forces or loyal subjects by me Discovered to any of his Majesties Officers contiguous, and it shall not exceed six hours before the said is discovered, if health and distance permit this. I do solemnly swear and promice to defend in all cases whatsoever.—so help me God.[3]

Recruiting Loyalist Regiments (1781)

Introduction

New England's Edward Winslow was the muster-master general of loyalist regiments during the war. In his 1781 letter to Governor John Wentworth of New Hampshire, Winslow emphasizes the folly of ignoring loyalists who were prepared to provide military assistance. He understood that the British neglected to equip and arm colonists because they seemed weak additions to professional soldiers. But in neglecting them, the British made them even weaker.

The nature of the present war in America is so peculiar, so different from what British armies have been formerly accustomed to, that experience acquired in other countries avails very little in this. Veterans who served campaigns in Germany and are perfectly acquainted with manoeuvering of armies in regular sieges and defences, find themselves novices when engaged against an army like the present, and bold as the assertion may appear I venture to affirm that the British have gained near as much from their observations of the Provincial and American Troops as the latter have acquired from them. I will only mention one circumstance by way of illustration, which does not in any degree derogate from the honor of the British (God forbid that I should say or write anything that did). When the British Light Infantry began their operations in this country they were almost compact in their movements, regular in their marching and from habit and general instructions they appeared averse to every attempt to screen or cover themselves from danger however imminent. Hence many of them were picked off in all the first skirmishes. It was observed that on all such occasions the enemy placed themselves behind trees and walls, etc., and it was apparently necessary to take them in their own way. In consequence a new word was adopted and the Flank Corps were on subsequent occasions ordered "To Tree"—a word of command as well known to them now as any other.

The theoretical part of military business is not so particularly intricate that a gentleman may not acquire a competent knowledge of it in a short time; much of the necessary knowledge of an officer is not what's generally understood by the term professional, and surely an acquaintance with the country in which he operates, with the temper of its inhabitants, their manners, &c., must be an essential qualification. I have the highest idea of the necessity of discipline and subordination myself but I will not subscribe to the doctrine that it requires a whole life spent in the service to give an officer a just idea of it. Many Provincial officers and very many young officers of the Line are proofs to the contrary. I know that experience is necessary to complete a military character, but that only men who have rose thro' all the gradations of military rank are fit to be trusted with military commands is an idea which I would hope was originally formed in the head of Sir Wm. [Howe] and would never descend farther than to his immediate successor. I would not detract one iota from the respect due to veterans, but in Heaven's name when a state is in danger should men of capability, liberal education and extensive knowledge remain unemployed until all the serjeants of the army are provided for? Surely this cannot be prudence or policy. This war has made many good soldiers for the rebels and it has added many good soldiers to the British. The discipline of the Americans is indisputably copied from the British, but the British in turn have in several instances profited by the examples of their enemies.

A General Burgoyne may contend that a regiment of raw recruits headed by inexperienced leaders cannot carry martial enterprises with success, he however ought to acknowledge that substitutes for discipline and experience were found in the American armies encountered by him, which more than compensated for the want of those qualities.

Having long since established in my own mind by this kind of reasoning the propriety and expediency of employing the gentlemen of this country, I readily declared my resolution to engage in the provincial service. Till the present time I have seen no fair opening. The anticipations of impediments in the recruiting business, had it not been for the discouraging partiality shewn to particular regiments, would never have discouraged me, but the necessity of contact with men whose ideas of service were different from my own was the obstacle that weighed most in my mind; for till very lately there have been to all the Provincial regiments recommendations of officers which were next to positive orders from the Commander in Chief. The present plan of Upham, Murray and myself is calculated to obviate all my objections. The task of recruiting a regiment is certainly arduous but perseverance in it will always ensure success. The progress which Murray has already made is a proof of this assertion, altho' he has had difficulties enough to encounter. In one instance a plan as well digested as ever a recruiting officer formed failed merely from the difficulty of obtaining a pass from Head Quarters to bring off the recruits, and 18 men who would have been doing duty as dragoons in the service are now suffering punishment in Simsbury mines. Another attempt of less consequence has failed in the Jerseys thro' very extraordinary delays—a third is now under consideration and it appears to me is of so much consequence that it must be adopted. There are, a sort of men here who with small pretensions affect a knowledge of this country that indulge themselves in very free observations on the nature of the recruiting business. They laugh at the idea of raising a regiment in the present situation of matters. * * *

We are anxious to exert our utmost endeavors to form a Brigade when we receive your consent to command it. I am sensible that in making this request we raise a proportion of difficulties for you, but I please myself with the consideration that the illiberal observations which may be made on giving the rank of Brigadier General may with equal propriety be let loose on the rank of Lieut. Colonel. * * * I venture to assert that were it necessary the signature of almost every man from the Eastern Provinces might be obtained to a request that you should command the proposed corps. I am sure it can need no additional motive but the public service to ensure your exertions. I need not increase this already extravagant epistle to convince you of that. I observed to you that I had not as yet obtained a warrant. I am in no hurry, nor have I the least objection to waiting until Murray's corps is completed and Upham's respectable. My situation is not exactly the same with theirs. Murray's all depends on the success of this business, and Upham (whose character must be given you by others less partial than myself) has at present little else to depend upon. My own appointment being at the Head of a Department is a very different one, and although the present emoluments of it have been screwed down to the last peg by the Strainer of Gnats and Swallower of camels who at present commands, I have less to complain of than my neighbors. I have no reason to suppose that I shall fail in my endeavors to secure appointment as Lieut. Colonel only that I have failed in every attempt that I have made since Sir Henry Clinton commanded here.

It was not till every mark of respect was shewn our first patron and every argument used to induce him to exert his influence that Upham, Murray and myself presumed to solicit for ourselves. To gratify that worthy man [Gen. Timothy Ruggles] and to facilitate a plan which was concerted by General Vaughan and himself, and which was afterwards objected to at Head Quarters, we cheerfully engaged with a party of Refugees from Rhode Island, with whom we every day risqued our reputation as well as our lives, presuming that the end of our toils would be an appointment to gratify our ambitions by raising the long talked of brigade. Although our successes were much beyond our most sanguine expectations, we found ourselves in the same predicament as before. In short it was evident that the General [Ruggles] had from the unpardonable inattention to him and from other causes contracted such a disgust to present men and measures here, that he could neither negotiate with confidence or serve with alacrity, and there was such a mixture of virtue even with his obstinacy that while we deprecated it as unfortunate for ourselves we dared not oppose it.[4]

Loyalist Military Decisions (1783)

Introduction

Zachary Gibbes's petition illuminates the war for the hearts and minds of the southern backcountry. Note his mention of mandatory loyalty oaths, rebel conscription, confiscation of loyalist property, and the role of Indians.

Petition of Colonel Zacharias Gibbes

4th Decr 1783.

Zacharias Gibbes—the Claimant—sworn.

He is a Native of America was born in Virginia. Has lived 20 Years in South Carolina. He took a very active part from the first. He sign'd a Protest in June 1775 agt a requisition made by Congress at that time that they would take up Arms agt the British Govt. They refused & he was the second Man who sign'd the Protest against it. In Septr 1775 they marched a force agt them. M Gibbes & his friends kept themselves embodied for a fortnight—they sent three Hostages into the Camp where Coll Gibbes & friends were but they would not accept them. However they came upon the terms of a 74 Days peace. Lord Wm Campbell was driven on board a Ship between June & Novr—provided the 74 Days truce was broken they were to be tried condemn'd &c. There was a battle in Novr 1775 between these people & the Rebels at Ninety Six which ended in Coll Gibbes & Co taking the fort. After this a Cessation of Hostilities was agreed upon for 20 Days at the end of the 20 Days Coll Gibbes's people broke into small parties & took to the Mountains & the Rebels were augmented to about 8000. He went into the obscure parts of Virginia & remain'd there 4 or 5 Months. He then returned & soon after that he was pursued & taken by Coll Brannan in the Spring 1776 who tender'd a Death Warrant to them which he & his Party sign'd consenting that if they ever took up arms again agt the Cause of America they should be put to death. After this time he remain'd in a very unpleasant Situation tho' they permitted him to go home they suspected him & watch'd him &c. He remain'd tolerably quiet until the State Oath was tender'd which was in 1776 this was the Oath of Abjuration. It was tender'd to him the Oath of Allegiance which he refused. His Situation was made then more unpleasant. However he still staid on his farm. He was taken Prisoner in July 1776 by the Americans upon the Indians breaking into the Province & they thought he had been instrumental in stirring up the Indians & he was carried into the Indian Nation. He was only kept for a fortnight. He then made his escape. He returned home but absconded at different times till the Year 1779. The 1st of Jany 1779 Genl Prevost & Coll Campbell took Savannah this Intelligence was sent to him & he took Steps to embody his Neighbours & raised 600 Men in two Days he was principally instrumental in this. On the 7th of Feby 1779 He marched with these Men. About 350 of them got to Savannah. They had two battles in their way. They repulsed the Rebels on the first Attack they took 13 Prisoners. Three Days after this they had another Engagement at Kettle Creek where Col¹ Gibbes was taken prisoner. 20 were killed on each side but Coll Gibbes's Party were defeated. He was marched down the River about 40 Miles & then he was put into Irons he was afterwards march'd 50 Miles further when he was brought before a Ct of Enquiry near Augusta. They asked him how he came to go out at the head of such a Banditti he said it was to join the British Army & to support the British Govt. They made a Minute of this & recorded it as a Confession And then he was taken to Ninety Six & tried. He lay about 30 Days in Gaol & then he was tried. He was one of 22 who were condemn'd without mercy. Of the 22 five were hanged. He was one of the pointed out to be robbed but he was let off & his Brother in Law was hanged. On the 17th of April there came a Habeas Corpus from the Govt to remove them 90 Miles to Orangebourg. A fortnight after this the were sent back to Ninety Six & were hanged. Then the Govr gave out an order that the remainder should be let off upon giving security for their good behaviour & that they would never return to Ninety Six. He gave three Securities to ye Amt of 15000 Currency that he should comply with this. For near 30 Days his Gallows & his Grave was in his Sight & he thought he really should have been executed. He went out of Gaol the 3rd Day of April & went into Camden District where he remain'd until June 1780 when Lord Cornwallis came there. He joined the Army & Lord Cornwallis & Coll Balfour both gave him Commissions. The Commissions are produced. Lord Cornwallis's is that of a Major & Coll Balfour's is the same. He was sent by them to raise a number of Loyalists in Ninety Six & he was to have the Command. He rais'd 500 Men. He went in the front of Lord Cornwallis's Army at the head of a body of Loyalists. Major Ferguson' sent him to raise 200 Men more. He went & did raise them & was bringing them back when he recd an Express from Major Ferguson not to join him which he produces. After he recd these Dispatches he went to Col¹ Cruger at Ninety Six from this time to the Evacuation, of Charlestown he served in the Militia & had in the meantime the Commission of Colonel given to him by Lieut Coll Balfour. He recd the pay of a Dollar a Day which was the Pay of a Captn & a Colonel had no more. Several very strong Certificates produced & read from Lord Cornwailis Coll Balfour Genl Leslie Coll Moncrief Coll Cruger Captn Douglas Coll Vernon Coll Campbell Major Chas Frazer & other Officers to the Loyalty & Services of Colonel Gibbes. They all speak of him & his Conduct in the highest terms. Col' Balfour is desired to attend at a future Day to speak to his Services.

Colonel Cruger—sworn.

He believes Coll Gibbes to have been a Man of Property but knows nothing of it but from hearsay. As to Loyalty he was frequently under Coll Cruger's command in different excursions & he executed all his Orders faithfully & as a good Officer. He believes him to be a very meritorious & decided Loyalist.

Colonel Balfour—sworn. 6th Decr 1783.

He was desired by the Board to speak to the Character & Loyalty of Coll Gibbes. He speaks in the highest terms of Coll Gibbes. He says that in the Month of June 1780 He was brought to the British Army with the strongest recommendation from all the persons in the Neighborhood saying that from his property & Loyalty he was a very proper person to be entrusted with a Command. In consequence of this he was sent into the District of Ninety Six in order to raise & embody the Militia there. He did do so & in about a Month he rais'd 600 Men. He afterwards had the Commission of Lieutt Col' Commandant & tho' as Coll Balfour says not a very good Soldier he is one of the truest Loyalists & an excellent Man. He says he must have been a Man of Property because if he had not He never would have been recommended to a Command. Coll Balfour does not know anything of his former Services excepting from hearsay but he believes them. Upon the whole Coll Ballour's Character of this Man added to his own testimony &c gives us the highest impression of his Loyalty & meritorious Conduct.

N.B. The Allowance was afterwards divided between Coll Gibbes & his Wife & £40 a Yr given to each.[5]

Introduction

The petition of Colonel John Philips reveals how some Irish-born colonists felt a deep commitment to the British empire. Colonel Philips refused to take an oath to the rebel government, rejected a commission as lieutenant colonel, and "staid tolerably quietly" until the British captured Charleston. He actively recruited loyalists for the British army after June 1780.

Petition of Colonel John Philips

10th Decr 1783.

Colonel John Philips—the Claimant—sworn.

He was born in Ireland & went to America in 1770. He settled on Jacksons Creek in South Carolina near Winsbourn. He first declared his Sentiments in July 1775—the principal people there at that time began to associate agt Govt & proposed resolutions to every person to sign & proposed it to the Claimant & he refused to sign it in the public Meeting House which prevented all (excepting two persons) from signing it. This first drew the Vengeance of the Rebels upon him. In Novr he was first fined for not going out to do Duty for them. He had then two Sons who were able to do Duty but they refused. There was no Oath tender'd to him until 1778. In 1777 He run a risque of his Life by swearing Allegiance to the King & by inducing others to take the same Oath & He was tried for this Offence in 1778. In 1775 the Rebels offer'd him a Lieutt Col's Commission if he would join them. In the Month of April or May they tender'd the Oath of Allegiance & Abjuration to him. He refused it. They in general gave 60 Days but they only allowed him 4 Days to go to Charlestown. He performed it within the time. He was afterwards deliver'd Prisoner to Genl Williamsburgh a Rebel Genl at Augusta. He was detain'd a Prisoner for two Months. The 3dl Day of December following he was tried & condemn'd to be hanged. They kept him for 15 Days with the Gallows before the Window & during the whole of that time He was fully persuaded that he should suffer. At this time one of his Sons died in Gaol at Orangebourg in consequence of their Cruelty. Coll Philips says the reason that he was not executed was that Coll Campbell had at that time taken Savannah & issued a Proclamation. In consequence of which near 100 of the people petition'd to save his Life upon an Apprehension that two of his Brothers who were with Coll Campbell would retaliate. He then went home & staid tolerably quietly until Charlestown was taken. He then came & joined the British Army at Camden in June 1780. He took 50 Loyalists with him when he first went & afterwards between 5 & 600 Men. In June 1780 Lord Cornwallis appointed him a Colonel in Ma. He cannot produce the Commn the Rebels took it from him from this time he served constantly with Lord Cornwallis until he went to North Carolina. He never recd Pay untill Lord Cornwallis went to North Carolina from Jany 1781. He had the Pay of a Colonel which was 20s. Sterg a Day. He recd this Pay until Charlestown was evacuated. Lord Cornwallis gave him for his Services at one time 50 Gas & at another 100 Dollars. He was very useful in transmitting provisions to the Army from Winsborough to Rocky Creek. He was in two or three Engagements. He was again taken Prisoner the 21st day of January 1781 & carried into No Carolina & very inhumanly treated. He was prisoner' about six weeks. Coll Philips's Son was taken by Colonel Hampton in

Augt 1781 & most inhumanly murder'd. About this time they drove his Wife & family off from their Plantation & they came in great Distress to Charlestown.

Several Certificates produced & read from the following persons Lord Cornwallis Lord Rawdon Several Officers of distinction & rank in that Army Colonel Balfour &c.

Colonel Balfour called—& sworn.

First knew Coll Philips in 1780 at Winsborough. He knows that Lord Cornwallis placed very great Confidence in Coll Philips & that he employed him to procure intelligence of the Enemy's movements & many other matters of importance. He trusted to this Man to discriminate between the friends of Govt & those who were not to be trusted & he relied entirely upon him. It is within Coll Balfour's knowledge that he came to Charlestown in 1781 as Coll of Ma that Coll Balfour relying perfectly upon his Integrity confided the whole of the District of Camden to his Direction. He considers him as an Active & Zealous Loyalist & a most honest & upright Man. He knew he had an Estate having been, upon it but does not know the Value of it. He says there cannot be a better Man in America than Colonel Philips.[6]

Introduction

When presented with the option of staying in jail or joining the rebel army, Alexander Chesney chose to join the rebels. He served with the rebels until 1780 when he joined the British army. He gave "material evidence" of his loyalty when he intercepted a rebel force of five hundred and defeated them. Note that the two previous petitioners, Virginia's Zacharias Gibbes and the Irish immigrant, Colonel John Philips, testified on his behalf.

Petition of Captain Alexander Chesney

11th Decr 1783.

Alexander Chesney—the Claimant—sworn.

He went from Ireland in 1772 & settled on Pacolet River in the district of Ninety Six in 1773. He lived with his father when the rebellion broke out. He was press'd to enter into the association in the Summer of 1775—but he refused it & went to Jackson's Creek to join the Loyalists under the Command of Captn Philips Brother to Coll Philips. He brought these Loyalists to his father's House where they staid about a fortnight. Soon after this in the beginning of 1776 He was made Prisoner by a Party of Rebels under Coll Steen. He was kept in prison about ten Days & then he was bail'd out. In the Summer following he was again taken Prisoner And he had the option of going to Gaol or going with them to Charlestown. He chose the latter & joined them & bore Arms for them. He was in Charlestown about three Months During which time he made an Attempt to get away with another Loyalist to join Sir Henry Clinton but fail'd. After this they marched agt the Indians. He staid with them till June 1777 when he got clear of them then the Corps in which he served was discharged & he came home. When the State Oath was made general in 1778 He agreed with a Party to go to Florida to avoid it but they could not accomplish it & so he staid at home till 1780 when Charlestown was taken. He says they never tender'd the State Oath to him. He join'd Genl Williamson a Rebel Genl with a view to join the British Army & staid two Months with him. He had leave to return home at that time. He & the other Loyalists who meant to desert from Genl Williamson's Army sent a Man to reconnoitre the British Army & he never returned. After Charlestown was taken in the Year 1780 He embodied with several Loyalists in Sugar Creek & he was one of the foremost. He afterwards join'd Coll Balfour & afterwards Major Ferguson took the Command of them. He was constantly with Major Ferguson till he was defeated ye 7th of Octr 1780. He wishes to mention some particular Services At a time when Major Ferguson apprehended he should be attacked he sent the Claimant with written & private Instructions to Captn Moore which he deliver'd. He afterwards gave material Evidence to Major Ferguson in consequence of which he intercepted 500 of ye Rebels at the Iron works & defeated them. He never recd any Compensation for his services. Major Ferguson gave him his thanks in writing he might have been paid but refused it. He was afterwards appointed Adjutant of many different Battalions & recd pay for it. He says he has undertaken many very hazardous services. He was taken Prisoner when [with] Major Ferguson And was offer'd by the Rebels that if he would serve one Month with them be should have all his possessions again. He refused it at the risque of his Life because they threaten'd him with death. They marched him about 150 Miles to Moravian Town he made his Escape from hence & went home where he remain'd very privately till he join'd Coll Tarleton. He raised a Company in Decr 1780 & obtain'd a Captn Commission from Coll Balfour which is produced. He was in an Action with Coll Tarleton in 1781. He soon afterwards went to Charlestown.

Several Certificates are produced & read from Lord Cornwallis Lord Rawdon Coll Balfour Coll Tarleton Major Doyle I. Cruden Commissary of sequester'd Estates &c &c to determined Loyalty & good Conduct.

Colonel Philips—sworn.

Knew Captn Chesney from his Infancy. Knew his father's plantation on Pacolet river. He confirms him in the Acct he gave of the first act of his Loyalty in bringing the Loyalists to his father's House. He says he believes him to have been loyal from the first notwithstanding he knows he bore

Arms for some time with them. But Coll Philips had an Opportunity when he was Prisoner of conversing with Mr Chesney & he knows that at that moment he was a true Loyalist & wished to serve the Cause of Great Britain. After Charlestown was taken he says be was particularly active & he knows he ran risques in carrying intelligence frequently. He believes he was paid for some of these services but not for others. He does not think the worse of him because he served in the Rebel Army many good Men were obliged to do it.

Colonel Zacharias Gibbes—sworn.

Knows Captn Chesney & has known him many Years. He was an Adherent to Govt from the beginning of the troubles. In 1776 when he was obliged to conceal himself he took refuge in old Mr Chesney's House & he thought himself safer there than anywhere on Acct of the loyalty of the family. He admits that Chesney did serve in the Rebel Army. He says he would not have done it himself but Chesney was a young Man & he imputes it to his Youth. He was a very active zealous Officer when under the Command of Major Ferguson. He says he believes that Chesney & several others whose Names are mention'd to him & who enter'd into the Rebel Service under Genl Williamson made & enter'd into a Combination at the time to desert the first Opportunity to the British Army & he believes them all to have been determined Loyalists. He says he does not know any Man for whom he can say more than he can for this Young Man.[7]

Introduction

Alexander Chesney immigrated to South Carolina from Ireland at the age of twenty. In many ways, Chesney's allegiances reflect the experience of other American loyalists. Imprisoned for serving the king's cause, twenty-year-old Alexander Chesney was given the choice of joining the rebels or standing trial. In this excerpted piece from his 1776 journal, Chesney details the ordeal he faced. He also describes how he helped to destroy thirty-two Indian towns. Ironically, these were towns inhabited by Cherokees, who had committed their loyalty to the British.

I was born in the townland of Dunclug near Ballymena in the County of Antrim Ireland the 16th or the 12th of September 1756 on Sunday; as appears by a register in my father's Bible. . . .

My father's family consisted of my father mother Alexander (myself) Ann, Martha, Jane, William, Robert, John, and Peggy about 8 months old who died of the small pox on the passage; in all eight children, my father and mother making ten, went on board & sailed from Larne the 25th. August 1772 and arrived safe in the Harbour of Charleston, South Carolina after a passage of seven weeks and three days which was I suppose about the 16 October 1772 . . .

My cousins Cooke came back with me to assist in moving the family, bringing with them two horses which being put into a pasture of Col Phillips' on Jackson's Creek strayed away and not found for 3 months after.

Our family lived at my Aunt Cooke's in the first instance whilst a Cabin was building by me and some land cleared which I did in part without any assistance; before planting time in 1773, when the family was established in the new residence and began the usual farming occupations increasing stock and clearing additional land without any particular occurrence save the birth of my brother Thomas and sister Eliza untill 1775 that resolutions were presented for signatures at the Meeting-house by the congress party and I opposes them.

. . . When the war broke out between England and America the congress party early in 1775 were sending a quantity of Ammunition and clothing as presents to the Indians; On which the loyalists who had not joined them assembled and went to Ninety-Six a wooden-fort after besieging the place for some days took it, and the stores; after distributing the Ammunition amongst the loyalists, both parties agreed to a Cessation of Arms for some weeks until several of the leading men could go and return from Charles-town to receive Lord William Campbell's directions on the business. . . . In the meantime the congress party sent to the neighbourhood of Ninety-Six an Army under the command of Colonel Richardson who seized the leading men of the loyalists and put them in goal and disarmed the rest; all this was accomplished before the expiration of the truce.

. . . I piloted all the loyalists who came in my way and amongst Capt Buchanan supposed to be of the Royal Navy who endeavoured to keep up the spirits of the loyalists amongst whom a regular correspondence was kept up. [1776] For which I was made a prisoner, my house ransacked, and Kept a prisoner in the Snowy Camp on Reedy River for about a week; Col Richardson released me, but the congress party held me at enmity and forced me either to be tried at Richardson's camp or to join the Rebel Army which latter alternative I chose in order to save my father's family from threatened ruin, he had been made prisoner already for harbouring some loyalists; and served from April 1776 until June 1777 as a private during which time I was at Charlestown and Bolton's landing place opposite Long-Island whilst the British army was encamped there under Sir Henry Clinton; going on a reconnoitring party one day towards the British lines on Long-Island a gun with grape shot was fired, one shot of which was within a few inches of killing me having struck the sand close by where I had squatted down to avoid the discharge; I endeavoured with some others to get to General [Henry] Clinton's Army but failed for want of a boat and returned to the Americans . . .

We then marched against the Indians, to which I had no objection, helped to destroy 32 of their towns under General Williamson with Col Sumpter. We had a severe battle with the Indians near the middle settlements; in the course of the engagement five or six of them concealed behind a log fired at me as I ascended the hill before the others, and one of their balls struck a saplin of about six inches diameter opposite my breast; fortunately the young tree broke the force of the ball and saved my life . . .[8]

Notes

1. Extract from the Reverend Charles Inglis's sermon to the troops at Bridgehead, New York, September 1777, in *The Life and Letters of Charles Inglis: His Ministry in America and Consecration as First Colonial Bishop, from 1759 to 1787*, ed. John Wolfe Lydekker (London: Society for Promoting Christian Knowledge, 1936), 257.

2. Articles of the Associated Loyalists under the Honourable Board of Directors, Broadsides, AAS, 1780 or 1781.

3. Lindley S. Butler, ed., *The Narrative of Colonel David Fanning* (Davidson: Briarpatch Press, 1981), 45–47.

4. George Athan Billias, ed., *Winslow Papers, A.D., 1776–1826* (Boston: Gregg Press, 1972), 67–70.

5. Hugh Edward Egerton, ed., *The Royal Commission on the Losses and Services of American Loyalists, 1783–1785* (New York: Arno Press and *The New York Times*, 1969), 45–46.

6. Egerton, *The Royal Commission*, 48–49.

7. Egerton, *The Royal Commission*, 49–51.

8. E. Alfred Jones, ed., *The Journal of Alexander Chesney, a South Carolina Loyalist in the Revolution and After* (Columbus: Ohio State University, 1921),1–9.

CHAPTER SIX

Loyalist Women

A Sister's Lament (1770)

Introduction

In a letter written from Castle William near Boston on July 25, 1770, Anne Hulton describes the violence her brother faced when "ruffians" attacked his home at midnight. Henry Hulton had arrived in Boston in 1767 as one of the commissioners of Customs in Boston, responsible for collecting the Townshend duties. Anne Hulton describes the attack as a contrived plot by designing men. She hopes the British government will intervene to protect Boston.

It is about Seven weeks ago that I did myself the pleasure of writing to Dear Mrs. Lightbody. Since that, you will have heard my Brother has been driven from his own Habitation and afterwards retired with his Family to this place [Castle William] for safety. I have often thought of what you said, that surely we did not live in a lone House. It's true we have long been in a dangerous situation, from the State of Government. The want of protection, the perversion of the Laws, and the spirit of the People inflamed by designing men. Yet our house in the Country has been a place of retreat for many from the disturbances of the Town, and though they were become very alarming, yet we did not apprehend an immediate attack on our House, or that a Mob out of Boston should come so far, before we had notice of it, and were fully persuaded there are Persons more obnoxious than my Brother, that he had no personal Enemy, and confident of the good will of our Neighbours (in the Township we live in) towards him, so that we had no suspicion of what happened the night of June the 19th—we have reason to believe it was not the sudden outrage of a frantic

Mob, but a plot artfully contrived to decoy My Brother into the hands of assassins. At Midnight when the Family was asleep, had not a merciful Providence prevented their designs, we had been a distressd Family indeed.

Between 12 and 1 o'Clock he was wakened by a knocking at the Door. He got up, enquired the person's name and business, who said he had a letter to deliver to him, which came Express from New York. My Brother puts on his Cloaths, takes his drawn Sword in one hand, and opened the Parlor window with the other. The Man asked for a Lodging—said he, I'll not open my door, but give me the letter. The man then put his hand, attempting to push up the window, upon which my Brother hastily clapped it down. Instantly with a bludgeon several violent blows were struck which broke the Sash, Glass and frame to pieces. The first blow aimed at my Brother's Head, he Providentialy escaped, by its resting on the middle frame, being double, at same time (though before then, no noise or appearance of more Persons than one) the lower windows, all round the House (excepting two) were broke in like manner. My Brother stood in amazement for a Minute or 2, and having no doubt that a number of Men had broke in on several sides of the House, he retired Upstairs.

You will believe the whole Family was soon alarmed, but the horrible Noises from without, and the terrible shrieks within the House from Mrs. H. and Servants, which struck my Ears on awaking, I can't describe, and shall never forget.

I could imagine nothing less than that the House was beating down, after many violent blows on the Walls and windows, most hideous Shouting, dreadful imprecations, and threats ensued. Struck with terror and astonishment, what to do I knew not, but got on some Cloaths, and went to Mrs. H.'s room, where I found the Family collected, a Stone thrown in at her window narrowly missed her head. When the Ruffians were retreating with loud huzzas and one cryd he will fire—no says another, he darn't fire, we will come again says a third—Mr. and Mrs H. left their House immediately and have not lodged a night since in it . . .

But there is no security from the virulence of Lying Tongues. Can you believe it, that a person shall suffer abuse, an attack upon his House, and attempt on his Life, and afterwards the reproach of having done it himself. This is really the case, the persons who are so vile as to be at the bottom of the Mischeif, have in order to remove the odium from themselves, and the Town, industriously spread this report, that Mr H. hired people to break his own Windows, for an excuse of his removal to the Castle, and to ruin this Country.

However ridiculous this Aspersion, yet it is believed or seemingly believed by one half of the people, as we are told. But the more sensible and moderate are ashamed of the absurdity, and freely say, that this outrage against Mr H. will hurt their Country more than anything which has been done yet. And for the honour of the Township we lived in, I must say, the principal People, have of their own accord taken up the affair very warmly, exerting their endeavors to find out the Authors, or perpetrators of the Villainy. They have produced above twenty witnesses, Men in the Neighborhood who were out a Fishing that night, that prove they met upon the Road from Boston towards my Brother's House, Parties of Men that appeared disguised, their faces blacked, with white Night caps and white Stockens on, one of 'em with Ruffles on and all, with great clubs in their hands. They did not know any of 'em, but one Fisherman spoke to 'em, to be satisfied whether they were Negroes or no, and found by their Speech they were not, and they answered him very insolently. Another person who mett them declares, that one of 'em asked him the way to Mr. H's house, and another of 'em said he knew the way very well. After all, you may judge how much any further discovery is likely to be made, or justice to be obtained in this Country, when I tell you that the persons who were thus active to bring the dark deed to light, were immediately stop'd and silenced, being given to understand (as I'm well informed) that if they made any further stir about the matter, they might expect to be treated in the same manner as Mr H. was. However, so much is proved as to clear Mr H. from the charge of doing himself the mischief, one would think.

. . . What Government intends doing to remedy these, We are yet strangers, or whether anything effectual will be done . . . If G[reat] Britain leaves Boston to itself, though its own honour will not be maintained thereby, it will certainly be the greatest punishment that can be inflicted on the place and people, but a cruelty to some individuals, who have shewn themselves friends to Government. The Town is now in the greatest confusion, the People quarreling violently about Importation, and Exportation. . . .[1]

Living with the British (1777)

Introduction

Born into a prestigious Philadelphia family, Elizabeth Drinker married a partner of a prominent shipping and importing firm, Henry Drinker. Both she and her husband were members of the Society of Friends. She lived in Philadelphia when the British governed the city between September 1777 and June 1778. Her two journal excerpts provide a glimpse of the relations between elite wives and British officers during the occupation, and also the rebel vengeance against two of the king's friends after the British army evacuated Philadelphia.

Oct. 11. . . . S. Emlen sent us word that he and ye other Friends, viz: Nicholas Waln, James Thornton, Wm Brown, Joshua Morris, and Warner Mifflin were returned from a visit to G. Washington. I apprehend they have no good news, or I think I should have heard it.

I have been more distressed in mind this day than for some time past—not from anything that I have heard, but my spirits seem much affected.

Oct. 12. Sister and ye children went to meeting this morning. Sam Emlen and Sam Smith called after dinner. S. E. related some particulars of their reception at Washington's Camp; as I had little expectations from their application, I am not much disappointed that little has come of it. Enoch Story and wife called; ye latter went to evening meeting with me, where Nicholas Waln appeared in Testimony and prayer. When I came home I found Hannah Sansom and her son William at our house.

H. D. Jr. called to let us know that he was to be on guard to night—I sent down for Chalkley, who is to be engaged on ye same business, so that Abel J. Junr lodges with us to night.

S. Smith's wife's Brother was taken by ye Americans bringing provisions to Town at the time of our Yearly meeting, and was carried to Washington's Camp, where, 'tis said, he is to be tried for his life . . .

Oct. 16. I stepped over to Neighbor Walns' this afternoon and drank Tea with them.

Last night one of ye Hessian Guards, who stood on Race street wharf was fired at from, or nearly from A. James' back store. The inhabitants have met today, and yesterday, to regulate a nightly watch, which has been dropped for some time, but which is thought to be again necessary . . .

Oct. 18. Ye Troops at Germantown are coming within 2 or 3 miles of this city to encamp. Provisions are so scarce with us now, that Jenny gave 2/6 pr lb. for mutton this morning. Ye people round ye country dare not come near us with anything; what little butter is brought is 7/6 per lb. Ye fleet not yet up, nor likely to be soon, I fear. Jenny and Billy went this afternoon with coffee and whey for the soldiers.

Oct. 19. First day. Ye troops have come this afternoon within a mile of us. J. Hunt's family, I hear, have moved to town, and many from Germantown. Ye Americans have stopped several who were out, and were returning home, and have sent them back again. M. Hains is one, we hear. A. James and wife, who went to Frankford to bring away their clothes &c., were told while there that some of ye Provincials were at J. Dickinson's place, which intelligence occasioned them to get into ye waggon and come home by the Point road as fast as they could. A great firing below to day.

Oct. 20. Dr Parke called to tell us of a letter he had received from his Father-in-law, James Pemberton, dated ye 10th inst four days since ye last—no fresh intelligence that concerns ye friends. Stepped into S. Pleasants; Polly has lost their waggon, 2 Horses, and negro boy; also a negro man who was hired to go with them to Germantown to bring some things away from Israel's place; they were all taken up by the Provincials. A waggon was stopped that was loaded at J. Hunt's door with his goods, and obliged to unload. A. Morris and son

Billy, who went to wait on R. Hunt were stopped, and their horses taken from them—they escaped themselves with some difficulty.

There has been a skirmish this morning between Germantown and Philadelphia, the particulars of which I have not learnt, and there was very heavy firing below a great part of ye afternoon, I know not yet upon what occasion. Last night, 16 or 18 flat bottom boats came up, and got safely by the Gondelows and Battery, but were fired upon by some of ye English who did not know them, and one man was killed.

If things don't change ere long, we shall be in poor plight; everything scarce and dear, and nothing suffered to be brought in to us. Tom Prior is taken up to day, on suspicion, as 'tis said, of sending intelligence to Washington's army.

Oct. 21. John Gracey who has been threatened has left his home on that account. 2000 of ye Hessians were landed in ye Jerseys this day. 'Tis supposed their intentions are against ye Mud-Island Battery. We saw a number of them crossing in ye flat bottomed Boats from our garret window. There has been application made by ye English for Blankets, as ye Fleet is at a distance, and they lost a number in ye Battle near Germantown. As I was not in ye way, sister came off with that excuse.

Oct. 22. Amos Taylor, (who was here trying on ye children's clothes), informs us that Richard Waln is taken up, and sent to New York. He had his choice of 3 things, either to go to Jail, take ye Test, or go within ye English lines. Ye latter was chosen.

Oct. 23. This day will be remembered by many. Ye 2500 Hessians, who crossed ye River, the day before yesterday, were last night driven back 2 or 3 times, in endeavoring to storm ye fort on Red bank; 200 were slain and great numbers wounded. Ye firing this morning seemed to be incessant from ye Battery, the Gondelows, and ye Augusta man-of-war, of 64 Guns. She took fire, and after burning near 2 hours, blew up. Ye loss of this fine vessel is accounted for in different ways. Some say she took fire by accident; others that it was occasioned by red hot Bullets from Mud Island Battery. Another English vessel, somewhat smaller, it is said is also burnt. Many of ye inhabitants of this city are very much affected by ye present situation and appearance of things while those on ye other side of ye question, are flushed, and in spirits. Count Donop is said to be among ye slain. It was between 11 and 12, near noon, when ye Augusta blew up many were not sensible of any shock others were. It was very plain to those who were at meeting, as this is fifth day, and appeared to some like an earthquake. Oswald Eve and Chalkley James went on ye top of our house this morning with a spy glass, but could discover nothing but smoke.

Ye Hessians, and other of ye British Troops are encamped in ye Jerseys this night; we can see their fires for a considerable distance along ye shore . . .

Oct. 24. We have heard a few cannon fired this day, but cannot tell ye occasion.

Oct. 25. An officer called to day to know if General Grant could have quarters with us. I told him my husband was from me, and a number of young children around me; I should be glad to be excused. He replied, as I desired it, it should be so. Tom Kite tells us that neigr Stiles' House near Frankford, was broken open ye night before last by ye Americans, and much plundered . . .

November 1. . . . Accounts in Town to day are that Gen Burgoyne with 5000 men, has surrendered. This account seems to gain credit. A poor soldier was hung this afternoon on ye commons for striking his officer. Ye Hessians go on plundering at a great rate; such things as wood, potatoes, turnips &c. Provisions are scarce among us.

Nov. 2. First day. The Hessian Count is not dead, but wounded.

Nov. 5. A soldier came to demand Blankets, which I did not in anywise agree to—notwithstanding my refusal he went up stairs and took one, and with seeming good nature begged I would excuse his borrowing it, as it was by G. Howe's orders. We have not bought a pound of butter for 3 or 4 weeks past. All we get is from our Cow, about 2 pounds a week, and very few of the citizens have any . . .

Nov. 13. I went this afternoon to G. Morgan's wife. She sets off tomorrow with Becky James Jr. for Frankford; to stay at Abel's place till her Husband comes back from Pittsburg, where, she says, he is called on extraordinary business. I called on Caleb Carmalt on my way home. He was here this evening; I paid him four dollars to renew ye Insurance on our House. J. Drinker, was here this evening, and tells us that a company of soldiers have taken possession of our House in Water street, near Vine street. Johnny called on them; they promised to take care that nothing was destroyed. No news from ye Battery. Fine, clear, cool weather . . .

Nov. 15. . . . I had the great satisfaction this evening of receiving two letters from my dearest Henry—ye first I have received from him since he left Reading. He mentions 2 others, written before these, which have not yet come to hand. If I can judge of my dear by his letters, he is in good Spirits, which thought is pleasing to me . . .

Nov. 21. I was awakened this morning before 5 o'clock by ye loud firing of cannon—my Head aching very badly. All our Family were up but little Molly, and a fire was made in ye Parlor more than an hour before day. All our neighbors were also up, and I believe most in Town. Ye Americans had set their whole Fleet on fire, except one small vessel, and several of ye Gondelows, which passed by ye city in the night. Ye firing was from ye Delaware, which lay at Coopers Point, on ye Gondelows—which they did not return. Billy counted 8 different vessels on fire at once, in sight; one lay near ye Jersey shore opposite our House; we heard ye explosion of 4 of them when they blew up, which shook our windows greatly. We had a fair sight of ye blazing Fleet from our upper windows . . .

An inferior Hessian officer; an elderly man, who lodges at the bakers next door, insisted on putting his Horse in our Stable, which I refused. He came in this morning, and asked for Harry. I called him into ye Parlor; he either could not, or pretended he could not, understand English, but told Harry in Dutch that he must and would put his Horse in our Stable. A. James, who came in some time afterward, was kind enough to go to Jos. Galloway, and get a few lines from him—which he took in next door, and had some talk with them, which I hope will settle ye matter . . .

Nov. 22. . . . There has been skirmishing to day, several times, between ye Americans and ye Piquet Guards, and 'tis said, 7 or 8 have lost their lives. Five vessels have turned ye Point this afternoon. One thousand men attacked ye Piquet Guard this morning, about 11 o'clock. They drove them of, when some took shelter in J. Dickinson's House, and other Houses thereabouts. Ye English immediately set fire to ye said Houses, and burnt them to ye ground. Ye burning of those Houses is said to be a premeditated thing, as they served for skulking places, and much annoyed ye Guards. They talk of burning all ye Houses within four miles of ye city without ye lines—J. Dickinson's House; that in which C. Thomson lived, Johnathan Muffin's; Widow Crawston's, and many others were burnt this afternoon. R. Waln and wife, Joshua Howell, and several others, went on top of our House to day, where they could see ye Houses burning, and ye Ships coming up. These two days past have been big with events, and alarms; until now, we have experienced great quiet since ye English came in; I have only heard ye noise of a Drum twice since they came . . .

Nov. 25. . . . We were very much affrighted this evening, before 9 o'clock. Jenny happened to go into ye Yard—where she saw a man with Ann. She came in and whispered to Sister, who immediately went out, and discovered a young officer with Ann. Sister held ye candle up to his Face, and asked him who he was. His answer was—"What's that to you?" Ye gate was locked, and he followed Ann and Sister into ye kitchen where he swore he had mistaken ye House, but we could not get him out. Chalkley James who, happened to be here came into ye kitchen, and asked him what business he had there. He damned him, and said, "What's that to you?" shook his sword, which he held in his Hand, and seemed to threaten, when Chalkley, with great resolution, twisted it out of his Hands, and collared him. Sister took ye sword from Chalkley, and locked it up in ye drawer in ye parlor—all his outcry was for his sword. He swore he would not stir a foot until he had it. I then sent in for. Joshua Howell, when he declared, that he knew we were peaceable people, and that he gave up his sword on that account, out of, pure good nature, which he had said to us before. He told Chalkley, in ye kitchen, that he would be the death of him tomorrow. Joshua got him to ye door, and then gave him his sword, expecting he would go off, but he continued swearing there. Joshua left him, and went to call Abel James; in ye meantime the impudent Fellow came in again, swearing in ye Entry, with ye sword in his hand. Sister had locked:

Chalkley up in ye middle room, and we shut ourselves in ye parlor where he knocked, desiring entrance. Our poor, dear children were never so frightened before-to have an enraged, drunken man-as I believe he was-with a sword in his hand, swearing about ye House. After going two or 3 times up and down ye Entry, desiring we would let him in to drink a Glass of Wine with us, he went to ye end of ye alley-when Harry locked ye Front door on him. He knocked and desired to come in, when J. Howell and A. James, whom Joshua had gone for, came to him. They had some talk with him, and he went off, as I supposed. I had all ye back doors bolted; ye Gate and Front door locked; when in about 10 minutes after, Harry came out of ye kitchen and told us he was there. I then locked ye parlor door, and would not let Chalkley out. Harry ran into Howells for Joshua, who did not come for some time after ye Fellow was gone, and Ann with him. He came over ye Fence, and they went out ye same way. 'Tis now near one o'clock in ye morning, and I have not yet recovered from ye fright. Ann called him Capt Tape, or John Tape . . .

Dec. 5. A number of Troops have gone out of Town, and 'tis said, they are this afternoon at Chestnut Hill.

Fine winter weather.

Dec. 6. Our neighbor Stiles sent over this morning to borrow our good Horse, Tomson, but as he was not shod we denied him; she sent again and we lent him to her to go to Frankford—her boy Sam with her. She returned in ye evening on foot, having lost her Chaise and our Horse; they were taken from her by ye English Light-Horse just as she was getting in ye Chaise at their place. They have been plundered at their country House lately of all ye valuable Furniture, Provisions, Coach, Chariot, Horses, 8 or 10 negroes, &c. &c. to a great amount.

Dec. 7. I drank Tea at neighbor Howells', who was last night robbed of a Bed from one of their 2 Pr stairs Chamber. The Fellow, being surprised, got off without ye rest of ye Booty, which he had laid out of ye Drawers ready to take away. There have been many robberies committed lately in Town. Dull, rainy weather to day tho' not very cold.

We have but 9 Persons in our Family this winter; we have not had less than 13 or 14 for many years past . . .

Dec. 9. I took a walk after dinner to Bartram's shop in Market street; called at Owen Jones'. Hannah Moore called while I was out to read some letters from George Dillwyn. Things seem to wear but an unpromising appearance at present, but ye absence of my dear Husband is worse to me than all ye rest put together.

Nothing will pass at this time, (unless with a Few), but Gold and Silver, which is hard upon those who have a quantity of ye old paper money by them.

The fence of Boards round our House in Water street is pulled down, and I suppose burnt. Neighbor Waln sent a Horse and Chaise here this afternoon to put into our stable—which Patterson's 2 sisters came with from Bristol. C.

James and Tommy lodge here again tonight, as H. D. Jr. is gone a foraging. I wrote to my dear Henry to day by I. Starr of Wilmington, who goes out of Town tomorrow . . .

Dec. 11 . . . These are sad times for thieving and plundering; 'tis hardly safe to leave the door open a minute. A number of Friends to Government, about ye country, have lately been plundered and ill-used by the British Troops; things wear a very gloomy aspect at this present time.

Dec. 13. I have heard it hinted today, that our friends, John Parish and John James were confined in Lancaster Jail.

Dec. 14. First day. Thomas Eddy called; he brought word that Drewet Smith was returned from Winchester, which news at first much surprised and fluttered me. I have not yet seen him, but am told that my dear Henry and those with him, have ye same liberty—but many of them are not free to take it, so that I know not yet what to think, but am loath to be too sanguine, or to give way to such pleasing expectations as would naturally occur on a certainty of their being set properly at liberty.

We were a little frightened about 11 o'clock by seeing 2 fellows peeping into Becky Jones's yard, and climbing on ye top of her Gate. Watch barked, and Harry went into ye yard. They went off. It causes me to recollect last night, at about one o'clock, I heard a noise against our fence; ye Dog barked violently. I awoke Jenny, who looked out of ye window, and saw 2 men in ye alley, who went out of sight. I often feel afraid to go to Bed.

Dec. 15. Last night about 11 o'clock, as we were going to Bed, we saw 2 soldiers in ye alley, standing by ye Fence. We went down stairs again, and into ye yard. We asked Harry aloud if John and Tom were yet in Bed? Harry answered, Yes. Sister ordered him to untie ye Dog and then come in. While we were contriving in this manner down stairs, Jenny saw them from my room window, move off with a large Bundle which she took to be a Bed. After we had been in Bed about an hour we heard a great noise in ye alley. Jenny, Sister and ye children ran to ye window, and saw ye Baker next door running up ye alley in his shirt, with only a little red Jacket on; ye rest of his Family were with him. We did not discover ye cause of ye uproar until this morning, when we found the Baker had been robbed of some of his wife's clothes—which we suppose was ye bundle ye Fellows went off with some time before . . .

Polly Reynolds, formerly Ritche, with 2 other women called before dinner. She is here to solicit ye General on account of her Husband, who has been a prisoner in ye Jerseys ever since last Christmas . . .

Friends have had several meetings lately, and have agreed to send orders to sundry merchants in London for a cargo of provisions and coal, as from ye present prospect, ye inhabitants will stand in need of such a supply. Ye officers and soldiers are quartering themselves upon ye Families generally. One with his Family is to be fixt at J. Howells. I am in daily expectation of their calling upon us. They were much frightened last night at Isaac Catheralls by a soldier who came into ye House, drew his Bayonet on Isaac, and behaved very disorderly. Anthony Morris, son of Samuel is said, to be dangerously wounded . . .

An officer who calls himself Major Crammond, called this afternoon to look for Quarters for some officer of distinction. I plead off; he would have persuaded me that it was a necessary protection at these times, to have one in ye House. He said that I must consider of it, and that he would call in a day or two. I desired to be excused, and after some more talk we parted. He behaved with much politeness, which has not been ye case at many other places. They have been very rude and impudent at some Houses.

I wish I may come off so; but at the same time fear we must have someone with us, as it appears likely to be a general thing. This has been a trying day to my spirit . . .

Dec. 19. Sister went out to inquire how Polly Pleasants had managed ye matter in respect to taking in officers, as they have had their doors marked. They had been to Jos. Galloway; but E. Story seems likely to settle ye matter with ye quarter master General Roberson. While sister was out, Major Crammond came to know if I had consulted any of my friends upon ye matter. I told him that my sister was out on that business; that I expected that we, who were at present lone women, would be excused. He said he feared not, for tho' I might put him off, (as it was for himself he applied); yet, as a great number of foreign Troops were to be quartered in this neighborhood, he believed they might be troublesome. We had a good deal of talk about the malbehavior of British officers, which he, by no means, justified. I told him how I had been frightened by ye officer, that thief-like stole my servant Girl over ye Fence, and of many other particulars of their bad conduct that had come to my knowledge. He said, that yesterday I had told him what sort of a man would suit in my Family; if I was obliged to take any, he was conscious that some of those qualities were his, (which were early hours, and little company); that there were very few of ye officers he could recommend; that W Galloway knew him very well; and that he would call again tomorrow to know my mind further. So he went off. I am straitened how to act, and yet determined. I may be troubled with others much worse, for this man appears to be much of a Gentleman—but while I can keep clear of them, I intend so to do. They have marked ye doors of Houses against their consent, and some of ye inhabitants have looked out for officers of reputation, (if any such there be), to come into their Families, by way of protection, and to keep off others.

E. Story called this evening; he says he thinks he shall be able to get us, whose Husbands are gone from us, clear of ye military gentlemen. He says they are much chagrined at the difficulty they find in getting quarters, and ye cool reception they have met with, or something to that effect; that several young Noblemen are at this time obliged to sleep at Taverns, on board Ship, or in ye Redoubts, for which I think they may, in great measure, thank themselves; tho', at the same time, it appears to me there was, perhaps too much backwardness shown towards them in ye beginning. We are told this evening that Owen Jones's Family has been very ill-used indeed, by an officer who wanted to quarter himself, with many others, upon them. He drew his sword; used very abusive language, and had ye Front door split in pieces. Mary Eddy has some with her, who, they say, will not suffer her to use her own Front door, but oblige her and her Family to go up and down the alley. Molly Foulke has been affronted, and so have many others. We have come oft as yet, wonderfully well. My resolution and fortitude have failed me much of late; my dear Henry's absence, and ye renewed fears on his account, and thoughts of our dear children, and my health but very middling—all together—it seems, at times, hard to bear up against . . .

Dec. 20. . . . Crammond called a third time with ye same story over again. I put him off as before; he said he would call again tomorrow. After he was gone, sister went down to consult Abel James. Abel went to Enoch Storys, and came here in ye evening. He believes we shall not be able to free ourselves from them. Mary Pernberton and M. Pleasants have been in trouble about it to day. J. Drinker went this evening to Mary Pemberton's, for our information, to find out how she had come off. She had promises of being excused, on account of her being an ancient woman, her Husband from her, and a Meeting held in her House, as ye Fourth street meeting house is taken up with ye poor, who are turned out of ye House of Employment, for ye Soldiers. For ye above reasons she was to be excused, provided it could be got from under ye hand of General Howe; so that on ye whole I fear we shall have our Family disagreeably encumbered. We must trust in Providence on that and on all other accounts . . .

Dec. 23. Monthly meeting. Sister and ye 4 children went to meeting this morning. Sister met Ann in ye street, who promised to pay for her time. Ye soldier's wife who lives in our House in Water street came to me this morning to inform that someone was tearing down ye shed &c. Sister went down after meeting and desired them to desist. They said they would not, for it was a Rebel's House. She assured them it was not, and after more talk, they promised, if she would let them take ye large Gate, they would desist; she agreed thereto, and came away . . .

Dec. 24. This is Christmas Eve, and the few Troops that are left in this city I fear are frolicking . . .[2]

Facing British Evacuation (1778)

Introduction

Elizabeth Drinker describes the aftermath of the British evacuation from Philadelphia. She notes the celebration of the Declaration of Independence on July 4, and of the French king's birthday on August 25. She laments the confiscation of loyalist property, the suffering of women, and the hanging of two prominent loyalists, John Roberts and Abraham Carlisle. In another document, "Mourning Loyalist Execution," another Quaker woman writes a poem about the execution of the two men mentioned in Drinker's journal.

June 17. Troops still crossing ye River. Vast numbers are gone over, and many continue with us yet.

H. D., T. P., I. Z., and S. S., endeavored to day to speak to ye General; he had not time to attend to them.

Captain Ford and Richard Waln took leave of us to day, as also did our John Burket. Sammy Shoemaker and Daniel Cox have gone on board one of ye Vessels, as have also many other of ye inhabitants. We engaged black Peter to take care of ye Cows.

June 18. Last night it was said there were 9000 of ye British Troops; left in Town; 11,000 in ye Jerseys. This morning when we arose there—was not one Red-Coat to be seen in Town, and ye encampment in the-Jerseys also vanished. Col. Gordon and some others had not been gone a quarter of an hour before ye American Light-Horse entered ye city—not many of them, but they were in and out all day.

A Bellman went about this evening, by order of one Col. Morgan to desire the inhabitants to stay within doors after night, and that if any, were found in ye street by ye Patrole, they should be punished.

Ye few that came in to day had drawn swords in their Hands; they galloped about ye streets in a great hurry. Many were much frightened at their appearance.

June 19. Ye English have in reality left us, and the other party taken possession. They have been coming in again all day, and ye old inhabitants, part of ye artillery, some soldiers &c. Washington and his army have not come; 'tis said they have' gone otherways.

June 22. Ye Store and Shop-keepers ordered to shut up, and to render an account of their goods.

June 24. Ye sun was eclipsed this morning 11½ Digits—almost total. It was not so obscure as I expected it would be.

Ye dealers are forbidden to sell their goods, so that it is almost impossible to get anything. We had this morning a very plentiful market, but as ye country People could not get goods for their produce, 'tis to be feared it will not be ye case much longer.

June 30. I went to meeting; Susanna Lightfoot and S. Emlen appeared in Testimony. James Bringhurst and Hannah Peters were married.

It is said there was a great Battle on First day last; that great numbers of ye British Troops were slain and taken.

A young soldier that is disordered in his senses, went up our stairs this afternoon; we had no man in ye House. Isaac Catheral came in, and went up after him. He found him in ye entry up two pr stairs, saying his prayers. He readily came down with him.

July 1. Ye thermometer this afternoon up to 91°. Joshua Howells is at 96½°.

July 2. Ye Congress came in today; firing of Cannon on ye occasion.

July 4. A great fuss this evening, it being the Anniversary of Independence; firing of Guns, Sky-Rockets &c. Candles were too scarce and dear to have an illumination, which perhaps saved some of our windows.

A very high Head-dress was exhibited thro' ye streets this afternoon, on a very dirty Woman, with a mob after her, with Drums &c., by way of ridiculing that very foolish fashion.

A number of prisoners brought in to day.

July 14. Wm Fisher was had up' yesterday before ye Council for saying something inimical, and security was given.

July 23. They have taken an account yesterday, or ye day before of Sammy Shoemaker's and Joseph Galloway's property, with design to confiscate.

August 1. Our neighbor Abraham Carlisle was yesterday taken up, and put into Jail.

Aug. 2. Billy helped to carry Miers Fisher's child to ye Burying Ground this afternoon, ye first time of his officiating in that manner.

Two of Oswald Eve's sons were yesterday put into Jail.

Aug. 3. Ann Carlisle called. She had been to ye old Prison to visit her Husband.

Aug. 7. Nancy and Billy went to Bush-Hill to see ye Aloes Tree, whose rapid growth, has lately been ye subject of much conversation.

Aug. 11. H. D., Israel Pemberton, and S. Hopkins waited upon Gen. Arnold, on account of some prisoners, for whom they procured a release.

Aug. 12. They are pressing waggons to day—for what purpose I know not. Ye lamps have not been lighted for some time past, nor does ye watchman call ye hour as usual.

Aug. 14. One. George Spangler was executed to day for some assistance he had given to ye British army. He has left a wife and several children.

Avg. 20. Grace Galloway turned out of her House this forenoon, and Spanish officers put in.

Aug. 21. Becky Shoemaker was again ordered out of her House last night.

Nobody is allowed to go to New York without a Pass from Congress.

Aug. 24. M. Pleasants was here this morning. She had been with Becky Shoemaker to Thomas McKean. Sammy Pleasants has had 6 good mahogany Chairs taken from him for ye substitute fine.

Aug. 25. Went to monthly meeting this morning; 3 couples passed, viz. Jonathan Knight and ye widow Baldwin, George Smith and Elizabeth Roberts, Dan Muffin and Debby Howell.

Firing of Cannon to day, and other demonstrations of joy on account of its being the anniversary of ye French King's Birth.

Joseph Yerkes was brought up yesterday before a magistrate for keeping school. His school is stopped, and our son Billy is at a loss for employment, as well as many others, in consequence of it. Sad doings.

September 2. Two men of ye names of Lyons and Ford, were shot about noon to day on board a Gondelow for desertion—2 were reprieved.

Sept. 4. H. D. received a letter yesterday from Rich Waln, dated from Walnford. We are pleased to find he is with his Family, but we do not yet know upon what terms.

Sept. 5. A letter received from General Sullivan with an account of a Battle in Rhode-Island.

Sept. 6. First day. Martha Harris made her appearance again to day, about 11 o'clock, at ye Bank, and Great meeting Houses, where she told Friends that a very trying time was near at hand &c.

A negro woman brought a letter this morning for Jane Sibal, (formerly Boon); so that Jennie is, I suppose, married to Philip, one of ye Majors orderly men.

Robert Waln, myself, my two sons, Bob Waln, Neddy Howell, and Anna Waln took a walk this afternoon to Springettsbury, to see ye Aloes Tree. We stopped on our return at Bush-Hill and walked in ye Garden. We came home after sunset, very much tired.

Sept. 8. Sammy Shoemaker's goods sold to day at Vendue. 'Tis said that Molesworth's Body is again taken up; I have not yet heard by whose direction.

Sept. 10. We are reduced from 5 servants to one, which won't do long, if we can help ourselves. It is the case with many at present. Good servants are hard to be had, such a time was never known here, I believe, in that respect.

Sept. 11. We have a new Cow come home to day for which H. D. paid £45 to Parson Stringer. We sent our two old Cows to day to ye Point meadow to fatten.

Sept. 15. Rebecca Waln came over. With her I went to ye Burial of my old Friend and acquaintance Nancy Potts, formerly Mitchell, whom I much valued. She died of a nervous fever.

Sept. 18. Oswald Eve's goods were sold yesterday for ye use of ye State.

Sept. 21. I spent this afternoon at Abraham Mitchell's.

H. D. had a summons sent to him this afternoon desiring him to meet ye 25th inst, with his arms and accoutrements &c.

Sept. 25. Abraham Carlisle's trial came on to day, and is not yet concluded. We are at a loss to judge how it will go with him.

Sept. 26. I went in this afternoon to visit our distressed neighbor Carlisle, whose Husband they, have brought in guilty of High Treason; though it is hoped by many he will not suffer what some others fear he will.

Old Benjamin Mason was yesterday buried at Fair-Hill. A year this day since ye British Troops entered.

Sept. 30. John Roberts' trial came on to day. I have not heard how it goes on. Abraham Carlisle is to be tried again, they say, on seventh day next as ye Lawyers have made a demur.

October 1. John Roberts' trial not yet over.

Oct. 2. John Roberts is brought in guilty, at which some are surprised as they did not expect it, of those who attended ye court. I understand this evening there is some demur in his case.

Oct. 3. There is talk that ye English Troops are at Egg Harbor, spoiling ye Salt Works, and that a number of ye Continentals are going off this afternoon towards them.

Oct. 17. Wm Hamilton was this Day tried for his life, and acquitted. John Roberts condemned to die—shocking doings!

Oct 18. First day. John and Abby Parish, Peggy Morris and Hannah Sansom came home with me from meeting—they stay'd to tea. 'Tis reported and credited that England and France have accommodated matters, and that ye French are called home. A. Carlisle's irons are taken off.

Oct. 19. Went this afternoon with H. Sansom to the funeral of Thos. Coomb's wife, Ye Corpse was taken to Church and afterwards to the burying ground in Arch street.

Oct. 20. H. D., C. West, and David Eastaugh visited John Roberts and A. Carlisle in, Prison. David Franks taken up and put into Jail for writing something they find fault with.

Oct. 21. A young man of the name of Latham, one of our Society, has appeared lately in, ye public streets, warning the People to repent &c.

Oct 24. John Roberts and Abm Carlisle's Death warrants were signed today and read to them. H. D. went to the burial of William Norton Jr. this afternoon. Peter Chavillear was buried two or three days past. 'Tis reported this Evening that the British Troops have evacuated. New York—it appears rather too sudden to be true.

Oct. 28. That New-York is evacuated proves a mistake; as also that France and Great Britain have accommodated matters; at least we have no proof of it.

Jane Roberts, wife of John Roberts, Owen Jones and wife, and James Thornton were here this morning. H. D. and self went with them to visit our neighbor Ann Carlisle when James had something to say to ye afflicted women, by way of Testimony, which I thought encouraging. Ye time for the execution of their Husbands is fix't ye 4th next month. Ye distressed wives have been with the men in, power, and several Petitions are signing by different people to send in to ye Council or Assembly—'tis hoped and believed that their Lives will be spared—'twould be terrible indeed should it happen otherwise. H. D. and sister went yesterday afternoon to ye Funeral of our ancient friend Mary Pemberton, ye Corpse was carried to meeting. She departed this Life on first day morning, ye 25th inst.

Ye prevailing report of this day is, that ye British Troops, who lately left Egg Harbour have returned there again with a reinforcement.

November 3. This afternoon I spent at Cat. Greenleafs, ye evening at S. Pleasants, where I was informed that preparations were making, this evening for the execution of our poor friends tomorrow morning Notwithstanding the many petitions that, have been sent in, and ye personal appearance of ye distressed wives and children before ye Council, I am still of ye mind that they will not be permitted to carry this matter to ye last extremity.

Nov. 4. They have actually put to Death, Hang'd on ye Commons, John Roberts and Abm Carlisle' this morning, or about noon—an awful solemn day it has been. I went this evening with my H. D. to neighbor Carlisle's; ye body is brought home and laid out—looks placid and serene—no marks of agony or distortion; ye poor afflicted widows are wonderfully upheld and supported under their very great trial-they have many sympathizing friends.

Nov. 5. Our back parlor was filled this afternoon with company who came to ye Burial, of our neighbor Carlisle; myself and four children went. Sister stayed at home; it was a remarkably large Funeral, and a solemn time; George Dilwyn and S. Emlen spoke at ye Grave, and ye former prayed fervently.

Nov. 27. I stepped in this evening to see neighbor Carlisle.

Nov. 28. 'Tis ye opinion of many that ye British are actually leaving New-York.

Nov. 30. Two men called for ye Lamp and watch tax.

December 1. Appearance of great rejoicing all day on choosing a President—Jos. Reed is said to be ye man; ringing of Bells and firing of Cannon &c.

Dec. 5. Chimney on fire this afternoon, next door but one, where Marshal lived. A vessel this afternoon from Nantz brings an account that England and France are likely to come to an accommodation &c.

Abijah Wright was executed this forenoon on ye Commons, for I know not what.

Dec. 14. About 130 Light Horse came into Town yesterday. G. Washington's wife in town, a grand entertainment at ye new Tavern.

Dec. 16. Talk of English being at Monmouth—and that ye Fleets arrived at Carolina.

Dec. 18. H. D. received a letter from J. Crammond. Our new maid had a visitor all day, and has invited her to lodge with her, without asking leave—times are much changed, and Maids have become Mistresses.

Dec. 19. P. Pemberton and M. Pleasants sent Molly this morning to ask my company with them to see G. Washington's wife; which I Declined.[3]

Stricken Smitten of God (1778)

Introduction

In this letter to her friend, Elizabeth Dering, on Shelter Island, an island in the eastern end of Long Island, on January 29, 1778, Anna Winslow looks to God to understand the sufferings in the colonies and hopes for an end to the war. Anna Winslow was a matron of the prominent Winslow family in Plymouth County, Massachusetts.

Dear Betsy

However old & old fashion I am I do assure you my dear I am all ways glad to hear from my young friends for although I may not expect quite so weighty & Serious letters from them I may my dear have some [illegible] sallies which from young fellows if duly restrained will always be agreeable

It gives me a very Sensible pleasure that you found yourself happy at Marshfield which in itself is one of the dullest places I believe on earth__ But you were with your aunt Thomas whose presence enlivens every place where She comes, & would ensure even [illegible] agreeable.

You need not refrain writing to me on account of any Superiority in me (that of years excepted)—I am no bodys superior but I need not tell you that more acquaintance will confirm you that herein I preach the truth

Thank you my dear for your kind invitation to See you at Shelter Island indeed Betsy I should greatly rejoice on such an occasion not only my dear in the pleasure I [illegible] have in seeing the place, but your good family again restored to their pleasure habitation with all their gardens & other pleasures round them it will not be long I hope eer the olive branch will be held up & peace upon honorable & equitable terms will be restored to our once happy [pgs 1] land__ But why are we thus let me offer my young friend__ Is it not for our iniquities that we are thus Stricken Smitten of God & afflicted Surely miss if so suffer a word of exhortation to myself as well as you let us each enquire seriously what hand we have had in helping on the trobles that now invade our land—& what ever we find amiss let us with full purpose of heart strive against that Action that troubles our camp—

I wont make you so ill a compliment as to Suppose you tired with a serious exhortation but as my letter is conveniently long you will allow me to present my best wishes in the most friendly terms to your good Pappa mama & brothers—write to me again soon & believe that a letter from you will always be a very great pleasure to your friend.[4]

Anna Winslow

Mourning Loyalist Execution (1778)

Introduction

Born into a Philadelphia family of Quakers, Hannah Griffitts' circle included other women who were either loyal to the Crown or objected to the war because of their pacifist principles. Between September 1777 and June 1778, when the British army stayed in Philadelphia, many colonists fled the occupied city whereas a minority chose to assist the British administration. Two men, John Roberts and Abraham Carlisle, faced rebel vengeance when the British, upon news of the French alliance with the rebels, evacuated Philadelphia to protect their interests in the Caribbean islands. Griffitts' poem expresses deep sorrow for the loyalist families.

"On the Death of John Roberts and Abraham Carlisle," November 4, 1778

In the sad Chambers of retir'd distress
The scenes of speechless woe, where widow's mourn
The Tender Husband lost; where orphan's weep
The Indulgent father, and sustaining friend
Th' Indulgent friend & father known no more;
Where the sad sister, faints beneath the stroke
That rent th' associate Brother from her heart;
Here, clad in solemn sympathy of woe,
My soul retire's to share my neighbour's grief,
Give sigh for sigh; & mingle tears with tears;
Or deeper still; beyond the gentle power,
Of words to Heal; or tears to mitigate
Deeper in the awful Center of the soul,
(Hid from the view of an unfeeling world,)
And wrap'd in fellow feeling of Distress
I still attend your melancholy steps,
And pay the Tender Tribute to your woes;
But words are vain; the Powers of harmony
Are useless here; ev'n friendship's soothing voice
Has lost its balm; in woundings like to your's;
Oh then from Heaven, from gracious heaven alone
Look for the strength to stand; the healing power,
The Balm of Comfort; the sustaining friend;
May He supply those soft Cementing bands,
Which Brutal Laws rent from your bleeding hearts
Direct your trenbling footsteps, and be found,

The Husband, Father, & the Brother lost;
And you, the guiltless victims of the day
(Who to a Timid City's late reproach
And blush of its Inhabitants,) have fallen,
A Prey to Laws; Disgraceful to the man
Fallen, on the Cruel shores, that gave you birth
Fallen, on th' ungrateful shores, your father's plan'd
"On the firm Basis of true Liberty,["]
"The Laws of justice; & the rights of man";
Long, shall your names, survive the brutal deed;
And fair, Transmitted down to better times
Stand the Reproach of our's; when Lawless power
And wealth, by Rapine gain'd; shall shroud its head
In Infamous oblivion; or be held
The warning, not example of mankind;

And you, whose mad ambition, Lawless grasp
Of Proud Dominion, and oppressive power
Have spread the flames of war around the shores
Where Peace once smiled & social union dwelt;
How will you stand the Retributive hour,
Or bear the Close of dread Decision's voice;
When, as you mingled deep the Cup of woe
For suffering souls; so will your souls partake
The deeply mingled Cup of woe again,
You have Dissolv'd the tender tyes of Nature,
And torn asunder, (by the barbarous hand
Of Cruel Laws) the Dear, the soft Connections
Which Heaven had Joynd & blest; till you arose
The sourge of Desolation on their peace;
To you, the widow & orphan look
With heartfelt anguish, as their source of woe,
And in the silent Pang, from you demand
The Tender Husband & the father lost;
Tho' here, the voice of nature breath'd in vain,
To Tig[e]rs fierce, and admantine rocks,
Or, hearts unfeeling, & as hard as theirs;
The day* will come, & wing'd with swift approach
When piercing deep, Armed in Tremendous power
The voice of God, & Conscience shall be heard
Oh, in "this day of Pleading," if His hand,
Mark you severe; as you, have other's mark'd,
How will your souls, sustain His dread Decision
Whose Laws are justice; & whose words are truth[5]

A Mother's Advice (1779)

Introduction

Daughter of a prosperous and prominent politician in Philadelphia, Grace Growden Galloway grew accustomed to ease, affluence, and respectability. In 1753, when she married the ambitious Joseph Galloway of a wealthy Maryland family, she continued her ascent in status. Outside of Benjamin Franklin, Joseph Galloway became the biggest force in Pennsylvania politics. Four children were born to Grace and Joseph Galloway, but only one, Elizabeth, survived beyond infancy. Joseph Galloway believed the colonial future lay along the constitutional path of the British connection rather than along the revolutionary one. When he and Elizabeth sailed for England in 1778, Grace Galloway dealt bravely and also bitterly with the enforced separation from her family, the confiscation of their property, and her comparative poverty.

May 15, 1779, Mrs. Galloway to her daughter, Elizabeth Galloway, afterwards Mrs. Roberts

My dear child,

I sent to you in February by Major West who is gone to Holland and I hope it got safe to hand your letter acquainting me of your safe arrival gave me great pleasure but yours to [sic] last letters makes one happy in hearing you are to wish the noble minded heroes on both sides would let us woman write without inspecting our scrawls I have been very much unwell the hole [sic] spring my nerves are very meek . . . But I am now about again and since my charriot is taken from me try to walk this in the fall I often did and one evening was coming home in such a storme of raine as I never was out in before in my life and just as I got home my own charriot drove by me this my dear made me feel but I drove it of in a moment knowing that all sublunary [sic] things have their viscitudes. And I am determined to wear with patience what I cannot prevent and not by opposition put it in the power of my enemies to hurt me in my mind or corrupt my manners and my mind may be affected and uncalled my mind shall not be subdued my soul is still my own and it will be my fault if it is made worse.

No rather let me bless that almightly being who can and has enabled me to conquer . . . unruly pations [sic] which if given way to would only aid my enemys in sinking me and my fortune. Nature has kindly formed my mind so as to be able to bear toils that are that is not to be loaded with. A sort of fortitude which on trifling ocations [sic] I have often wanted therefore know my dearest child I am not otherways unhappy but by being separated from you and seeing your fortune in the possession of others for all is gone. But let me treat you not to let your spirits sink or act anyways unworthy of yourself. A coward by disposition counts fell usage at least it is in fine measure one of life's for it is a proof that the bountys of heaven was not properly bestowed for tho you meet with ill-fourten [sic] convince the world that you do not deserve it and by your conduct force it to give you its esteem the only way to do this is to put your trust in God. I loan [sic] implore his protection and fear nothing but disobeying his law and let me perswaid [sic] you to rely on his goodness who never forsaked them that call upon him and aloan [sic] can defend you from all harms attend closely to your duty to him and then you will be happy in this world and to come my mind is now so releaved [sic] on account of your health and wellfair [sic] that it has lille moor to wish but to be with you. I trimble [sic] lest you should vintune hear had you not liked England I should have been compleatly wretched for know my dear, warr with its iron hand corrupts the manners and invads the mind as much as it destroys the body and all ranks of people are moor or less affected by it.

Truth and simpliscity [sic] fled to their native skyes. In short America is not the same the very element seems changed nor do I wish to see my child on this side the Atlentick [sic] . . . is would be my advice to your Papa also for reasons I must not now give . . . Your letter I can answer in no other way but to tell you wishing I could take you in my arms and assure you that you have one friend that will never forget you one moment and has happyness as inseparable from your own let me know how I must proceed. I long to see my sister and relations nothing else is worth my notice. Be polite to all but intimate with none an easey [sic] deportment is the best recommendation do that which is just and right and leave the rest neither be arrogant nor servill [sic] both are the marks of a mean mind. Your wants not much cultivation. Adieu my dear child.

Grace Galloway.[6]

Unhappy Widow Seeking Relief (1779)

Introduction

In July 1779, Mary Price, widow of a loyalist surgeon, petitioned for British assistance. Her petition was one of hundreds received by the British commander-in-chief in New York City. The loyalist women asked for shelter, wood, and food for their parents, children, and sometimes, servants. Note Mary Price's understanding of the revolution as an "unnatural rebellion" and also the endorsement from prominent men at the bottom of the petition.

That your memorialist is one of the numerous unhappy persons who have suffered by the unnatural rebellion of this country. That she possesses property sufficient in the city of New Brunswick, a province of Jersey, to support herself, a mother, and two small children with decency in the comforts of life till deprived of the same by the rebels, who have lost everything of value she had in said city and to add to her misfortune the house she lived in, in this city was last summer burned to the ground with all her household furniture, wearing apparel, &c.

That your memorialist has for some time past been enabled to live by the kind assistance of friends with the aid distributed by your Excellency's order to the unfortunate but although she has been greatly relieved by such distribution she is still under the unavoidable necessity of observing that, it is far from being sufficient in these times of distress for the care, support of a helpless widow, her mother, and children.

Your memorialist therefore requests your Excellency will be pleased to consider her situation and afford her such relief as you shall judge proper assumed that whom a faithful servant . . .

Endorsed by Stephen Skinner and Sam Kemble: We are well acquainted with Mrs. Price and believe the foregoing narrative to be true. [Also signed by William Franklin][7]

Receiving Allowance from the British (1783)

Introduction

Margaret Reynolds received compensation from the British based on her husband's military service with the British military. She emphasizes that her husband had remained steadfastly loyal since the beginning of the rebellion.

9th Decr 1783.

Margaret Reynolds—the Claimant—sworn.

Her Husband died in Charlestown in Feby 1781. Before that he lived in Ninety Six District but he was obliged to quit his property. His Property Her lay upon Long Cane Creek. Her Husband was a Planter & afterwards Captn of Ma in Coll King's Regt. He was appointed a Captn in the Ma after the British took Ninety Six. She says he never took the Oath to the Rebels they offer'd it to him but he refused it they did not molest them they only threaten'd him. He lived upon the farm till Ninety Six was taken.

M Reynolds has an Allowance of £20 a Year from the Treasury.[8]

Seeking Compensation for Slave Property (1786)

Introduction

Of the 3,225 loyalists who presented claims to the British government between 1783 and 1788, 468 were women. In this excerpted petition, sub-mitted on November 13, 1786, Mrs. Mary Webb, widow of James Webb, the commissary of musters in the province of East Florida, describes the circumstances that led her from St. Augustine, Florida, to New York City and finally to England. Webb hopes the British government will compensate her for her two slaves, a box of wearing apparel, and her passage to England.

that your memorialist formerly resided at St Augustine in the province of East Florida, but now of the parish of St James London. That she the widow of the abovementioned James Webb is left entirely destitute by the death of her husband, having no provision made for a commissary's widow by government, your memorialist with her family was obliged to make the best of her way to New York and took with her two women slaves the one named Sarah and the other Asserina, with one box of apparel and provisions necessary for the voyage and embarked them on board a packet commanded by Capt. Hunter bound for New York with dispatches from Governor Tonyn, Your memorialist being taken suddenly ill was obliged to go ashore again and lost her passage but sent the two negroes in the above packet, which was taken on their passage by an American privateer and carried into Boston. The above slaves she values at eighty pounds sterling, the box of apparel and sea stores in the abovementioned packet she values at eighty pounds sterling . . .[9]

Notes

1. Ann Hulton to Elizabeth Lightbody, July 25, 1770, in Neil Longley York, *Henry Hulton and the American Revolution: An Outsider's View* (Boston: Colonial Society of Massachusetts, 2010), 246–49.

2. Henry D. Biddle, ed., *Extracts from the Journal of Elizabeth Drinker, from 1759 to 1807* (Philadelphia: J. B. Lippincott Company, 1889), 58–78.

3. Biddle, *Extracts from the Journal of Elizabeth Drinker*, 106–13.

4. Sol Feinstone Collection No. 1687, Anna Winslow to Elizabeth Dering, January 29, 1778, Marshfield, MA; transcribed by W. P. Tatum III, March 2012.

5. Hannah Griffitts, "On the Death of John Roberts and Abraham Carlisle," in *Milcah Martha Moore's Book: A Commonplace Book from Revolutionary America*, ed. Catherine La Courreye Blecki and Karin A. Wulf (University Park: Pennsylvania State University Press, 1997), 317–18.

6. Papers of Joseph Galloway, 1717–1874, mssHM 36839-36895, Huntington Library Manuscript Collection.

7. Sir Henry Clinton Papers, July 1779, Memorial of Mary Price, widow of Joseph Price, late surgeon of the 2nd Battalion of his majesty's 60th Regiment of Foot.

8. Hugh Edward Egerton, ed., *The Royal Commission on the Losses and Services of American Loyalists, 1783–1785* (New York: Arno Press and The New York Times, 1969), 47–48.

9. Wilbur Henry Siebert, *Loyalists in East Florida, 1774 to 1785: The Most Important Documents Pertaining Thereto, edited with an Accompanying Narrative* (Boston: Gregg Press, 1972), 61–63.

CHAPTER SEVEN

Slaves

Escaping to the British (1775)

Introduction

Boston King's excerpted memoir shows how the guerrilla war in the South translated into a transatlantic journey for some black loyalists. Slave to a Mr. Richard Waring of South Carolina, King fled his master to enter British lines in the hope of freedom. Like many other southern slaves, King found refuge in British-held New York City. He established life as a freeman, got married, and obtained employment as a boatman. In the summer of 1783, he, along with three thousand other free blacks, embarked for Nova Scotia. In 1792, disillusioned by the treatment from white loyalists and the British government, King joined an expedition of free blacks who hoped for a better life in Freetown, Sierra Leone. Curiously, his name, Boston King, may have been a name he gave himself, an amalgamation of patriot city and British loyalty. His spiritual visions and connection to Christianity shaped his life and his memoir.

> It is by no means an agreeable task to write an account of my Life, yet my gratitude to Almighty GOD, who delivered my affliction, and looked upon me in my low estate, who delivered me from the hand of the oppressor, and established my goings, impels me to acknowledge his goodness: And the importunity of many respectable friends, whom I highly esteem, have induced me to set down, as they occurred to my memory, a few of the most striking incidents I have met with in my pilgrimage. I am well aware of my inability

for such an undertaking, having only a slight acquaintance with the language in which I write, and being obliged to snatch a few hours, now and then, from pursuits, which to me, perhaps are more profitable. However, such as it is, I present it to the Friends of Religion and Humanity, hoping that will be of some use to mankind.

. . . My master being apprehensive that Charles-Town was in danger on account of the war, removed into the country, about 38 miles off. Here we built a large house for Mr. Waters, during which time the English took Charles-Town. Having obtained leave one day to see my parents, who had lived about 12 miles off, and it being late before I could go, I was obliged to borrow one of Mr. Waters's horses; but a servant of my master's, took the horse from me to go a little journey, and stayed two or three days longer than he ought. This involved me in the greatest perplexity, and I expected the severest punishment, because the gentleman to whom the horse belonged was a very bad man, and knew not how shew mercy. To escape his cruelty, I determined to go Charles-Town, and throw myself into the hands of the English. They received me readily, and I began to feel the happiness of liberty, of which I knew nothing before, altho' I was much grieved at first, to be obliged to leave my friends, and reside among strangers. In this situation I was seized with the small-pox, and suffered great hardships; for all the Blacks affected with that disease, were ordered to be carried a mile from the camp, lest the soldiers should be infected, and disabled from marching. This was a grievous circumstance to me and many others. We lay sometimes a whole day without any thing to eat or drink; but Providence sent a man, who belonged to the York volunteers whom I was acquainted with, to my relief. He brought me such things as I stood in need of; and by the blessing of the Lord I began to recover. . . .

By this time, the English left the place; but as I was unable to march with the army, I expected to be taken by the enemy. However when they, came, and understood that we were ill of the small-pox, they precipitately left us for fear of the infection. Two days after, the waggons were sent to convey us to the English Army, and we were put into a little cottage, (being 25 in number) about a quarter of a mile from the Hospital.

. . . Soon after I went to Charles-Town, and entered on board a man of war. As we were going to Chesepeak-bay, we were at the taking of a rich prize. We stayed in the bay two days, and then sailed for New-York, where I went on shore. Here I endeavoured to follow my trade, but for want of tools was obliged to relinquish it, and enter into service. But the wages were so low that I was not able to keep myself in clothes, so that I was under the necessity of leaving my master and going to another. I stayed with him four months, but he never paid, me, and I was obliged to leave him also, and work about the town until I was married. A year after I was taken very ill, but the Lord raised me up again in about five weeks. I then went out in a pilot-boat. We were at sea eight days, and had only provisions for five, so that we were in danger of starving. On the

9th day we were taken by an American whale-boat. I went on board them with a cheerful countenance, and asked for bread and water, and made very free with them. They carried me to Brunswick, and used me well. Notwithstanding which, my mind was sorely distressed at the thought of being again reduced to slavery, and separated from my wife and family; and at the same time it was exceeding difficult to escape from my bondage, because the river at Amboy was above a mile over, and likewise another to cross at Staten-Island. I called to remembrance the many great deliverances the Lord had wrought for me, and besought him to save me this once, and I would serve him all the days of my life. While my mind was thus exercised, I went into the jail to see a lad whom I was acquainted with at New-York. He had been taken prisoner, and attempted to make his escape, but was caught 12 miles off: They tied him to the tail of a horse, and in this manner brought him back to Brunswick. When I saw him, his feet were fastened in the stocks, and at night both his hands. This was a terrifying sight to me, as I expected to meet with the same kind of treatment, if taken in the act of attempting to regain my liberty. I was thankful that I was not confined in a jail, and my master used me as well as I could expect; and indeed the slaves about Baltimore, Philadelphia, and New-York, have as good victuals as many of the English; for they have meat once a day, and milk for breakfast and supper; and what is better than all, many of the masters send their slaves to school at night, that they may learn to read the Scriptures. This is a privilege indeed . . .[1]

Competition among the King's Subjects (1779)

Introduction

Thousands of refugees swarmed into the British headquarters of New York City. The population of the city increased from five thousand in 1776 to more than thirty-five thousand by 1783. This unusual petition from Judea Moore to the British commander in chief shows the rivalry between white and black loyalist refugees.

I Judea Moore [rent] a seller kitchen from Mr. Brasier and I pay him 8 pounds a year and the gentleman is willing for me to stay in the seller while I do pay my rent and none the same John Harrison wants to get the seller from me and he offered to pay 15 pounds to the landlord to get me out. But the landlord is willing for me to stay in the place while I do pay and Sir General I was at the Mayor's office and he told me that it was a pity that all we black folk that came from VA was not sent home to our master's which sir I do think it very hard that I can't have satisfaction and sir it is very hard for me to stay and be abused so by this man and his journeyman and sir if you please to give me some satisfaction I shall be ever obliged to you . . .[2]

Envisioning God with Empire (1781)

Introduction

Lieutenant Murphy, leader of the Black Pioneers, was one of few slaves who performed active military duty during the war. Most others who escaped to the British did strenuous and time-consuming work. In this excerpt, Lieutenant Murphy believes that God himself had spoken against the rebel cause.

> A fortnight ago when he was at the barracks of the company in Water Street he heard a voice like a man's (but saw nobody) which called him by his name and desired him to go and tell the commander in chief Sir Henry Clinton to send word to General Washington that he must surrender himself and his troops to the King's army and that if he did not the wrath of God would fall upon them.
>
> That if Gen. Washington did not surrender the commander in chief was then to tell him that he would raise all the Blacks in America to fight against him. The voice also said that King George must be acquainted with the above. That the same voice repeated the aforesaid message to him several times afterwards and three days ago in Queen Street insisted that he should tell it to Sir Henry Clinton upon which he answered that he was afraid to do it, as he did not see the person that spoke—that the voice then said that he must tell it that he was not to see him, for that he was the Lord and that he must acquaint Sir Henry Clinton that it was the Lord that spoke this; and to tell Sir Henry also that he and Lord Cornwallis was to put an end to this rebellion for that the Lord would be on their Side.[3]

Negotiating Slave Return (1783)

Introduction

The following excerpts reveal General George Washington's attempts to catch his runaway slaves before British evacuation. Washington also tried to retrieve the slaves of Virginia's Governor, Benjamin Harrison. Washington argued that the Peace Treaty stipulated the return of all rebel property. The British commander-in-chief, Sir Guy Carleton, replied that the Negroes freed by the British proclamations could no longer be considered property. General Carleton agreed to record the names of all freed blacks leaving for Nova Scotia so that rebel slave owners could later make claims to the British government (see excerpts from the Book of Negroes). In frustration, Washington argued that the slaves would provide false names and lie about their owners to prevent re-enslavement. Carleton did not budge.

To Daniel Parker, Head Quarters, April 28, 1783

Sir: Being informed by Colo Humphry as well as by your Letter to me, that you have been induced to accept, for the present the superintendence of the Embarkation from N York of the Tories and Refugees who are leaving the Country, and to prevent if possible, their carrying off any Negroes or other property of the inhabitants of the United States; [and having seen Sir Guy Carleton Orders on this Head] I take the Liberty of inclosing to you a List and description of Negroes which has been sent me by Govr. Harrison of Virginia, and to beg that you will improve the Opportunity you will have, of obtaing [sic] and securing them agreeable to the Govr's Request, if they are to be found in the City. Your Endeavours will not only be very obliging to the Governor, but will be thankfully acknowledged by me.

Some of my own slaves [and those of Mr. Lund Washington who lives at my Ho] may probably be in N York but I am unable to give you their Descriptions; their Names being so easily changed, will be fruitless to give to you. If by Chance you should come at the knowledge of any of them, I will be much obliged by your securing them, so that I may obtain them again.

This Business which you have undertaken, altho troublesome to yourself and as I imagine, very difficult in the Execution; yet, as I am persuaded you have accepted it from the best motives, will I hope, be of utility to the Subjects of the United States, and therefore cannot I think involve any impropriety of Conduct in your being concerned, untill Measures are adopted by Congress, for the Appointment of persons for this purpose. With much regard, etc.

[PS. Since writing the above I have received a Letter from Mr. Lund Washington respecting some of his Negroes, a list of which with my own is herewith inclosed.][4]

To Governor Benjamin Harrison, Newburgh, April 30, 1783

. . . Immediately, upon the receipt of your letter of the 31st. Ulto, I transmitted the list of your slaves to a Gentleman; a worthy active Man, of my acquaintance in N York and requested him to use his endeavors to obtain and forward them to you. All that can be done, I am sure he will do, but I have but little expectation that many will be recovered; several of my own are with the Enemy but I scarce ever bestowed a thought on them; they have so many doors through which they can escape from New York, that scarce any thing but an inclination to return, or voluntarily surrender of themselves will restore many to their former Masters, even supposing every disposition on the part of the Enemy to deliver them. With great truth. etc.[5]

To Governor Benjamin Harrison, Tappan, May 6, 1783

My dear Sir: A few days ago I wrote to you from Newburgh; and informed you (if I mistake not of the meeting I was to hold with Sir Guy Carleton consequent of the resolve of Congress directing me to make arrangements with him for delivery of the posts, Negroes and other property belonging to the Citizens of the United States.

This meeting I have had; but the indisposition of Genl. Carleton has taken him back to New York this Morning before the business could be brought to a close: I have discovered enough, however, in the course of the conversation with was held, to convince him that the Slaves which have absconded from their Masters will never be restored to them. Vast numbers of them are already gone to Nova Scotia, and the Construction with he (Sir Guy) puts upon the 7th article of the provisional treaty differs very widely from ours; but as I have given him my Sentiments in writings and have not yet received his in that way I cannot be more explicit at this time on this Subject. I could not, however altho' I am hurried, and upon the point of returning to Newburgh forbear giving you this concise acct. of my interview and the little good which I think is to be expected from the aforesaid article respecting the Negroes.[6]

Substance of a Conference Between General Washington and Sir Guy Carleton, Orange Town, May 6, 1783

General Washington opened the Conference by observing that the heretofore had transmitted to Sir Guy Carleton the Resolutions of the Congresss of the 15th. Ulto, that he conceived a personal Conference would be the most speedy and satisfactory Mode of discussing and settling the Business and that therefore he had requested the Interview. That the Resolutions of Congress related to three distinct Matters namely the setting at Liberty the Prisoners, the receiving Possession of the Posts occupied by the British Troops and the obtaining the delivery of all negroes and other property of the Inhabitants of the States in the possession of the Forces or Subjects of or adherents to his Brittanic Majesty. . . .

General Washington therefore expressed his Surprize that after what appeared to him an express Stipulation to the Contrary in the Treaty Negroes the Property of the Inhabitants of these States should be sent off; to which Sir Guy Carleton replied that he wished to be considered as giving no Construction to the Treaty that by *Property* in the Treaty might only be intended Property *at the time* the Negroes were sent off, that there was a difference in the Mode of Expression in the Treaty Archives Papers &c. were to be restored, Negroes and other Property were not only to be destroyed or carried away but he principally insisted that he conceived it could not have been the intenion of the British Government by the Treaty of Peace to reduce themselves to the necessity of violating their Faith to the Negroes who came into the British Lines under the Proclamation of his Predecessorts in Command, that he forebore to express his Sentiments on the Propriety of these Proclamations but the delivering up the Negroes to their former Masters would be delivering them up some possibly to Execution and others to severe Punishment which in his Opinion would be a dishonorable Violation of the public Faith pledged to the Negroes in the Proclamations that if the sending off the Negroes should hereafter be declared an Infraction of the Treaty, Compensation must be made by the Crown of Great Britain to the Owners, that he had taken Measures to provide for this by directing a Register to be kept of all the Negroes who were sent off specifying the Name Age and Occupation of the Slave and the Name and Place of Residence of his former Master.

General Washington again observed that he conceived this Conduct on the part of Sir Guy Carleton a Departure both from the Letter and Spirit of the Articles of Peace and particularly mentioned a Difficulty that would arise in compensating the Proprietors of Negroes admitting this infraction of the Treaty could be satisfied by such compensation as Sir Guy Carleton had alluded to, as it was imposing to ascertain the Value of the Slaves from any Fact or Circumstance which may appear in the Register, the value of a Slave consisting chiefly in his Industry and Sobriety and General Washington further mentioned a Difficulty which would attend identifying the Slave supposing him to have changes his own Name or to have given in a wrong Name of his former Master. In answer to which Sir Guy Carleton said that as the Negro was free and secured against his Master he could have no inducement to conceal either his own true Name or that of his Master. Sir Guy Carleton then observed that he was not by the Treaty held to deliver up any Property but was only restricted from carrying it away and therefore admitting the Interpretation of the Treaty as given by Genl. Washington to be just he was notwithstanding pursuing a Measure which would operate most for the Security of the Proprietors for if the Negroes were left to themselves without Care or Control from him Numbers of them would very probably go off and not return to the parts of the Country they came from, or clandestinely get on board the Transports in Manner which it would not be in his power to prevent in either of which Cases and inevitable Loss would ensure to the Proprietors but as the Business was now conducted they had at least a Chance for Compensation; and concluded the Conversation on this Subject by saying that he imagined that the Mode of compensating as well as the Accounts and other Points with respect to which there was no express Provision made by the Treaty must be adjudged by Commissioners to be hereafter appointed by the two Nations. (Signed by Egbert Benson, George Clinton, Jonathan Trumbull, Jr., and others present at conference)[7]

Evading Re-enslavement (1783)

Introduction

The following excerpts show the enormous difficulties that slaves faced at the end of the war. Since 1775, British proclamations had promised rebel-owned slaves freedom if they fled their masters and joined the British army.

In 1783, Dinah Archey and others hoped that the British would honor their promise when slave owners entered British garrisons to recapture their property. The sources do not specify whether Dinah Archey received permission to leave the American colonies.

> From August 2, 1783
>
> William Farrer claims a Negro woman named Dinah Archey lately embarked to go to Nova Scotia and brought on shore for examination. She produced a certificate from Brig. Gen. Birch . . . dated May 1, 1783 that the bearer Dinah Archey being a free Negro has the commandant's permission to pass from the garrison to whatever place she may think proper.
>
> She now acknowledges that she was formerly the property of John Bains of Grane island, Norfolk County Virginia and that he sold her as he then said to the claimant with whom she lived about three years and until he was obliged to leave the country on account of the war and went to England leaving this negro woman behind him and she further says that the said John Bains afterwards told her that he had never given the claimant a bill of sale for her and compelled her to return to him where she remained until the expedition up the Chesapeake under Sir George Collier and Gen. Mathews when she came with them to New York.
>
> The claimant upon being asked declares himself to be a British subject whereupon The Board are of opinion that they are not authorized to determine the question between the claimant and the Negro woman and therefore refer the matter to the commandant and police of the garrison.
>
> The Petition of Dinah Archey humbly sheweth that your poor petitioner embarked with her husband Daniel of Virginia has she says been here five years and came in agreeable to his Excellency General Howe Proclamation but was claimd by a certain William Farray and brought on shore has is said been before the Police. . . . Neither did said William Farray shew a Bill of Sale.
>
> Your poor petitioner therefore humbly prays that William Farray has taken her pass from her that he may prove his Property which she firmly believes he cannot & your poor petitioner as in Duty Bound will ever pray & c.
>
> Signed,
> Dinah Archey.[8]

Retrieving Stolen Children (1783)

Introduction

On September 18, 1783, Judith Jackson tried desperately to prove her service to the British so she could be one of the refugees allowed to embark for Nova Scotia. But her pleas were denied and her child forcibly "stolen" from her.

On September 20, the British upheld the claims of her master and returned her to slavery.

> I came from Virginia with General Ashley When I came from there I was quite Naked. I was in Service a year and a half with Mr. Savage the remaining Part I was with Lord Dunmore. Washing and ironing in his Service I came with him from Charlestown to New York and was in Service with him till he went away My Master came for me I told him I would not go with him One Mr. Yelback wanted to steal me back to Virginia and was not my Master he took all my Cloaths which is Majesty gave me, he said he would hang Major Williams for giving me a Pass he took my Money from me and stole my Child from me and Sent it to Virginia.
>
> And as in Duty Bound Your Petitioner shall Ever Pray, Judith Jackson[9]

Black Petitions (1784)

Introduction

At the end of the war, forty-seven free blacks petitioned the British for compensation for their losses on behalf of empire. These three excerpted memorials emphasize the range of black experience during the revolution. Significantly, two of the petitioners wanted compensation for lost property.

> Memorial of John Twine—a Black
>
> 13th of Septr 1784.
>
> John Twine—the Claimant—sworn.
>
> Was Christen'd about four Months ago & knows the Nature of an Oath. Does not know how old he is. When the troubles broke out he lived at Petersburgh in Virginia. He swears that he is free born & that his free papers are left at the Treasury. They were given to him by Coll Balinghall. In 1775 He lived with Mr Bradley who kept a Tavern. Six Years ago he join'd the British at Trentown. Before that he was in the rebel Service. He drove a Waggon for the rebels. Since he join'd the British he has served with the Army & been a Servt to an Officer. He was wounded in the Thigh at Camden.
>
> Property.
>
> One Lot of Land containing one Acre & a Dwelling House. He got this from his father. It is in a small Island. One Peters lived in the House. He paid him 7s. per week Virginia Money. But he afterwds says that he lived with Peters & that he the Claimt was a Lodger. However he continues to swear that the House was his own. Says Col[1] Bannister who wanted to buy it said it was not worth more than £150 including some few Articles of furniture. Says that nobody knows this to be his property but one Mr Dudley who is gone to America. But if he returns soon he will bring him.

Memorial of Samuel Burke—Black
13th of Septr 1784.
Samuel Burke-the Claimant—sworn.

He is a Native of Charlestown & was Christen'd in Ireland. When the troubles broke he was Servt to Govr Brown who was then on the Missisippi. He swears that he was born free. He had free papers but he has lost them. He took no Notice of them. He remain'd with Govr Brown whilst he was raising a Regt. He bore Arms. He has been twice wounded. He has remain'd ever since with the Army. He never recd pay. Swears that he killed at least ten Men at the Hanging rock.

Certificate produced from Govr Brown in which he speaks of his Loyalty & says that he was a free Man & has been twice wounded.

Property.

He married a Dutch Mulatto Woman at New York & he got about £40 with her & an House & Garden. His Wife got this from her former Husband This was in Dutch Street No 5. He left it to her & she had the papers & gave them to the Claimt. He has lost them. He says it was valued at £350 by the Genls Aid de Camp. Besides this He had furniture which he values at £7 9s. This was used as a Barrack House. He has no Witnesses here. He desired a person to attend who had seen him in his House but he does not attend & Govr Brown he is afraid will not live to attend. He has recd the Sum of £20 from the Treasury.

Memorial of Scipio Handley—a Black
13th of Septr 1784.
Scipio Handley—the Claimant—sworn.

He has been Christen'd here about a Year ago & knows the Nature of an Oath. He lived in Charlestown & was free born. He was carrying on trade for himself as a fisherman. He never carried Arms or took any Oath for the Americans. He was taken by the rebels when he was carrying things to Lord Wm Campbell on board. They took his Boat. He was put in Irons & confined for this six weeks. He left the province at that time & never returned. He came to Georgia with the British Troops.

Property.

He had no Land. He Lost some furniture & a few other Articles which are contain'd in the Schedule which he values at £97 9s. He kept his House with his Mother but says the furniture was his own. £28 Cash left in the House. Two Trunks valued at £15. He had, 7 Hogs Valued at 8 Gas. He has recd in full from the Treasury.

Ellenor Listor—Widow—sworn.

Knew Scipio Handley at Charlestown. Knows his Mother to have been a free Woman. The Mother sold Gingerbread. Knows that he carried things to Lord Wm Campbell & the Americans confined him for it. She believes him to have been loyal. There was some furniture used both by the Mother & the Son but she does not know to whom it belonged She never saw any Mahogony furniture. She left Charlestown in Easter 1782 & she believes the Mother is in possn of the furniture.[10]

Book of Negroes (1783)

Introduction

When the British evacuated New York City, three thousand black loyalists embarked for British North America. Between April and November 1783, the British inspected and qualified the blacks who could lawfully leave the city. As this excerpt from the Book of Negroes shows, the British inspectors recorded the details of successful applicants. They noted the name, details of escape or claim to freedom, military record, and the name of former masters. Ship captains could only carry the person if the name was listed on the roll. If the owner of a slave was a loyalist, the blacks had no chance of winning their freedom because the property rights of British subjects remained protected. Two-thirds of the loyalists listed in the Book of Negroes had escaped from the South.

Ship *Aurora* bound for St. John's

Billy Williams, 35, healthy stout man, (Richard Browne). Formerly lived with Mr. Moore of Reedy Island, Carolina, from whence he came with the 71st Regiment about 3 years ago.

Rose Richard, 20, healthy young woman, (Thomas Richard). Property of Thomas Richard, a refugee from Philadelphia.

Daniel Barber, 70, worn out, (James Moore). Says he was made free by Mr. Austin Moore of little York nigh 20 years ago.

Sarah Farmer, 23, healthy young woman, (Mrs. Sharp). Free negress indented to Mrs. Sharp for one year.

Barbarry Allen, 22, healthy stout wench, (Humphry Winters). Property of Humphrey Winters of New York from Virginia.

Elizabeth Black, 24, mulatto from Madagascar, (Mr. Buskirk). Free, indented when nine years of age to Mrs. Courtland.

Bob Stafford, 20, stout healthy negro, (Mr. Sharp). Taken from Mr. Wilkinson in Virginia by a party from the Royal Navy about four years ago.

Harry Covenhoven, 24, [stout healthy negro], (Mr. Buskirk). Came in two years ago from Mr. Covenhoven in Jersey.

John Vans, 39, healthy, blind of his right eye, (Mr. Buskirk, Jr.). Taken in Pennsylvania by a party of the British Army about 6 1/2 years ago; lived there with Sam Barber who he says had eight months before given him his freedom.

Anthony Haln, 27, stout negro, (Nicholas Beckle). His own property willed to him by his father.

Joyce, 12, healthy negress, (James Moore). Lived with James Moore for 6 years; her father died in the King's service.

Simson McGuire, 23, stout healthy negro man, (John Buskirk). Came in to General Arnold in Virginia from Benjamin Hill.

Bristol Cobbwine, 14, stout negro boy, (Richard Browne). Came from Woodbury, Charlestown, South Carolina, with Major Grant of the King's American regiment about 4 years ago.

Paul, 19, [stout] mulatto, ([Richard Browne]). [Came from Woodbury, Charlestown, South Carolina, with Major Grant of the King's American regiment.][11]

Notes

1. Susanna Ahston, ed., *I Belong to South Carolina: South Carolina Slave Narratives* (Columbia: University of South Carolina Press, 2010, originally in *The Methodist Magazine*, March, June 1798).

2. Letter from Judea Moore (black) to Sir Henry Clinton from New York, Clinton Papers, February 10, 1779.

3. Clinton Papers, August 16, 1781, Lieutenant Murphy of Black Pioneers, Clements Library, Ann Arbor.

4. John C. Fitzpatrick, ed., *The Writings of George Washington from the Original Manuscript Sources, Volume 26, January 1, 1783 to June 10, 1783* (Washington DC: United States Government Printing Office, 1938), 364–65.

5. Fitzpatrick, *The Writings of George Washington, Volume 26*, 370.

6. Fitzpatrick, *The Writings of George Washington, Volume 26*, 401–2.

7. Fitzpatrick, *The Writings of George Washington, Volume 26*, 402–6.

8. "Negroes Stay or Leave," August 2, 1783, British Headquarters Papers; Dinah Archey, August 8, 1783, Antislavery Collection, Clements Library.

9. *Carleton Papers*, PRO 30/55/81, September 9, 1783, to September 18, 1783.

10. Hugh Edward Egerton, ed., *The Royal Commission on the Losses and Services of American Loyalists, 1783–1785* (New York: Arno Press and *The New York Times*, 1969), 197–98.

11. Graham Russell Hodges, *The Black Loyalist Directory: African Americans in exile after the American Revolution* (New York: Garland Publishers, 1996), 5–6.

CHAPTER EIGHT

Indian Allies

Relations with Indians (1774)

Introduction

Born in Ireland, Sir William Johnson was British Indian agent and an adopted Mohawk for more than three decades until his death in 1774. This excerpt shows Johnson as a semifeudal ruler whose life included the Mohawk woman Mary Brant, his partner from the late 1750s until his death; their eight half-breed children; his white servants; and slaves. The will testifies that Johnson benefited enormously—in land, relationships, and income—from his trusted position among the Mohawks. After his death, Mary Brant swayed Mohawk warriors to join the British side during the rebellion.

In the name of God amen,—I, Sir William Johnson, of Johnson Hall, in the county of Tryon and Province of New York, Bart., being of sound and disposing mind, memory and understanding, do make, publish and declare, this to be my last will and testament, in manner and form following:

First and principally, I resign my soul to the great and merciful God who made it, in hopes, through the merits alone of my blessed Lord and Saviour, Jesus Christ, to have a joyful resurrection to life eternal; and my body I direct to be decently interred in the place which I intend for it; and I would willingly have the remains of my beloved wife, Catharine, deposited there, if not done before my decease; and I direct and desire my hereinafter mentioned executors to provide mourning for my housekeeper, Mary Brant, and for all her children; also for young Brant and William, both half-breed Mohawks, likewise for my servants and slaves; it is also my desire that the sachems of both Mohawk villages be invited to my funeral, and there to receive each a black stroud blanket, crape and gloves, which they are to wear, and follow as mourners, next after my own family and friends. I leave it to the discretion of my executors, to get such of my friends and acquaintances for bearers as they shall judge most proper, who are to have white scarves, crapes and gloves, the whole expense not to exceed three hundred pounds currency. And as to the worldly and temporal estate, which God was pleased to endow me with, I devise, bequeath and dispose of in the following manner: Imprimis. I will, order and direct, that all such just debts as I may owe, at the time of my decease, together with my funeral expenses of every kind, to be paid by my son, Sir John Johnson, Bart. Item. I give and bequeath to the following persons the sums of money hereafter mentioned which several sums of money are to be paid to them, by my executors, out of the money I may have in the three per cent consolidated annuities, of which the heir of the late Sir William Baker has the management, and that in six months after my decease. And first, to the children of my present housekeeper, Mary Brant, the sum of one thousand pounds sterling, to wit: to Peter, my natural son by said Mary Brant, the sum of three hundred pounds sterling, and to each of the rest, being seven in number, one hundred pounds each; the interest to be thereof duly received and laid out to the best advantage by their guardians or trustees, and also the income of whatever other legacies, &c., as are hereafter to be mentioned, until they come of age or marry, except what is necessary for their maintenance and education. Item. To young Brant, alias Keghneghtaga, and William, alias Tagcheunto, two Mohawk lads, the sum of one hundred pounds York currency to each or the survivor of them.

After paying the before mentioned sums of money, I bequeath to my dearly beloved son, Sir John Johnson, the remaining part of what money I may then have left in the before mentioned, and the other half to be equally divided between my two sons-in-law, Daniel Claus and Guy Johnson, for the use of their heirs. Item. I bequeath to my son, Sir John Johnson, my library and household furniture at the Hall, except what is in my bedroom and in the children's rooms or nursery, which is to be equally divided among them; I also bequeath to him all my plate, except a few articles which I gave to the children of my housekeeper, Mary Brant; he is also to have one-fourth part of all my slaves, and the same of my stock of cattle of every kind. To my two daughters, Anne Claus and Mary Johnson, two-fourths of my slaves and stock of cattle; the other fourth of my slaves and stock of cattle of every kind, I give and bequeath to the children of Mary Brant, my housekeeper, or to the survivors of them, to be equally divided amongst them, except two horses, two cows, two breeding cows, and four sheep, which I would have given before any division is made to young Brant and William of Canajoharie, and that within three months after my decease. I also give and devise all my own wearing apparel, woolen and linen, &c., to be equally divided among the children of my said housekeeper, Mary Brant, share and share alike.

In the next place, I dispose of my real estate, all of my own acquiring, in the following manner, and as I maturely weighed the affair, and made the most equitable division which my conscience directed, I expect all who share of it, will be satisfied, and wish they may make a proper use of it. And first, to my son, Sir John Johnson, Bart., I devise and bequeath all my estate, at and about Fort Johnson, with all the buildings, improvements &c., thereunto belonging, to be, by him and his heirs, forever peaceably possessed and enjoyed. Also a small tract of land on the south side of the river, opposite Fort Johnson; fifty thousand acres of King's land or Royal Grant, all in one body, except the few lots which I have otherwise disposed of; also my share in a patent called Klock & Nellis, jr. on the north side of the Mohawk river. I also devise and bequeath to my son, Sir John Johnson, all my right and title to the Salt Lake, Onondaga, and the lands around it, two miles in depth, for which I have a firm deed, and it is also recorded in the minutes of council at New York; I likewise devise and bequeath to my said son lot No. 10 in said meadow, or patent Sacondaga containing two hundred and sixty-three acres, to be by him and his heirs, of his body lawfully begotten, forever quietly and peaceably possessed and enjoyed; lastly, I do most earnestly recommend it to my son to show lenity to such of the tenants as are poor and of upright conduct in all his dealings with mankind, which will, upon reflection, afford more satisfaction and heart-feeling pleasure, to a noble and generous mind, than the greatest opulency.

In the next place, I devise and bequeath to my son-in-law, Colonel Daniel Claus, and to his heirs, the tract of land whereon he lives, to wit: from Dove Kill to the creek which lies about four hundred yards to the northward of the new dwelling house of Colonel Guy Johnson, together with all the islands thereto belonging; also the house and lots in Albany which I purchased of Henry Holland, together with the water lot adjoining thereto, which I purchased of the corporation of Albany, together with all the buildings and other improvements thereon.

I further devise and bequeath unto the said Daniel Claus and the heirs of his body, all my right in the patent adjoining the German Flatts, on the south side of the Mohawk river, containing about sixteen hundred acres; also three lots in the patent of Kingsborough, to wit: no. thirteen, fourteen and fifty-seven, in the western allotment of three lots in Sacondaga patent, to wit: No. 29, sixty-six, and twenty-seven, containing each two hundred and fifty acres; a third part of a lot in Schenectady, which exchanged with Daniel Campbell, Esq.; also ten thousand acres of land in the Royal Grant, next to that of Sir John Johnson, which is never to be sold or alienated. And lastly, I devise and bequeath unto the said Daniel Claus and the heirs of his body, nine hundred acres, the half of that land that was Gilbert Tices, in the nine partners patent, between Schoharie and the Mohawk; the whole of the several tracts, lots and houses and before mentioned, to be by him and his heirs, of his body lawfully begotten, forever quietly and peaceably possessed and enjoyed. Item. I devise and bequeath to my son-in-law, Colonel Guy Johnson, and the heirs of his body lawfully begotten, the farm and tract of land whereon he now lives, together with all the islands, buildings, and other improvements thereon; also the house and lot of land on Schenectady, purchased by me of Paul Cowes, and now in the possession of the said Guy Johnson, all my right in the Northampton patent, which I purchased of one Dewey; two lots in Sacondaga patent containing one thousand acres, to wit: lot No. 1 and two, near to the river and on both sides of Sacondaga creek; three lots of land in Kingsborough, No. eighty-seven, eighty-eight, and eighty-nine, containing each one hundred acres of land, and one in the eastern allotment; ten thousand acres of land in the Royal Grant, now called Kingsland, adjoining to the ten thousand acres given to Colonel Daniel Claus, which is never to be sold nor alienated on any account; and lastly, nine hundred acres in the half of that land which was Gilbert Tice's in the nine partners patent between Schoharie and the Mohawk village; all the above-mentioned farms, tracts of land and houses with their appurtenances, to be by him and his heirs, of his body lawfully begotten, forever peaceably and quietly possessed and enjoyed. I devise and bequeath unto Peter Johnson, my natural son by Mary Brant, my present housekeeper, the farm and lot of land which I purchased from the Snells in the Stoneraby patent, with all the buildings, mill and other improvements thereon; also two hundred acres of land adjoining thereto, being part of Kingsborough patent, to be laid out in a compact body, between the Garoge and Caniadutta Creeks; also four thousand acres in the Royal Grant, now called Kingsland, next to the Mohawk river, and another strip or piece of land in the Royal Grant, from the Little Falls or carrying-place to lot No. one, almost opposite the house of Hannicol Herkimer, and includes two lots, No. three and No. two, along the river side, and which are now occupied by Ury House, &c. I devise and bequeath unto Elizabeth, sister of the aforesaid Peter, and daughter of Mary Brant, all that farm and lot of land in Harrison's patent, on the north side of the Mohawk river, at No. nineteen, containing near seven hundred acres, bought by me several years ago of Mr. Brown, of Salem, with all the buildings and appurtenances thereunto belonging; also two thousand acres of land in the Royal Grant, now called Kingsland, and that to be laid out joining to that of her brother Peter, both which she and the heirs of her body, lawfully begotten, are to enjoy peaceably forever.

To Magdalene, sister of the two former, and daughter of Mary Brant, I devise and bequeath that farm near to Anthony's Nose, No. eight, containing about nine hundred acres of land, and on which Mr. Brant now lives, with all the buildings and improvements and other appurtenances thereunto belonging; also two thousand acres of land in the Royal Grant now called Kingsland; adjoining to that tract of her sister Elizabeth.

To Margaret, sister of the above named Magdalene, and daughter of Mary Brant, I devise and bequeath two lots of land, part of Stoneraby patent, the one to wit: No. twenty-five, which I bought of William Marshall, contains one hundred acres, the other, No. twelve, contains one hundred and thirty-one acres and a half, or thereabouts, which I purchased of Peter Weaver; also two thousand acres in the Royal Grant now called Kingsland, to be laid out next to her sister Magdalene.

To George, my natural son by Mary Brant, and brother to the four before-mentioned children, I devise and bequeath two lots of land, part of Sacondaga patent, known by Nos. forty-three and forty-four, and called New Philadelphia, containing two hundred and fifty acres each; also a small patent or tract of land called John Brackans, lying on the north side of the Mohawk river, almost opposite to the Canajoharie castle, and contains two hundred and eighty acres or thereabouts; and lastly, three thousand acres in the Royal Grant now called Kingsland, next to the two thousand acres given to his sister Margaret. The said farms or tracts of land with all the buildings and other appurtenances belonging to them, are to be by him, and the heirs of his body lawfully begotten, forever quietly and peaceably possessed and enjoyed.

To Mary, daughter of Mary Brant, and sister of the before-mentioned five children, I devise and bequeath two thousand acres in the Royal Grant, now called Kingsland, adjoining those of her brother George; also two lots in Stoneraby patent, No. thirty-six and thirty-eight, containing about one hundred and fifty acres, which I bought of Peter Davis and Hannes Kilts.

To Susannah, daughter of Mary Brant, and sister of the foregoing six children, I devise and bequeath three thousand acres of the Royal Grant now called Kingsland, laid out adjoining to them of her sister Mary.

To Anne, sister of the foregoing seven children by Mary Brant, I devise and bequeath three thousand acres of the Royal Grant now called Kingsland, to be laid out next to that of her sister Susannah, and to be by her, and the heirs of her body lawfully begotten, forever quietly and peaceably possessed and enjoyed.

To young Brant alias Kaghneghtaga of Canajoharie, I give and bequeath one thousand acres of land in the Royal Grant, now called Kingsland, to be laid out next to and adjoining the before-mentioned land of Anne, daughter of Mary Brant. Also to William, alias Tagawirunte, of Canajoharie, one thousand acres of land in said Royal Grant, alias Kingsland, adjoining that of Brant, to be by them and the heirs of their body, lawfully begotten, forever quietly and peaceably possessed and enjoyed.

It is also my will and desire, that in case any of the before mentioned eight children of mine by Mary Brant should die without issue, their share or shares, as well of my personal as real estate, be equally divided amongst the survivors of them by their guardians.

To my prudent and faithful housekeeper, Mary Brant, mother of the before-mentioned eight children, I will and bequeath the lot No. one, being part of the Royal Grant now called Kingsland, and is opposite to the land whereon Honnicol Herkimer now lives, which she is to enjoy peaceably during her natural life; after which it is to be possessed by her son Peter, and his heirs forever; I also give and bequeath to my said housekeeper one negro wench named Jenny, the sister of Juba; also the sum of two hundred pounds, current money of New York, to be paid to her by my executors within three months after my decease; I also devise and bequeath to Mary McGrah, daughter of Christopher McGrah, of the Mohawk country, two hundred acres of land in the patent of Adageghteinge, now called Charlotte river, to be by her and her heirs forever peaceably possessed and enjoyed.

I give and bequeath to my brothers, John and Warren Johnson, to my sisters Dease, Sterling, Plunkett, and Fitzsimons, the following tracts of land, which I would have sold by my executors to the best advantage, and moneys arising therefrom to be equally divided among them and their heirs, to wit: whatever part of the patent called Bymes at Schoharie, may remain unsold at my decease; also my fourth part of another patent at Schoharie called Lawyer & Zimmer's patent; also that of Adageghteinge or Charlotte river; and lastly, the five thousand acres which I have in Glen and Vrooman's patent; also the thirteen thousand acres which I have in the patent called Peter Servis near General Gage's or whatever part of the aforesaid tracts may be unsold at the time of my decease; this, (from the many losses which I have sustained, and the several sums expended by me during the war which were never paid), is all I can possibly do for them without injuring others, which my honor and conscience will not admit of. As his present majesty, George the third, was graciously pleased as a mark of his favor and regard, to give me a patent under the great seal for the tract of land now called Kingsland, and that without quit rent, except a trifling acknowledgment to be paid yearly, it is my will and desire that no part of it be ever sold by those to whom I have devised it, as that would be acting contrary to my intentions and determined resolution.

I devise and bequeath to my much esteemed nephew, Doctor John Dease, the sum of five hundred pounds current money of New York, to be paid to him within six months after my decease by my executors out of such moneys as I may have in this country at that time, or by my son, Sir John, for which he, my said son Sir John Johnson, shall have and forever enjoy that lot of land in Sacondaga Patent, whereon Martin Lafflet and two more tenants now live, viz: No. eighty-four, containing two hundred and fifty acres. I also devise and bequeath unto my said nephew, John Dease, Esq., two thousand acres of land lying near to South Bay, or Lake Champlain, which tract was purchased by me of Lt. Augustine Prevost, and which was formerly the location of Ensign or Lt. Gorrel, with all the advantages thereunto belonging; or should he, my said nephew, prefer or rather choose to have the value of it in money; in that case it is my will and desire, that my executors dispose of said land to the best advantage, and pay the amount of it to my said nephew.

To my faithful friend, Robert Adems, Esq., of Johnstown, the dwelling house, other buildings, and the lot and one acre whereon he now lives, the

Potash laboratory, and one acre of land with it; also the farm which he holds by deed from me, all free from rent during his natural life, except the quit rent.

To Mr. William Byrne, of Kingsborough, I give the lot of land whereon he now lives and improvements; also that part of the stock of cattle which was mine, free of rent or demand, as long as he lives, the quit rent excepted.

I also will and bequeath to Mr. Patrick Daly, now living with me, for whom I have a particular regard, the sum of one hundred pounds current money of New York, to be paid unto him within three months after my decease, by my executors. It is also my will and desire that all the white servants I may have at the time of my death, be made free and receive from my son ten pounds each.

I also devise and bequeath unto my much esteemed friend and old acquaintance, Joseph Chew, Esq., now of Kingsborough, in the county of Tyron, during his natural life, fifty acres of land, which I purchased from Matthias Link, with all the buildings and other improvements thereon belonging; and after his decease, to his son, William, my god-child, and to his heirs forever. In case of the death of my said god-son William without issue, then to be possessed and enjoyed by Joseph Chew, junr., elder brother of my said god-son William, and his heirs forever. I also devise and bequeath unto the said Joseph Chew, Esq., two hundred acres of land in the patent called Preston's, now Mayfleld, to be laid out in one piece next to the lots already laid out by John Collins, Esq., for the township; the same two hundred acres with all the appurtenances thereto belonging to be by him, the said Joseph Chew and his heirs, forever peaceably and quietly possessed and enjoyed.

It is also my will and desire, that in case my son Sir John Johnson should (which God avert) die without issue, the following disposition be made of the personal and real estate, which is by the foregoing part of this will bequeathed to him, to wit: all the lands of Kingsborough containing above fifty thousand acres, the few lots excepted which I have otherwise disposed of, to be by my grandson William Claus, and the heirs of his body, quietly and peaceably possessed and enjoyed; also twenty thousand acres of the Royal Grant, now called Kingsland, which is never to be sold or alienated from my family.

It is likewise my will and desire, that in the above case, viz., of my son's death without issue, that the lands, houses, &c., at Fort Johnson, and a small tract on the opposite side of the Mohawk river, called Babington's, together with twenty thousand acres of the Royal Grant now called Kingsland, be possessed and enjoyed by the first male heir which my daughter Mary Johnson may have by Guy Johnson, and by his heirs lawfully begotten forever; and in case of her having no male heir to possess it, then it is my will that the before-mentioned lands be equally divided between her daughters and their heirs, in consideration of which my two sons-in-law, Daniel Claus and Guy Johnson shall (within a year) pay unto my executors and trustees for the use of my children by Mary Brant, my housekeeper, the sum of eight hundred pounds current money of New York: that is to say, Colonel Daniel Claus shall pay the sum of five hundred pounds, and Colonel Guy Johnson the sum of three hundred pounds, which sums are to be (as well as the rest devised and bequeathed to them), put out to interest for their support and emolument until they come of age or marry, when equal division is to be made by their guardians or trustees. All the remainder of my son's estate, except what remains of his share in the Royal Grant alias Kingsland, shall be sold by my executors to the best advantage, and the monies arising from the sale thereof to be equally divided between my brothers and sisters as before named, the remainder of his share in Kingsland to be equally divided between his two sisters' children, who are never to dispose of it.

Lastly, I do hereby make, constitute and appoint my beloved son Sir John Johnson, Kt., my two sons-in-law, Daniel Claus and Guy Johnson, Esqs., my two brothers John and Warren Johnson, Esqs., Daniel Campbell, of Schenectady, John Butler, Nelles Fonda, Captain James Stevenson, of Albany, Robert Adems, Samuel Stringer of Albany, Doctor John Dease, Henry Frey and Joseph Chew, Esqs., or any six of them, executors of this, my last Will and testament. And it is also my will and desire that John Dease, Nelles Fonda, John Butler, James Stevenson, Henry Frey and Joseph Chew, Esqs., be, and act as guardians and trustees of my before-mentioned eight children by Mary Brant, my present housekeeper, in full confidence that from the, close connection of the former, and the long uninterrupted friendship subsisting between me and the latter, they will strictly act as brothers, and inviolably observe and execute this my last charge to them; the strong dependance on, and expectation of which unburthens my mind, allays my cares, and makes a change the less alarming. And as I would willingly, in some measure (although trifling), testify my regard and friendship for the above-mentioned gentlemen, I must request their acceptance of three hundred pounds currency to purchase rings as a memento for their once sincere friend, which sum is to be immediately paid to them by my son, Sir John Johnson. And I do hereby revoke, disannul and make void all former wills, bequests and legacies by me heretofore at any time made, bequeathed, or given; and I do hereby make and declare this only to be my last will and testament. In witness whereof I have (with a perfect mind and memory), hereunto set my hand and seal this 27th day of January, 1774, one thousand seven hundred and seventy-four, and my name at the bottom of each page, being thirteen.[1]

British Recruiting Northern Indians (1775)

Introduction

The Earl of Dartmouth was American secretary of state from 1772 to 1775. Colonel Guy Johnson took over Sir William Johnson's post as British Indian agent for the northern colonies when the latter died in 1774. In the following excerpted letter, written on July 24, 1775, Dartmouth encourages John-son to induce Indians to "take up the hatchet" against the rebels.

The Earl of Dartmouth to Colonel Guy Johnson.

Whitehall, 24, July 1775

I have already in my letter to you of the 5th inst. hinted that the time might possibly come when the King, relying upon the attachment of his faithful al-lies, the Six Nations of Indians, might be under the necessity of calling upon them for their aid and assistance in the present state of America.

The unnatural rebellion now raging there calls for every effort to suppress it, and the intelligence His Majesty has received of the Rebells having excited the Indians to take a part, and of their having actually engaged a body of them in arms to support their rebellion, justifies the resolution His Majesty has taken of requiring the assistance of his faithful adherents the Six Nations.

It is therefore His Majesty's pleasure that you do lose no time in taking such steps as may induce them to take up the hatchet against His Majesty's rebel-lious subjects in America, and to engage them in His Majesty's service upon such plan as shall be suggested to you by General Gage to whom this letter is sent accompanied with a large assortement of goods for presents to them upon this important occasion.

Whether the engaging the Six Nations to take up arms in defence of His Majesty's Government is most likely to be effected by separate negociation with the chiefs or in a general council assembled for that purpose, must be left to your judgement, but at all events as it is a service of very great importance, you will not fail to exert every effort that may tend to accomplish it, and to use the utmost diligence and activity in the execution of the orders I have now the honor to transmit to you.[2]

British Recruiting Southern Indians (1776)

Introduction

George Germain replaced the Earl of Dartmouth as American secretary of state in 1775. In his letter of November 6, 1776, Germain urges John Stuart, the British Indian agent for the southern colonies, to exploit rebel mistreat-ment of the Creek and Choctaws.

Lord George Germain to John Stuart, Indian Agent.

Whitehall, 6th November, 1776

I expect with some impatience to hear from you of the success of your nego-ciation with the Creeks and the Choctaws and that you have prevailed with them to join the Cherokees who I find have already commenced hostilities against the Rebels in Carolina and Virginia. The Rebel government in the former province have, I also learn, not only offered considerable rewards for the scalps of those Indians but declared their children of a certain age which may be taken prisoners the slaves of the captors, a measure which I am sure must inflame the enmity of that nation to the highest pitch against them and excite the resentment of all the other Indians in so great a degree that I cannot doubt of your being able under such advantageous circumstances to engage them in a general confederacy against the Rebels in defence of those liberties of which they are so exceedingly jealous and in the full enjoyment of which they have always been protected by the King.

At this distance and before the issue of the campaign to the northward can be known here it is impossible to give you any instructions for the employment of the savages. General Howe will no doubt give you full directions when he has formed his plan of operations against the Southern Colonies. In the mean time as the Cherokees have declared for us they must be supported and it will be your duty to procure them all the aid in your power from the other Indian nations and to supply them with arms and ammunition and other necessaries to enable them to carry on the war. I am not without hopes that Governor Sawyer will find means of assisting them with a detachment of his numerous garrison, and if the well affected inhabitants in the back countries could be collected and embodied to conduct and support the Indians, the Rebels on the sea coast would soon feel the distress from the want of the accustomed supplies, the discontent of the people with the new mode of government would increase with that distress, and resentment against the authors of their calamities would be the necessary consequences.

Inclosed I send you by the King's command printed copies of His Majesty's most gracious speech at the opening of the session together with the addresses of both Houses of Parliament to His Majesty in return, which I have the pleasure to acquaint you were passed in both Houses by very great majorities.[3]

Vying for Indian Support (1778)

Introduction

As much as the British, General George Washington worried about garnering Indian support. In this excerpted letter to the commissioners of Indian Affairs, written from Valley Forge on March 13, 1778, Washington explains the importance of "procuring" Indians. Washington also expresses confidence in the loyalty of the Oneidas.

To the Commissioners of Indian Affairs.

Head Quarters, Valley Forge, March 13, 1778

Gentlemen: You will perceive, by the inclosed Copy of a Resolve of Congress, that I am impowered to employ a body of four hundred Indians, if they can be procured upon proper terms. Divesting them of the Savage customs exercised in their Wars against each other, I think they may be made of excellent use, as scouts and light troops, mixed with our own Parties. I propose to raise about one half the number among the Southern and the remainder among the Northern Indians. I have sent Cob Nathl. Gist, who is well acquainted with the Cherokees and their Allies, to bring as many as he can from thence, and I must depend upon you to employ suitable persons to procure the stipulated number or as near as may be from the Northern tribes. The terms made with them should be such as you think we can comply with, and persons well acquainted with their language, manners and Customs and who have gained an influence over them should accompany them. The Oneidas have manifested the strongest attachment to us throughout this dispute and I therefore suppose, if any can be procured, they will be most numerous. Their Missionary Mr Kirkland seemed to have an uncommon ascendency over that tribe and I should therefore be glad to see him accompany them. If the Indians can be procured, I would choose to have them here by the opening of the Campaign, and therefore they should be engaged as soon as possible as there is not more time between this and the Middle of May than will be necessary to settle the business with them and to March from their Country to the Army. I am not without hopes that this will reach you before the treaty which is to be held, breaks up. If it should, you will have an Opportunity of knowing their sentiments, of which I shall be glad to be informed, as soon as possible. I have the honour, etc.[4]

Hessian View of Indians (1777)

Introduction
In one of the first treaties with the Germans, the British government hired Brunswick troops under the command of Baron von Riedesel. In a treaty with the Duke of Brunswick on January 9, 1776, the British negotiated a supply of approximately four thousand soldiers who would be paid the same rate as their own soldiers and officers. In addition to an annual subsidy, the Duke would receive thirty crowns for each soldier and compensation for each wounded or killed soldier. The first Brunswick soldiers landed in Quebec in the summer of 1776. The following excerpted journal from February 14, 1777, describes a Hessian officer's distrust of the Indians and of Mohawk leader Joseph Brant in particular.

The misunderstanding with the savage nations is not yet entirely over; however, it is hoped that this can soon be put to order. The issue is actually that some refuse to continue the war against the Rebels this year under the command of foreign officers and would rather go against them independently under their own leaders so that they might rob, lay waste, and kill in their savage way with less hindrance, which the English commanders could never have permitted them. An Iroquois named Joseph, who recently returned from England and to whom the interests of the wild nations are only too well known, has incited them to this. Since they abhor deeply the daily expansions of Europeans, they regard the present war against the Rebels as a splendid means of taking their revenge against the poor Colonists who live isolated and closest to them. This Joseph is said to have had circulars sent to all the wild nations living beyond the English provinces in which he criticizes exceedingly their deportment of the previous year and recommends that they declare to the English generals their willingness to fight against the Rebels this year for the King, however, with the express proviso that they be permitted to act independently from all other commanders but their own. At the same time the aforementioned Joseph offers himself as their general leader. This proposal is said to have pleased many nations uncommonly and enabled them to go so far as to indicate this to the English commanding generals. It can easily be imagined how unfortunate the Colonies would be if these wild nations were permitted such a ferocious war, and therefore all effort is being expended to direct their thoughts elsewhere.[5]

Accusing Savages of Scalping Europeans (1777)

Introduction

Jane McCrea was engaged to a loyalist officer in General John Burgoyne's army. In 1777, during Burgoyne's campaign in upstate New York, Jane Mc-Crea was captured by some of Burgoyne's Indian allies. She was shot and scalped, and the clothing was stripped from her body. Fearful of losing Indian allies, Burgoyne allowed the culprit to go unpunished. Rebel leaders such as George Washington used this incident to circulate rumors about the tyranny of the British government, which not only hired Hessian mercenaries, but recruited savages to commit murder. The following excerpted exchange between the rebel officer, Horatio Gates, and the British officer, John Burgoyne, highlights the troubled place of Indians in a war between Europeans and their descendants.

GENERAL HORATIO GATES TO BURGOYNE
U. S. Headquarters, September 2, 1777
Last Night I had the honor to receive Your Excellencys letter of the 1st instant. I am astonished you should mention inhumanity, or threaten retaliation; nothing happened in the action at Bennington but what is common when works are carried by assault.

That the savages of America should in their warfare mangle and scalp the unhappy prisoners who fall into their hands, is neither new nor extraordinary;

but that the famous Lieutenant General Burgoyne, in whom the fine Gentleman is united with the Soldier and the Scholar, should hire the savages of America to scalp Europeans and the descendants of Europeans, nay more, that he should pay a price for each scalp so barbarously taken, is more than will be believed in Europe, untill authenticated facts shall, in every Gazette, convince mankind of the truth of the horrid fate.

Miss McCrea, a young lady lovely to the sight, of virtuous character and amiable disposition, engaged to be married to an officer in your Army, was with other women and children taken out of a house near Fort Edward, carried into the woods, and there scalped and mangled in a most shocking manner. Two parents, with their six children, were all treated with the same inhumanity, while quietly residing in their once happy and peaceful dwelling. The miserable fate of Miss McCrea was particularly aggravated by her being dressed to receive her promised husband, but met her murderer employed by you. Upwards of one hundred men, women and children have perished by the hands of the ruffians to whom it is asserted you have paid the price of blood. [The next sentence, crossed out but still clearly legible, reads: "The law of retaliation is a just law, and you must expect to feel its force."] . . .

GENERAL BURGOYNE TO GATES

September 6, 1777

I received your letter of the 2: instant and in consequence of your compliance with my proposal of sending a surgeon to visit the wounded officers in your hands, and some servants to carry money and necessaries to their masters and to remain with them, I have now to desire the favor of you to dispatch the officer you design with a drum. . . .

It has happened that all my transactions with the Indian Nations, last year and this, have been open; clearly heard; distinctly understood; accurately minuted by very numerous and, in many part, very unprejudiced audiences. So diametrically opposite to truth is your assertion that I have paid a price for scalps that one of the first regulations established by me at the great Council in May, and repeated and enforced and invariably adhered to since, was that the Indians should receive compensation for prisoners because it would prevent cruelty, and that not only such compensation should be withheld, but a strict Account demanded, for scalps—those pledges of conquest, for such you well know they will ever esteem them—were solemnly and peremptorily prohibited to be taken from the wounded and even the dying, and the persons of aged men, women, children and prisoners were pronounced sacred even in assaults.

In regard to Miss McCrea, her fate wanted not of the tragic display you have labored to give it to make it as sincerely abhorred and lamented by me as it can be by the tenderest of her friends. The fact was no premeditated barbarity. On the contrary two chiefs who had brought her off for the purposes of security, not of violence to her person, disputed which should be her guard; and in a fit of savage passion in the one from whose hands she was snatched, the unhappy woman became the victim. Upon the first intelligence of this event I obliged the Indians to deliver the murderer into my hands; and tho to have punished him by our laws or principles of justice would have been perhaps unprecedented, he certainly should have suffered an ignominious death had I not been convinced by circumstances and observation, beyond the possibility of a doubt, that a pardon, under the forms which I prescribed and they accepted, would be more efficacious than an execution to prevent similar mischiefs.

The above instance excepted, your intelligence respecting cruelties of the Indians is false.[6]

Mohawks Side with the British (1778)

Introduction

Writing on June 27, 1778, Reverend Dan Claus's excerpted letter explains why the Mohawks chose to remain loyal to the British. Claus also defends Indian warfare as primarily defensive and praises the Mohawk chief, Joseph Brant, for his moderation.

Indeed the Generality of Indians on this Continent saw it their political Interest from the Beginning of this Rebellion to oppose the Rebels as much as in their Power, being sensible of the Americans having always had so great a Propensity of encroaching upon their Lands by foul Means & otherwise, and in particular became more & more troublesome to them in that Respect since the Conquest of Canada, and in short clearly foresaw that should they succeed in their rebellious Plan & become Masters of the Continent they would soon overrun their hunting Territory allotted them by His Majesty in 1768, and expel them. However this Endeavour of theirs was greatly checked by an ill judged Delicacy in the Rulers of this Country the two first Years, which had it not been the Case the Rebellion in my We Opinion must have been check'd in its Bud and Thousands of Lives thereby saved.

Now the Rebels having openly threatened the Indians to extirpate them whenever in their Power & take Possession of their Lands, they are detirmin'd to carry on the war against them to the last Extremity, And I apprehend if Matters were settled to Morrow on Governmts side they could not be brought so easily to make Peace with the Rebels after such Threats, being in general of an unforgiving, jealous & savage Temper. Yet notwithstanding this Conduct of the Indians in their own Cause as it were, the Rebels in Conformity to their gen[l] Character do their utmost to persuade & influence the public agst Government of their being the Instigators & Employers of Savage Exploits & Cruelties; & which are published in their Papers with the most unjust & false Exaggerations, as I myself read in one of them touching our Affairs at Fort

Stanwix, of which they published that enormous Untruth of Numbers having been murdered in cold Blood, when it can be made to appear with the greatest Truth that we merely acted defensively in preventing an Enemy to attack, dislodge & if in their power cut us to pieces; and not a Rebel was killed after being taken & brought to Camp, but as soon as possible purchased & released from the Indians & sent to this Place . . .

The Mohawk Chief Joseph Brant that was in London in 1776, has since his Return to his Country and Nation proved & distinguished himself the most Loyal and firmly attached Friend to His Majesty's Cause & Interest; he harangues his Warriors unweariedly to defend their Lands & Liberty against the Rebels, who in a great measure began this Rebellion to be sole Masters of this Continent and only for the Great King their father's interposing & protecting them they must have perhaps e'er now been deprived of everything that was dear to them, wherefore they could not sufficiently exert themselves to espouse the King's Cause, that was so nearly connected with theirs. He was the most active Chieftain in the last Campaign under me, & by my Directions has all last Winter prepared them, & the other day attacked a rebel post called Cherry valley in Tryon County & cut off a party of upwards [of] 300 entirely. I am sure he must occasion some Diversion in favor of Sir Henry Clinton coming up Hudson's River as he keeps the whole Country alarm'd. And altho' he is a thorough Indian born, he allows of no Cruelties in his Exploits; his Proficiency in Christianity is amazing and incomparable, he has acquired the English Language so perfectly that he is the best Interpreter from that into ye Iroquois Language, and has translated [a] great part of the New Testament . . .[7]

Mohawks Seek Assistance in Canada (1786)

Introduction
Joseph Brant rose as a Mohawk leader due to his connections with British officials such as Sir William Johnson. A devout Anglican, Brant translated the prayer book into the Mohawk language. In his letter to the American secretary of state, Lord Sydney, written on January 4, 1786, Brant reminds the British of Indian sacrifices during the rebellion. He pledges loyalty to the king and asks the government to assist his people in Canada.

My Lord,

The claims of the Mohawks for their losses having been delivered by Sir John Johnson, His Majesty's Superintendent General for Indian affairs, to General Haldimand, and by him laid before your Lordship, who cannot but be well informed that their sufferings, losses, and being drove from that country which their forefathers long enjoyed, and left them the peaceable possession of, is in consequence of their faithful attachment to the King, and the zeal they manifested in supporting the cause of His country against the rebellious subjects in America.

From the promises made by the Governor and Commander-in-chief of Canada, that their losses should be made good, and that soon, when I left them, I was desired to put His Majesty's ministers in mind of their long and sincere friendship for the English nation, in whose cause their ancestors and they have so often fought and so freely bled,—of their late happy settlements, before the rebellion, and their present situation,—and to request their claims might be attended to, and that orders may be given for what they are to receive to be paid as soon as possible, in order to enable them to go on with the settlement they are now making; in some measure stock their farms, and get such articles and materials as all settlements in new countries require, and which it is out of their power to do before they are paid for their losses.

On my mentioning these matters, since my arrival in England, I am informed orders are given that this shall be done; which will give great relief and satisfaction to those faithful Indians, who will have spirit to go on, and their hearts be filled with gratitude for the King, their father's, great kindness, which I pray leave, in their behalf, to acknowledge, and to thank your Lordship for your friendship.[8]

JOSEPH BRANT, Captain, or
Thayendanegea.

Indians as Beasts of Prey (1783)

Introduction

The two excerpted letters, written on May 10, 1783, and September 7, 1783, illuminate General George Washington's desire to advance frontier settlement without instigating another "Indian War." Throughout, Washington remains clear about rewarding the efforts of American "warriors" through granting them Indian land. Washington's comparison of Indians with wolves, both beasts of prey, highlights the continuing Indian resistance to American expansion.

To Chevalier de Chastellux, Newburgh, May 10, 1783

At present, both Armies remain in the Situation you left them, except that all Acts of hostility have ceased in this quarter and things have put on a more tranquil appearance than heretofore. . . .

We look forward with anxious expectation for the Definitive treaty to remove the doubts and difficulties which prevail at present, and our Country of our Newly acquired friends in New York, and other places within these states of whose Company we are heartily tired. Sir Guy, with whom I have had a meeting at Dobbss ferry for the purpose of ascertaining the Epoch of this event, wd.

give me no definitive answer; but general assurances, that he has taken every preparatory step for it, one of which was that a few days before, he had shipped off for Nova Scotia upwards of 6000 Refugees or Loyalists; who apprehending they would not be received as Citizens of these United States he thought it his duty to remove previous to the evacuation of the City by the Kings Troops.

. . . The Indians have recommenced hostilities on the Frontiers of Pennsylvania and Virginia; killing and scalping whole families, who had just returned to the habitations from which they had fled, in expectation of enjoying them again in Peace; these people will be troublesome Neighbours to us unless they can be removed to a much greater distance and this is only to be done by purchase, or Conquest; which of the two will be adopted by Congress I know not. the first, I believe would be cheapest, and most consistent perhaps with justice. the latter most effectual.

To Marquis de Lafayette, Head Quarters, Newburgh, May 10, 1783

. . . The Indians on the Frontiers of Virginia and Pennsylvania have lately committed Acts of hostility, murdering and Scalping many of the innocent Settlers, who were returning to thier former habitations in hopes of possessing them in Peace. It is much to be doubted whether these wretches will ever suffer our Frontiers to enjoy tranquility till they are either exterminated, or removed to a much greater distance from us than they now are.[9]

To James Duane, Rocky Hill, September 7, 1783

Sir: I have carefully perused the Papers which you put into my hands relative to Indian Affairs.

My sentiments with respect to the proper line of Conduct to be observed towards these people coincides precisely with those delivered by Gen. Schuyler, so far as he has gone in his Letter of the 29th. July to Congress (which, with the other Papers is herewith returned), and for the reasons he has there assigned; a repetition of them therefore by me would be unnecessary. But independent of the arguments made use of him the following considerations have no small weight in my Mind.

To suffer a wide extended Country to be over run with Land Jobbers, Speculators, and Monopolisers or even with scatter'd settlers, is in my opinion, inconsistent with the wisdom and policy which our true interest dictates, or that an enlightened People ought to adopt, and besides, is pregnant of disputes both with the Savages, and among ourselves, the evils of which are easier, to be conceived and then described; and for what? but to aggrandize a few avaricious Men to the prejudice of many, and the embarrassment of Government. for the People engaged in these pursuits without contributing in the smallest degree to the support of Government, or considering themselves as amenable to its Laws, will involve it by their unrestrained conduct, in inextricable perplexities, and more than probable in a great deal of Bloodshed.

My ideas therefore of the line of Conduct proper to be observed not only towards the Indians, but for the government of the Citizens of America, in their Settlement of the Western Country (which is intimately connected therewith) are simply these.

First and as a preliminary, that all Prisoners of whatever age or Sex, among the Indians shall be delivered up.

That the Indians should be informed, that after a Contest of eight years for the Sovereignty of this Country G: Britain has ceded all the Lands of the United States within the limits described by the arte. of the Provisional Treaty.

That as they (the Indians) maugre all the advice and admonition which could be given them at the commencement; and during the prosecution of the War could not be restrained from acts of Hostility, but were determined to join their Arms to those of G Britain and to share their fortune; so consequently, with a less generous People than Americans they would be made to share the same fate; and be compelled to retire along with them beyond the Lakes. But as we prefer Peace to a state of Warfare, as we consider them as a deluded People; as we perswade ourselves that they are convinced, from experience, of their error in taking up the Hatchet against us, and that their true interest and safety must now depend upon *our* friendship. As the country, is large enough to contain us all; and as we are disposed to be kind to them and to partake of their Trade, we will from these considerations and from motives of Compn., draw a veil over what is past and establish a boundary line between them and us beyond which we will *endeavor* to restrain our People from Huting or Settling, and within which they shall not come, but for the purposes of Trading, Treating, or other business unexceptionable in its nature.

In establishing this line, in the first instance, care should be taken neither to yield nor to grasp at too much. But to endeavor to impress the Indians with an idea of the generosity of our disposition to accommodate them, and with the necessity, we are under, of providing for our Warriors, our young People who are growing up, and strangers who are coming from other Countries to live among us. and if they should make a point of it, or appear dissatisfied at the line we may find it necessary to establish, compensation should be made them for their claims within it.

It is needless for me to express more explicitly because the tendency of my observns. evinces it is my opinion that if the Legislature of the State of New York should insist upon expelling the Six Nations from all the Country they Inhabited previous to the War, within their Territory (as General Schuyler seems to be apprehensive of) that it will end in another Indian War. I have every reason to believe from my enquiries, and the information I have received that they will not suffer their Country (if it was our policy to take it before we could settle it) to be wrested from them without another struggle. That they would compromise for a part of it I have very little doubt, and that it would be the cheapest way of coming at it, I have no doubt at all. The same observations, I am perswaded, will hold good with respect to Virginia, or any other state which has powerful Tribes of Indians on their Frontiers . . .

At first view, it may seem a little extraneous, when I am called upon to give an opinion upon the terms of a Peace proper to be made with the Indains, that I should go into the formation of New states; but the Settlemt. of the Western Country and making a Peace with the Indians are so analogous that there can be no definition of the one without involving considerations of the other. for I repeat it, again, and I am clear in my opinion, that policy and oeconomy point very strongly to the expediency of being upon good terms with the Indians, and the propriety of purchasing their lands in preference to attempting to drive them by force of arms out of their Country; which as we have already experi-enced is like driving the Wild Beasts of the Forest which all return as soon as the pursuit is at an end and fall perhaps on those that are left there; when the gradual extension of our Settlements will as certainly cause the Savage as the Wolf to retire; both being beasts of prey tho' they differ in shape. In a word there is nothing to be obtained by an Indian War but the Soil they live on and this can be had by purchasing at less expence, and without that bloodshed, and those distresses which helpless Women and Children are made partakers of in all kinds of disputes with them.

P.S. A formal Address and memorial from the Oneida Indians when I was on Mohawk River, setting forth their Grievances and distresses and praying relief, induced me to order a pound of Powder and 3 lbs. of Lead to be issued to each Man, from the Military Magazines . . .[10]

Notes

1. Arthur Pound, "Appendix," in *Johnson of the Mohawks: A Biography of Sir Wil-liam Johnson, Irish Immigrant, Mohawk War Chief, American Soldier, Empire Builder* (New York: Macmillan Company, 1930), 489–502.

2. F. B. O'Callaghan, *Documents Relating to Colonial History of New York*, vol. 8 (Albany: Weed, Parsons, 1853–1887), 596.

3. William L. Saunders, ed., *Colonial Records of North Carolina*, X (New York: AMS Press, 1968), 893–94.

4. John C. Fitzpatrick, ed., *The Writings of George Washington from the Original Manuscript Sources, Volume XI* (Washington, DC: United States Government Print-ing Office, 1938), 76–77.

5. V. C. Hubbs, "Journal of the Brunswick Corps in America under General Von Riedesel," in *Sources of American Independence: Selected Manuscripts from the Collec-tions of the William L. Clements Library*, ed. Howard H. Peckham (Chicago: University of Chicago Press, 1978), 244.

6. Originally in Gates Papers, Box XIXb; and Gates Papers, Box VII, no. 223; both in the New York Historical Society. These excerpts are also included in Henry Steele Commager and Richard B. Morris, *The Spirit of Seventy-Six: The Story of the American Revolution as Told by Participants* (New York: Harper & Row, 1967), 558–61.

7. John Wolfe Lydekker, ed., *The Faithful Mohawks* (Cambridge: The University Press, 1938), 154–56.

8. William L. Stone, ed., *Life of Joseph Brant-Thayendanegea, including the border wars of the American Revolution and sketches of the Indian campaigns of Generals Harmar, St. Clair, and Wayne; and other matters connected with the Indian relations of the United States and Great Britain, from the peace of 1783 to the Indian peace of 1795,* Volume 2 (St. Clair Shores, MI: Scholarly Press, 1970), 252–53.

9. John C. Fitzpatrick, ed., *The Writings of George Washington from the Original Manuscript Sources,* Volume 26, *January 1, 1783 to June 10, 1783* (Washington, DC: United States Government Printing Office, 1938), 419–20, 421.

10. John C. Fitzpatrick, ed., *The Writings of George Washington from the Original Manuscript Sources,* Volume 27, *June 11, 1783 to November 28, 1784* (Washington, DC: United States Government Printing Office, 1938), 133–40.

CHAPTER NINE

Loyalist Losses

Loyalists in the Peace Treaty (1783)

Introduction

Shockingly, the clauses in the Treaty of Paris provided no protection for Indians, slaves, or white loyalists. The Treaty did not mention Indian allegiance or Indian land and offered generous land and political concessions to the United States. Article 7, which assured Americans that the British would not carry off slaves or other rebel property outside of the new nation, remained a sore point for years to come. In recommending that the states restore the property of returning loyalists, the British government left white loyalists to deal with legal and extralegal punishment from local leaders who despised the loyalists as traitors.

Article 5:

It is agreed that Congress shall earnestly recommend it to the legislatures of the respective states to provide for the restitution of all estates, rights, and properties, which have been confiscated belonging to real British subjects; and also of the estates, rights, and properties of persons resident in districts in the possession on his Majesty's arms and who have not borne arms against the said United States. And that persons of any other description shall have free liberty to go to any part or parts of any of the thirteen United States and therein to remain twelve months unmolested in their endeavors to obtain the restitution of such of their estates, rights, and properties as may have been confiscated; and that Congress shall also earnestly recommend to the several states a reconsideration and revision of all acts or laws regarding the premises, so as to render the said laws

197

or acts perfectly consistent not only with justice and equity but with that spirit of conciliation which on the return of the blessings of peace should universally prevail. And that Congress shall also earnestly recommend to the several states that the estates, rights, and properties, of such last mentioned persons shall be restored to them, they refunding to any persons who may be now in possession the bona fide price (where any has been given) which such persons may have paid on purchasing any of the said lands, rights, or properties since the confiscation.

And it is agreed that all persons who have any interest in confiscated lands, either by debts, marriage settlements, or otherwise, shall meet with no lawful impediment in the prosecution of their just rights.

Article 6:

That there shall be no future confiscations made nor any prosecutions commenced against any person or persons for, or by reason of, the part which he or they may have taken in the present war, and that no person shall on that account suffer any future loss or damage, either in his person, liberty, or property; and that those who may be in confinement on such charges at the time of the ratification of the treaty in America shall be immediately set at liberty, and the prosecutions so commenced be discontinued.

Article 7:

There shall be a firm and perpetual peace between his Brittanic Majesty and the said states, and between the subjects of the one and the citizens of the other, wherefore all hostilities both by sea and land shall from henceforth cease. All prisoners on both sides shall be set at liberty, and his Brittanic Majesty shall with all convenient speed, and without causing any destruction, or carrying away any Negroes or other property of the American inhabitants, withdraw all his armies, garrisons, and fleets from the said United States, and from every post, place, and harbor within the same; leaving in all fortifications, the American artillery that may be therein; and shall also order and cause all archives, records, deeds, and papers belonging to any of the said states, or their citizens, which in the course of the war may have fallen into the hands of his officers, to be forthwith restored and delivered to the proper states and persons to whom they belong.[1]

Despair and Distraction (1782)

Introduction

Written on August 7, 1782, this excerpted memo from the British commander-in-chief, Sir Henry Clinton, describes loyalist response to the preliminary peace treaty.

The situation in which the unfortunate adherents of the Crown are left by the late resolution of independence to this country is such that your feelings tho at the distance of 3,000 miles must be greatly hurt—never was despair or distraction stronger painted than in the countenance I momently see; and I do declare that I am often obliged to retire to my room to avoid hearing aspersions against my country too justly founded.

The militia who have been performing the military duties of the Crown have declined further service, and so exasperated were they that before Troops could arrive in town, they left their posts and went to their different homes to condole their wretched fates. . . . while the people of the garrison were protected by the military they did not wish but on particular occasions to share the service with them; but now I verily believe (except a very few) the whole would attempt any enterprise sooner than become the servants of a tyrant Congress—papers are every night stuck up in every quarter of the town with the most vindictive fury against those who advised our sovereign to accede to the independence of this country—some I have seen copies of which I send you—but others I could not procure –[2]

Dreadful Tidings (1782)

Introduction
Written on August 8, 1782, this excerpted letter from Beverly Robinson expresses loyalists' disbelief at the possibility of American independence. Robinson raised a loyalist military corps, the Royal American Regiment, and served with the British administration since 1777. Robinson knew that his public support for reunion with Britain would mean exile from his home and community.

Everything in this country has continued in a state of suspence and nothing of any consequence has happened since you left us until Wednesday 31st July on which day a packet arrived from England—on my dear Sir what dreadfull & distressing tidings does she bring us; the independence of America given up by the King without any condition whatsoever; the loyalist of America to depend on the mercy of their Enemeys for the restoration of their possessions, which we are well assured they will never grant; the greatest part of the estates that have been confiscated by them are already sold, this is the situation of most of the loyalists that had an estate to loose; but what my good sir is to become of me & my family you well know I can expect no mercy from them—my wife, my eldest son and myself being among those proscribed by an act of assembly of this state passed in Oct., 1779 by which act we are condemned to be hanged without further tryal or ceremony if ever we are catched within this state . . . I have been too active against their measures from the beginning & had too good an estate were to expect forgiveness from them, besides all my personal & the greatest part of my real estate is already sold; I must prepare to go England with my wife and daughters (the boys must follow the fate of their regiments);

On Sunday last, many people read a note (myself among them) from the commander in chief and Admiral Digby to attend at head at one o'clock on the subject of the packet—many people were informed of it verbally and a great number attended when a letter from the commissioner to Gen. Washington was publickly read—this you may be sure made many a heavy heart; the shock at first was so great that we thought every thing was lost past recovery but upon reading the letter over coolly & reflecting upon it I for my part think there is still some hope left, and cannot persuade myself that England means or intends to give up all connections with or command over this country. I hope this has only been a political finesse to answers some good purpose; why should England give up America (in a manner this letter mentions) the very thing she went to war for at a time when her arms are victorious every where and I assure you sir that the Kings cause in this country was gaining every day, a general discontent to the war & the heavy burthens it occasioned prevailed almost universally throughout the colonies, & the people were never so ripe for a general revolt against Congress measures as at present . . .³

Unwavering Devotion (1782)

Introduction

In this excerpted petition, the Reverends Charles Inglis, Samuel Seabury, Isaac Browne, and fifty-nine other loyalists express effusive devotion to George III and pray that the empire would not abandon them.

New York December 18th 1782

The Solemn Declaration, and humble Petition of the American Loyalists, to their *Most August Monarch, George the Third*, of Great Britain, France & Ireland, *King, Defender* of the *Faith*, &c. &c. &c.

Most Gracious Sovereign!

We, Your Majesty's Loyal & Faithful American Subjects, humbly pray your Regal Permission, to approach Your Throne with the most profound Deference, & with Hearts replete with the warmest Gratitude to Your Royal Person, for the gracious Protection Your Majesty has ever granted us.

And we do beg Leave, also, Solemnly to declare to Your Most Gracious Majesty, that we do hold the horrid Attempt of Your ungrateful, revolted Subjects, and their Abettors, to despoil Your Crown of one of the most invaluable Gems that adorns it, Your American Colonies & provinces,) in utter Detestation, as being, in the very highest Degree, unwarrantable & nefarious; and that we *will, therefore*, contribute every Thing within our Power, to prevent their carrying this *most iniquitous Attempt* into Execution.

We do crave, Moreover, in the humblest Manner, to Declare to Your Regal Majesty, that we are so very far from conceiving ourselves aggrieved or injured by Your Majesty, or by the Parent Country, that, contrariwise, we are fully assured, that all Your American Subjects have been highly favoured & indulged, not only by Your Most Excellent Majesty, & by Your Regal Predecessors, but also by the Parent Country: For Annual Requisitions have been made on, and liberally granted by our European fellow Subjects, Whereas Such Annual Requisitions have not been made on, nor granted by Your American Subjects, for the Protection of the Whole English Empire. So that we are perfectly convinced, from Matters of Stubborn & undeniable fact, that Your Majesty's American Subjects, are not merely an uninjured, but a highly favoured people: Since Your Majesty's Colonies & Provinces have cost the Parent Country, even before the Commencement of the present unprovoked Rebellion, more than Three Hundred Millions of Pounds, New York Currancy, besides *Much Blood.*

Furthermore, we also desire, with all Humility, to Declare to Your Most Excellent Majesty, that we, Your Majesty's American Loyal Subjects, from the above Mentioned Considerations, from the Principles of Natural Equity, & innate Generosity, are not only willing, but also most ardently *desirous*, that for the Future, Your Royal Majesty would be most graciously pleased, to make Requisition on us, as well and as *frequently*, as on our Transatlantic, or European Fellow Subjects, by the Medium of our Legal Representatives: For, that Your European Subjects, Most gracious Sovereign, Should bear the Public Burdens *alone*, and that for the Common Protection, Defence, Security and Felicity of the *Whole British, or English Empire*, (as hath hitherto in a Manner been the Case,) gives us an Idea, which *Strict Equity*, and *natural Generosity*, *nòt to Say Sound policy*, utterly disables us to Suffer and endure *any longer*, we do own, not without Confusion & Colouring, it has been brooked and Suffered *too long*, by Your Majesty's Collonial Subjects of North America, by Means of Some designing Men.

We have thus humbly presumed, *gracious Sovereign*, to Declare our Sentiments, and pray to add, that we can with Truth assert, that a vast Majority of Your American Subjects, (many of whom now groan under the unparalleled Tyranny of Lawless Usurpers & their Abettors, deaf to every Overture So generously made and held forth to them by Your Majesty,) exactly coincide with ours.

In Consequence of those our Loyal Sentiments, & of our inviolable Attachment to Your Royal person & Government, We beg Leave to beseech Your gracious Majesty, not to withdraw Your Royal Protection from us, Your American Loyal Subjects, as Such a Measure would render the Calamities & Distresses of Your Majesty's American Loyal Subjects, *absolutely Insupportable, absolutely Ineffable!*

We do also pray, that Your Most excellent Majesty would be graciously pleased, to publish to all the Courts of Europe, this our Solemn Declaration & humble Petition.

In Fine, We Send up our most ardent Petition to the awfully glorious Monarch of the Universe, the *King* of Kings, that he may for a long, very long Series of Years, preserve & Keep Your Most excellent Majesty, the grand

Ornament of the British Throne, the first Pillar of the English Constitution, (which breaths nothing but Liberty, Equity & Impartiality,) The Father of all Your Subjects; And that Your Royal Successors may fill and adorn the British Throne till Time Shall be no more. That You, Most August & gracious Monarch, having very long, & in a most Supereminent Manner, promoted the Glory of the *King* of Kings, & the Felicity of Your Subjects, may be raised from a Terrestial Throne & Crown, to a Throne and Crown celestial and eternal!

Endorsed:—

Loyalists—18th Dec.r 1782

To GENERAL SIR GUY CARLETON[4]

Irrecoverable Debts (1783)

Introduction

Written on November 15, 1783, this petition from Rhode Island's John Maudesley shows the vulnerable situation loyalist merchants faced when British troops withdrew protection from cities such as Newport. The British army variously occupied and evacuated Boston, Newport, Philadelphia, Savannah, and Charleston. In November 1783, New York City was the last port to be evacuated.

A situation of real distress and a duty, which I owe a suffering family from the basis of that confidence which I assume in addressing your Excellency by letter.

I was long an inhabitant of Newport, on the late colony of Rhode Island, and before his Majesty's troops took possession of that place . . . Was appointed captain of one of the associated companies at a time when safety of the garrison required such an exertion.

When the majesty's ships were withdrawn from the Island, I accompanied them in this place, where I have since resided. The circumstances attending my removal were peculiarly unfortunate and greatly enhanced by the capture of a vessel [New York] with a valuable cargo which were carried into New London—the remains of my fortune which I had brought from Rhode Island having been totally annihilated by a succession of losses which no human prudence could foresee, I was constrained from necessity to ask the assistance of his Majesty's bounty which was extended to me in the beginning of the year, 1782 by an allowance of a dollar a day.

. . . My object extends no further than to repossess much of my property recover my debts and afterwards to remove my family and the proceeds in money to some place still in allegiance to his Majesty. My contempt for republican government contracted by education and since informed in experience and observation forbid the idea of becoming a citizen of either of the American states, more especially as their authority, now recognized by Great Britain, can be considered in no other point of view than the effect of political necessity, and which by the unnatural separation must, to the inhabitants of this country, be ultimately, productive of anarchy and confusion.

But this intention is not in my power to prosecute without your Excellency's assistance. I declare in the province of that God whom I lust for and adore that at present I have not the means of removing myself and family to Rhode Island . . .[5]

Rebel Retaliation (1783)

Introduction

Written on October 30, 1783, this testimony from Joshua Booth, wagoner, from Orange County in New York, shows the plight of ordinary loyalists after the war. Significantly, the men who ridiculed Booth were not strangers but neighbors.

> [When he went to visit his family in Orange County] . . . a party imprisoned him and . . . eyebrows slashed with a pen knife—his head was tarred and feath-ered—and a sheepskin cap put on it—inscription on this head said "Look yo Tory Crew, and see what George your king can do." He was then driven by a party on horseback and himself on foot about four miles, a drum beating and fife playing—then he was set on a horse bare backed and taken to Newburgh where he was dismounted and driven about the streets with much mockery and insult till near midnight and then conveyed on board of a sloop to New York—the parties in this abuse and violence were Zebulon Hughson, Thomas Delap . . . about forty persons.[6]

Damages in Property and Slaves (1783)

Introduction

Submitted in March 1784 to the Commission of Loyalists Claims, this petition from South Carolina's Anglican loyalist James Stuart shows how southern loyalists adjusted to wartime circumstances. Stuart requested com-pensation for his losses in income, property, and slaves.

> The Memorial of James Stuart, clerk.
>
> Sheweth
>
> That he was Rector of George Town Parish South Carolina when the late Troubles began in America, but for his Loyalty and Attachment to his Coun-try, was violently assaulted by a Savage Mob, and when he appealed to the Justice of the Country for Redress, the very Judge applauded the Brutality of

the Banditti, and encouraged the Aggressors even after Conviction, to insult him in their Court of Justice.

Finding there was no Law, Justice or Protection for Loyal or even neutral Men, and reasonably apprehending his Life to be in danger, he betook himself to the West Indies in 1777 where he remained (borrowing Money for his Support) til the reduction of Georgia by His Majesty's Troops, an event which he flattered himself was preparatory to that of South Carolina: Accordingly he quitted the West Indies, and after a long circuitous passage, wherein he experienced the greatest Hardships, a few weeks before it was besieged by D'Estaing, he arrived at Savannah, where he got a small appointment in the Army. The following spring he attended the Forces to the Siege of Charlestown, and upon its reduction, was enabled once more to return to his Family and Property; but, unhappily, by another Revolt, of the people, he was obliged to quit them at a Moment's Warning, without being able to carry with him the smallest Article of Property, and to take Refuge within the Lines of Charlestown, and at the final Evacuation of it, to bid an everlasting adieu to that Country.

He afterwards had the additional Misfortune to be taken in the Channel by a French Privateer, and carried with his Family into Dunkirk, a circumstance truly distressing and expensive.

As to his Services, and personal Sufferings in the Cause, they have not he presumes, been inferior to those of many, as is well known to many Gentlemen; Col. Balfour & Captn. Ardesoif of the Navy, can testify some instances thereof.

As to his Losses, his private Property used to be worth to him about £400 Sterling and his parish £200 per Annum the latter is irrecoverably lost, and also a great part of the Former; and as to the remainder he is totally unacquainted with its Situation having not, since he left America, had the Satisfaction of hearing from those, on whom he depended for its care and preservation, but hopes it is not confiscated, as he was informed, before he left Charlestown, that Mrs. Stuart's Relations, by their Influence, got it erased from the confiscation list.

The Income of his Parish arose thus, £760 Currency, i. e. £108 "11 Sterling (the Salary) was paid half Yearly out of the Publick Treasury; the Parsonage House &c he let for £25—and his Fees (it being a very wealthy and extensive Parish) about £80—which to him and in that cheap country and where his Property and Connections lay was better than £400 would be here. This Loss is of public Notoriety, but if it is doubted, the late Ordinary Lt Gov: Bull, or Doctr Fyffe, one of his parishoners can certify it.

His other Losses occasioned by the War cannot be so publickly known but he can conscientiously state the whole thus—

His Parish 7 years: £1400.

Upwards of 4 years he had nothing from his private property: £1600.

By near 20 years labour and virtuous conduct he had saved about £2300 Sterling, which he let at Interest; it is now reduced by their iniquitous depreciation to about £1100

Lost then by Depreciation : £1200.

But unfortunately about £700 of the £1100 was Lent to Loyalists of considerable property, but whose Estates are now confiscated; whether the confiscators will pay the Debts out of the confiscated Property he knows not; if not the Commissioners will, he hopes, allow it to be a just claim, as it undoubtedly would has [sic] been paid but for the part he took.

His Expenses in the West Indies where he had no Support from Government, as those of his Description had here—the consequence truly of Loyalty: £230.

Expenses and Losses in coming home, and being taken and carried into France: £75.

A Negro Carpenter, Horses &c &c plundered and carried off.

Your Memorialist therefore prays that his Case may be taken into Consideration, that your Memorialist may be enabled under your Report to receive such Aid and Relief as his Losses and Services may be found to deserve. London. March 23, 1784.[7]

Forsaking Britain (1781)

Introduction

Born into one of the most prestigious families in Prince George's County, Maryland, Anglican Reverend Henry Addison was an exile in London during the revolutionary years. In this excerpted letter of May 30, 1781, to his fellow exile and brother-in-law, Jonathan Boucher, Addison explains the reasons for his disillusionment with Britain and his acceptance that the two sides could not be reconciled. Addison returned to the American colonies after the revolution.

You will be surprized a little perhaps when I tell you my Friend that I shall embark very shortly for America, & that I shall take my son with me. I have several reasons wch have determin'd me to this later Measure; with a few onlly of wch I shall at present trouble you . . .

I have a thousand Things to say to you; & they crowd so upon me, that I know not how to give them Utterance, they must be reserved, I believe, for the subject of a conversation, whch shall be in a few days. To-morrow I must be down in the City, as I have been today; from whence I have returned most heartily fatigued, with my Zeel [sic] terribly ? Of the motives by which I was prompted in the commencement of this wretched Business;—of the sentiments I held, & brought with me hither, You need not be inform'd;—they were such in wch we both heartily & sincerely, I trust, concur'd. I have called my Heart to a strict account for them. I find nothing there of wch to accuse myself. If I were in the same situation again I cd—I wd take no other part. The God within the Conscience acquits me, & so, I trust will the God of that God . . .

But I must honestly confess to you, that looking forwards, my sentiments have undergone much change. . . . From the oppy wch the resident of near five years have given men, to take a nearer view . . . I am persuaded that their Govt is, of all others, the most unfit for ruling distant Colonies. Rent as they are into endless factions, the fatal effects of whch have appear'd in the Field & now on the Ocean, there is neither uniformity or stability in their counsesl or actions. It is one ceaseless round of contest for office & the emoluments of office. . . . there is no plan or system; or if any such imperfect one there were, it is reprobated & damned, if for no other reason, for that alone that it was the plan of their predecessors.

Too much blood hath likewise, I think, been spilt to leave any Room even for hope that a cordial Reconciliation can ever again take place. . . . The business has also been fatally drawn out into such a length, that what at first might have been attributed to that of Blood has had time to subside into a settled hatred & rancour.

And to this that animosities are observed to be strongest betwixt those who are allied by kindred & blood—& in proportion to the affecn wch has formerly prevailed. . . . there is so much combustible matter on each side the Atlantic, that the least spark would kindle into a Flame, wch all the waters of that ocean wd be insufft to quench. Eternal jealousies & animosities will prevail, & offences be given & taken where they were not meant to be given.

The Degree of power, wch at any event, can remain with this kingdom, will be so feeble, as just to serve to give Life to those Jealousies & Disorders but not to subdue or correct them.

Both parties will remain so sore from the contest that an Eternal Divorce with respect to Govt I mean, appears to be necessary for both: as in the marriage state, small dissentions if they be taken in the beginng., & these may be any sense in either of the Parties may be suppressed; when they have arisen to a degree as to exclude all reasonable hope of future peace; 'tis best for both to part.[8]

Seeking Refuge in Britain (1783)

Introduction

A loyalist son of New York's royalist lieutenant governor Cadwallader Colden, David Colden served as superintendent of the police on British-governed Long Island in 1780 during the war. David Colden returned to England after the war and died shortly after in 1784. (However, his son, another Cadwallader Colden, after a brief sojourn in Canada, would return to New York. An eminent lawyer, Colden served as a mayor of New York City, as a congressman, and as state senator.) The excerpted letter, written by David Colden to his niece, Mrs. Henrietta Maria Colden, on September 15, 1783, shows Colden's worries about Britain's compensation to loyalists.

SPRING HILL 15th September 1783

Dear Madam:

I am sorry to have been in any degree accessory to the painfull anxiety under
which you waited six months, expecting a letter from me. I hope one I wrote
in April, would reach your hands in a few weeks after the date of your last to
me, of the 30th of the same month. You would, however, even then, receive
little satisfaction from my letter, respecting your affairs in this country; but it
might convince you that I do not forget you. Be assured I would write oftener,
if I could ever communicate any thing, either new or satisfactory to you about
your affairs . . .

The legislature of this State have not passed any act, immeadiatly affecting
the title of any part of the estate belonging to you or your children. No act of
theirs yet passed, mentions your husband's estate, his fathers or his grandfather
Colden's, either directly or by implication. That part of my fathers estate only,
which belongs to me, is involved as being part of mine. But as you desire me
to give you the most particular information of any act passed that may affect
you, I will transcribe abstracts of some clauses of the act of attainder, passd in
1779, which renders every man's estate who was within the British lines at any
time of the war, liable to be yet involved in the destruction it works.—It is
enacted that, the Grand Jurors at any Supreme Court of Judicature, Oyer and
Terminer or General Joal Delivery, to be held in and for any county of this
state, on oath of anyone or more creditable witness, that any person, whether
in full life or *deceased*, has been guilty of the offence aforesaid (adhering to the
enemy) shall prefer bills of inditments against such persons.—Sheriffs are to
give notice of the inditements by publishing advertisments,—and it is then
enacted that, on neglect to appear and traverse the inditement, agreeable to
the sheriff's notice, the several persons charged in such inditement whether in
full life or *deceased* to be adjudged guilty and forfeit all and singular their estate
real and personal.—In case a person *deceased* is indited his representative is to
appear and traverse.—Some hundred Freeholders, Merchants and Inhabitants
of Long Island, New York and Staaten Island have been indited, under this Act,
since the cessation of hostilities. So little effect have the preliminary articles
yet had!—I do not know that they have proceeded against any person not in
full life, altho' they might under this very extraordinary act, declared by the
preamble to be made in order to work a confiscation of estates for the use of
the State.—Tyrannical Law! made to take a man's life for the express purpose
of getting his estate. Be not surprised at the warmth of my expressions; it af-
fects me to the quick. But you wish to have me say what predicament I think
your children's estate stands in. I believe it safe from confiscation. The law
is too severe to be continued. Hitherto it has lain unnoticed. It must now be
annimadverted upon, and stigmatised with such censure by the world, that for
the credit of a national character, it must be blotted out. I believe there is a tax
laid upon all uncultivated lands; if it is so your son's estate cannot be exempted

from the effects of such a law; but what method is taken to get money for the tax, I am not informed.

McLean, the tenant your husband left on the farm near Newburgh. I hear is yet in possession of it: and Haasbrook, of the lands he rented.—The back rents, when they can be collected, must amount to something considerable.

. . . I must endeavor to give you some idea of the state of this country, which will at the same time be answering some other queries in your letter. . . . We have pass'd a twelve month, in the most perplexing state of uncertainty that ever a people did. Long waiting for the portionary articles, expecting they would certainly provide some security for the unfortunate loyalists, they have only increased our distress and cause of anxiety, and to this hour we do not know that they will have the smallest effect in our favour. No measures have yet been taken by Congress, except the release of prisoners, or by any of the states, that we know of, in consequence of the treaty. Even the recommendation of Congress, to which the English Ministry have devoted the lives and fortunes of thousands, whose virtuous attachment to Government shall render their characters immortal, while that of the ministers shall be execrated, I say, even this recommendation has not yet come forth. The spirit of persecution and violence against the unhappy loyalists does not appear to abate in any degree, since the cessation of hostilities. They are not suffered to go into the country even to take a last farewell of their relations. Committees are formd throughout the country, who publish the most violent resolves against the loyalists, and give instructions to the legislative bodies, directly repugnant to the treaty. We are told that these committees have allarmd the people in power, who wish to suppress them, but know not how. The people have been taught a dangerous truth, that *all power is derived from them.* Nothing can now render the country tolerably happy but the strength and firmness of the Governors: the Legislative Bodies; those in whom the Constitution have placed the Power of Governing. The most dread full anarchy must ensue, should the new Government prove unequal to the Task. An event most devoutly to be deprecated by every good Man! The Legislature of the State of New York have not been convened since the preliminary Treaty came [over?]. It is said, that by the Constitution, Peace having taken place, they cannot meet till representatives are elected for Long Island and that part of the state that has been within the British Lines. The election cannot be made while the British Army is here. General Charlton has informed Congress by letter of the 17th of last month, that he has received the Kings orders for the final evacuati[on] of New York, but that the infractions of the Treaty, and violences committed in the country upon the loyalists, has driven such multitudes of them to apply to him to be removed to some place of security, that he cannot say when he shall be able to leave the place being determind not to leave any loyalist behind, who choses to go away. Above 30,000 men women and children, have already been transported to Nova Scotia etc. and a very large number are still waiting for ships to carry them. Many substantial farmers of Long Island, and inhabitants of New York are gone and going, freightend away by inditements, and menaces, the fear of taxes, and an abhorrence of a republican government.

What I have now writen will be sufficient to convince you that this country is by no means yet in such a situation, that private affairs can be lookd into and settled.

You must allow my dear Niece that if I do not write frequently, you get very long epistles from me. The present has got to an enormous length, and yet I have said very little of the friends you inquire after. This will fill every corner of my paper. I have nothing to add to what I have already said of Antill and his family. Hamilton says he will abide on his farm in my neighborhood with his children. It is generally thought that he will be made very unhappy, as soon as the British army leaves us, and that he had much better go to some other place. My sister Delancey has had many severe tryals to encounter. Her son James included in the same act of attainder with me, has no expectation of recovering his estate: he is gone to England. She has parted with him, never expecting to see him again. Her daughter Barclay is gone with her husband and four children to Nova Scotia, where they must be reduced to a kind of life neither of them have ever before been acquainted with. The half pay allowed them will make their situation tolerable, which I apprehend would otherwise have been much otherwise. Her son Stephen lately sailed with his wife and four children for Quebec, to look out for the means of living when he gets there. Her son Oliver has been turnd off of the old family estate at West Chester since the cessation of hostilities, by commissioners acting under authority of the state, who gave him and several others a severe whiping, lest they should forget the Orders they had got to remove. Oliver had given his Mother a great deal of uneasiness not long before by a most foolish and disagreable marriage. My sister herself was threat-end with the loss of her estate at West Chester, Union Hall, and to secure it has been obliged to remove there with her Daughter Nancy. It is a most horrid place to be in at present. They have been very quiet since they got there, now about three weeks, under the protection of some of the American Army who are sta-tiond there to curb the lawless Bandittie who had got possession of the Country. Her son John is in New York, but I immagine he will not remain behind the British Army. Warner you recollect is in the 17th Dragoons. My brother Cad'r is in New York, his wife and family returnd to his estate at Coldingham after the peace, where they were well received and have met with no disturbance. He cannot go home himself to [till] the banishing act is repeald, and is advised to go out of the way, somewhere, when the evacuation takes place, till the act is repeald. His son Thomas and his wife intended going to Nova Scotia, with the Regt. who saild a few days since, but Thom has been ill, and is not sufficiently recovered to undertake the voyage, and the difficulties they must encounter, not having the least corner prepard, or a spot of cleard ground, where they are going. Capt. Willett has got leave to go to England.

Now for myself, here am I, condemnd to suffer death, if ever I am found in the State of New York; and yet my determination is to put them to the test. They have condemnd me, while living at my usual place of residence, without calling on me to appear and take a tryal. I am not guilty of the treason alledged against me. My going or staying will not I conceive affect the recovery of my estate. If they are determined to have it, they surely will let me off with my life at any time. My family will be inerted [?] in certain distress if I leave them, which they may escape if I stay with them. This, and a consciousness of innocence, determines my present resolution to keep possession of that part of my estate where I lived before and during the war.

I am glad to close this gloomy letter with a subject of another kind, the marriage of one of your connections. Rich'd Harrison 29 was married last week to Miss Ludlow, eldest daughter of the Judge; she went to England in June. I am happy to hear of the progress your sons make in their learning. My wife and children join in very affectionate remembrance of you and them. Please to present my respect full compliments to your father, and do not forget to give me credit for the length of my letters, tho' you cannot for their frequency . . .

Your affec't Uncle and most humble Serv't
DAVID COLDEN[9]

Notes

1. http://www.earlyamerica.com/earlyamerica/milestones/paris/text.html.

2. Clinton Memo, August 7, 1782, Clinton Papers, Clements Library, Ann Arbor.

3. Beverly Robinson, August 8, 1782, Clinton Papers.

4. British Headquarters Papers, December 18, 1782; also available in John Wolfe Lydekker, ed., *The Life and Letters of Charles Inglis: His Ministry in America and Consecration as First Colonial Bishop, from 1759 to 1787* (New York: Macmillan, 1936), 258–60.

5. Sir Guy Carleton Papers, November 15, 1783.

6. British Headquarters Papers, October 30, 1783.

7. Harry D. Bull, "A Note on James Stuart, Loyalist Clergyman in South Carolina," *The Journal of Southern History* 12, no. 4 (November 1946): 573–75.

8. Henry Addison to Jonathan Boucher, May 30, 1781, Henry Addison Papers, Clements Library.

9. E. Alfred Jones, "Letter of David Colden, Loyalist, 1783," *The American Historical Review* 25, no. 1 (October 1919): 80–86.

CHAPTER TEN

Loyalist Exiles

British Nova Scotia (1783)

Introduction

Written on July 12, 1783, this excerpted letter from a successful merchant in London, Brook Watson, shows how some British imagined the loyalists' new settlement in British North America. Watson anticipated that townships in Nova Scotia, as representations of constitutional stability, would invite the "envy" of their American neighbors.

The people of this independent country are run amuck, and will soon become objects of compassion. The unfortunate people who are now driving to seek refuge in Nova Scotia will soon be envied by the lawless wretches who now persecute them. In Europe we see the spirit of freedom Burning from the flames of Discord as Montesque [sic] says, but in America, the flames of Discord from the seeds of liberty too soon at maturity.

. . . The loyalists of this country are all preparing to leave it to settle in Nova Scotia. Port Roseway and St. Johns River seem the favorite destinations; the former will immediately become a great settlement, at least 3,000 souls will sail hence the beginning of next month, & carry with the [sic] a Body of troops with cannon, stores &c and a very considerable Property, a like number will probably sail for St. Johns at the same time/thus you see my dear friend, the province will be at last be settled, and that with good People of Property carry-ing in their hearts, the most settled love to the Constitution of England, they will form a barrier against those of opposite principle, and become the envy of

all their Neighbors; if you mean to sell your property in the Province, I do hope
you have followed my orders & sent your orders to that end.[1]

Loyalist Nova Scotia (1784)

Introduction

Written on April 26, 1784, from Halifax, Edward Winslow's letter expresses
his hopes for Nova Scotia to his longtime friend Ward Chipman. Winslow
explains his rationale for the partitioning of Nova Scotia and particularly
how loyalist refugees could not coexist peacefully with large numbers of established New Englanders. He also expresses confidence in Nova Scotia as a
supplier of provisions, lumber, horses, and fish required by the British sugar
islands. Finally, he echoes Watson. The Nova Scotian community created
by the "immense multitude" of like-minded gentlemen refugees would indeed
excite the "envy of the American States."

You are not to start at the appearance of this letter. I feel that it will be a long
one. The importance of the subject will justify even circumlocution and pro-
lixity. Writing to you is like having a tete a tete with myself. I am not shackled
by any vulgar rules, I throw aside all ideas of method and connection and
perfectly satisfied that you will find out my meaning I give you the unadorned
language of my heart. You know how zealously I have express'd myself on the
subject of dividing the province of Nova Scotia and forming a government on
the north west side of the Bay of Fundy.

I have seen, my dear Chipman (in the country which I have formerly described to you), a vast collection of valuable men of different orders,—men,
respectable for their conduct, with their families and the little remains of
their property—unattended to, and ungoverned. I saw all those Provincial
Regiments, (which we have so frequently mustered) landing in this inhospi-
table climate, in the month of October, without shelter and without knowing
where to find a place to reside. The chagrin of the officers was not to me so
truly affecting as the poignant grief of the men. Those respectable Serjeants
of Robinson's, Ludlow's, Cruger's, Fanning's, &c., (once hospitable yeomen of
the country) were addressing me in a language which almost murdered me as
I heard it.

"Sir we have served all the War. Your Honor is witness how faithfully. We
were promised land, We expected you had obtained it for us,—We like the
country—only let us have a spot of own, and give us such kind of *regulations* as
will hinder bad men from injuring us.—

Think you Chipman that it could be possible for me to retreat from a scene
like this? Or do you think affecting as it was, that it would discourage me from
exertions—No! It had a contrary effect—it stimulated me to propose to Gen-

eral Fox (who was also witness to their distress) the plan of forming a separate Government, as the only possible means of effectual relief—and to contribute to that relief was my ambition and my motive.

That matter being settled I shall go on.

You have already received all the arguments (in favor of this plan) which arise from local considerations. Since our first proposal vast numbers of settlers have arrived in that country. Almost all the people who composed the Garrison of Penobscot, are now at Passamaouoddy. The late Fencible Americans, D'cr. Paine with a large party; Sam Blisst with another party—are there; in short the numbers are astonishing. All these men are waiting with the most eager impatience for some regulations in their favor. All agree that nothing short of a separate Government can effectually serve them. Surely it must happen. It must be for the interest as well as the honor of the British Government, to save from despair so many of its faithful subjects. Consoled with this idea we are determined to expect it. The encouragement given in your letter has revived us beyond all description. For Heaven sake don't suffer us to be disappointed.

It has been a question here, and perhaps may be the subject of enquiry in England—Whether the British West Indies can be supplied with the articles they want from Nova Scotia. I have occasionally, since my arrival here, had much conversation with merchants and other well inform'd Gentlemen on this subject, and I am perfectly satisfied in my own mind, that the Countries of Nova Scotia and Canada can supply the British West Indies with every article they want. But as an ipse dixit, in a business of this sort cannot be satisfactory, I will endeavor to give some reasons for this opinion.

The articles usually exported from the American Provinces to the West Indies are Lumber, Fish, Horses, & some Provisions.

To form a judgment of the quantity of Lumber which the country produces, consider what has been the last year's consumption in this province. The towns of Shelburne, Digby, and those on St. John's River, and many inferior towns have been built in the course of last Year and they now contain many thousand houses. The materials for building those houses have been supplied without any great assistance from the New Settlers, and the importation from the States has been very inconsiderable, because in most of those places the New Settlers have (injudiciously) refused to traffic with them. It is fair reasoning to say—If such considerable quantities of Lumber could be supplied (on an emergency) by the former inhabitants (who God knows are not remarkable for their industry) Surely it will increase immensely when a multitude of spirited men shall find it an object worth their attention. The fund of timber is literally inexhaustible. Take the plan of the River St. John's, trace it from the Entrance, observe the prodigious branches from it, the vast lakes in the vicinity of it, from whence those streams run, Consider the extent of country between that & Passamaquoddy, and the other way to Pitcoudiac. Realize that the borders of those lakes & rivers are covered with timber of almost every kind, and that the interior country as far as has been explored furnishes timber in the same proportion. Look also at Passamaquoddy Bay and the rivers which empty into that.

Omnipotence cannot effect the creation of more perfect streams for mills than are to be found in all these places, and the transportation of lumber from the places of sawing to the places of Export is rendered perfectly easy because the currents always sett towards the latter. There was nothing wanting but labourers, to procure almost any quantity of lumber. The late acquisition of inhabitants—obviates that difficulty. The kind of lumber which is used for building, and which is most essential, such as Frames, Joists, Plank, Boards, Clap Boards, & Shingles will be exported in great abundance from hence—immediately. And so will Hoops, the Birch hoops it is agreed are as durable and valuable as any in the World. Staves, are the only article about which there is a doubt, & staves I am told may be had in Canada. In my observations on this business you'l recollect that I have confined myself principally to the propose'd new province, and you will take it into consideration that there are many places on the peninsula of Nova Scotia from which large quantities of lumber have been usually exported, and that the exports from those places will increase in proportion to the increase of inhabitants Sawmills are erecting & other improvements making in places where the old Nova Scotians never trod. A Capt. Taylor, of Stephen Delancey's regiment, has commenced his operations at St. Mary's Bay, and he now supplies all the people who are settling about that Bay & the Sissiboo river. New Mills are building in the neighborhood of Annapolis and Granville, almost in every other considerable town.

I shall say but little on the subject of Fish because it must occur to every man of common sense, that if the New England Traders could find a profit in sending their vessels to this coast for Fish,—those who inhabit its borders can carry on the business to much greater advantage. The exertions now making are very spirited and I have no doubt that the exports of Fish from Shelburne & the other new places added to the former usual exports from the old ports will be an ample supply for the West Indies this year.

Horses are reared with more facility in Canada & about St. John's than in any country I ever saw, and they are the best Hacks in the world.

Beef & Pork is produced in great abundance on the peninsula of Nova Scotia, more than is necessary for the inhabitants. Witness the quantities that were brought to us during the siege of Boston.

I cannot speak or write of that country about the river St. John's without making use of such extravagant expressions as have a tendency to lessen the weight of my testimonies in its favor. I acknowledge myself to be a little romantic, but I will appeal to General Fox & others who have observed it without being so much in raptures, whether they ever beheld a more delightful grass country, better cattle, or better grain, or more abundant crops.

What then in the name of wonder should hinder us from supplying the West India Islands with all the articles they want especially as the privilege of doing it is effectually secured to us by the navigation Act. There has been an idea sported here that there would be either a suspension or a relaxation of that act but this 1 think can never happen. I cannot imagine on what principle of politics such a measure could be adopted. If the apprehension of inconvenience to the islands from the operation of the act is the argument in favor of relaxing it, it must have been suggested without due consideration. For (if the necessary attention which the new settlers are obliged to give to their private matters during the first Year, prevents any great speculations) the islands can't suffer. The Americans (if advantages result from the traffic) will bring their commodities to our ports sell them to us—or make their vessels British Bottoms—give a spring to our commerce, and not greatly enhance the price of the articles at the final market. This consideration will hold good with respect to any other article which in future we may not be able to supply. All these circumstances considered it appears to me there can be no danger even of a relaxation of the act. Such an event would greatly check the progress of our settlements.

Let me impress on your mind, my dear fellow, the necessity of the immediate exertion of every friend to this country to effect the new government. You call have no idea of the strange situation which those people on the St. John's side are now in. The difficulties which attend a communication between that country & the present metropolis have been severely experienced this season. The unfortunate Provincial Officers & others, who have from a concurrence of unaccountable accidents been prevented from the possession of their lands, and have business of other kinds to negotiate with the officers of Government here, have been led into expenses which has deprived them of the small remains of their hard earn'd money, and many of them who have been obliged to make the tour, are reduced to distress from the necessary expences: Some of 'em reside 100 miles from the mouth of St. John's, they have of course (after performing that journey) to pass the Bay of Fundy and to travel by land from Annapolis 130 miles more, and they arrive at a place where expences are enormous, and the worst part of the story is that they have generally returned without effecting their business. They invariably complain of the want of an efficient and regular system of Government—they say, "their property is insecure & the spirit of enterprize check'd." They also say that there are suggestions of claims in consequence of former assignments of lands, and the people are frighten'd at the idea of fixing a residence on a property which is liable to contest. There are no attempts to remedy these inconveniences—the feeble effort of sending the Chief Justice with a Mr Elias Hardy to enquire into their grievances, can't possibly be attended with any salutary consequences. In short Chip, the relief must be speedy. The clamour is now so great that (altho' not warranted by the information I received) I thought it necessary to send off an express to Coffin & my other friends, to acquaint them of the prospect of a government being established there. Late letters received from men not accustomed to enumerate grievances, are filled with such melancholy anticipations that I could not avoid endeavoring to relieve them.

As I don't care how long my letter is, I'll introduce another argument in favour of dividing this province, which (if not of equal weight with others) is of some consequence. You will I think enter into the spirit of it. A large proportion of the old inhabitants of this country are natives of New England, or descendants from New Englanders, they, from their situation, never experienced any of the inconveniences which resulted from the violence of political animosity, they remained quiet during all the persecutions in the other provinces—they retained a natural (perhaps laudable) affection for their country. The rebel party were more industrious, and their doctrines and principles were more greedily adopted, than those of the other side, by degrees the Nova Scotians became firmly persuaded of the justice of their cause. Of this complexion are the public officers, generally. On our side the principal people are men who have served in a military line—irritable from a series of mortifications scarcely cooled from the ardor of resentment jealous to an extreme, some of 'em illiberally so. Either of these kinds of men may form useful societies among themselves—but they can't be mixed—separate them, and this very difference of opinion will increase the emulation and contribute to the general good; together—wrangles and contests would be unavoidable.

Lord Sydney's declaration quoted in your letter, "That he will make Nova Scotia the envy of the American States," has excited a kind of general gratitude, I cannot describe it. Other ministers and Great men have by their patronage of new settlers, relieved individuals from distress, and rendered services to their country, but it is a Godlike task that Lord Sydney has undertaken. Such an event as the present, never happened before—perhaps never will happen again. There are assembled here an immense multitude (not of dissolute vagrants such as commonly make the first efforts to settle new countries,) but gentlemen of education—Farmers, formerly independent—& reputable mechanics, who by the fortune of war have been deprived of their property. They are as firmly attached to the British constitution as if they never had made a sacrifice. Here they stand with their wives and their children looking up for protection, and requesting such regulations as are necessary to the weal of society. To save these from distress, to soothe and comfort them by extending indulgencies which at the same time are essentially beneficial to the country at large, is truly a noble duty. By heaven we will be the envy of the American States. The obligation which we—St. John's men feel for the proposal of giving us a government is greatly enhanced by the consideration that the man proposed to be placed at the head is perfectly calculated for the performance of the duty. General Fox is of a character so dignify'd he is so truly respectable for his services—has discovered such brilliant abilities, such an enterprizing spirit & indefatigable industry, that we anticipate the most important benefits from his exertions. When the people of the neighboring states shall observe our operations—when they see us in the enjoyment of a regular system of Government protected by the mother country—not saddled with enormous taxes, and compare their state with ours, Will not they envy us? Surely they will. Many of their most respectable Inhabitants will join us immediately. You have abilities my friend of a superior kind, if there are yet obstacles in the way, exert all your talents to remove them. The nobleman whose heart suggested an idea so benevolent, cannot be inaccessible to men of sense. See Lord Sydney, expatiate to him on the importance of the object convince him by fair reasoning, of the necessity of adopting the plan. I am so confident of your success in the business that I have been enquiring where will probably be the boundaries of our province . . . Most cordially & uncommonly yours, Ed. Winslow.[2]

Predicting the Collapse of the United States (1785)

Introduction

Although the document does not include a title or a date, William Smith Jr. probably wrote this in early 1785, when he was in England awaiting a position as chief justice of Quebec in British North America. Smith expected the colonies to have a short history; without the ballast of the British constitution, there was little hope for stability. Past experience had shown that republican government was weak. Democracy, its logical concomitant, brought with it the rule of the poor and the evils of egalitarianism.

The Conduct of the Colonies in the War, to the Eye of a distant Spectator, favors the Separation had been the general wish of *the Continent*. But better informed observers on the Spot, know how account for its Progress without any such Hypothesis—The Americans were never united, but when the Defence of Liberty against British Taxation was the Object; They were divided from the moment that Independency was declared. But then the Congress had an Army, and the Discontented were *disarmed*; and on the Part of Great Britain there was a failure of all the means to avail herself of the Aid of the Friends to the unity of the Empire—She did not make war—She pursued a double System of irritating Coercion and imperfect Concession—She fed the Hopes of the Rebels that they found. Too often they plundered their Friends as well as their Foes and in the Districts from which the latter were expelled no government took Place grateful to the wishes or adequate to the Security of the Inhabitants attached to the British Interest. The Civil Authority was not erected nor the Loyalists armed—on every Evacuation therefore they were at the mercy of their Enemies.

But be this as it may, the Question is *now* not worth a Discussion; the Calamities induced by the War, and by the Peace itself (of which perhaps very wrong Conceptions are abroad as Time will discover) have made great and material Changes, both in the Condition and Temper of the Country.

The first Leaders in America were not all of them Republicans, tho the Mask was expedient to feed the Hopes & obtain the Concurrence of a great Part of the Multitude; and they who *really are such at this Day*, are but a Handful to the Hosts arrayed against them, converted by Disappointments and Distress.

The Republican Independents (for it is very material to distinguish the Commonwealths man at Heart from others, who judging by their Feelings, abhor a Frame of Government that renders them unhappy) form the Party, that *by Principle mean Evil to Great Britain*—and their Object, and indeed their Hope of Defence, against the rising wrath of a Country they have ruined, is

The Erection of a Constitution, to become a Nation not in Name but Reality—to have but *one* will, & the Power to carry that will into Execution, *under a model perfectly Republican*.

But a Thousand Obstacles are already in the Way of this Enterprise; because Malcontents, of various Classes are shooting up in all Parts of America from the Hotbeds of selfish Contention—The opposers to the Commonwealth Project, are innumrable [*sic*] & distinguished by general Descriptions, are:

1. The Loyalists to a Man; who in some of the Provinces are nearly half (as both Parties in Pensilvania avowed last August, on the Secession from the Assembly) and in others (as New York for Instance) a larger Proportion of the Inhabitants.
2. The converts to their opinions, from disappointed Expectations, and the *Paper-money* Frauds—Scores of Thousands have been ruined by the Millions of Paper Dollars, now not worth a Shilling, because not intended to be redeemed. The Bills issued by the Congress were near 200 millions and the respective State Emissions many millions more. The holders are creditors but creditors in Despair.
3. The great Landlords and the Opulent; who contemn the Equality, hate the Insolence, and dread the Rapacity of the Poor under Democratic Frames.
4. The Debtors to British Subjects; left by the Treaty to the Mercy of their Creditors, liable to Demands they joined in the War to elude, and now are breaking the Treaty to avoid, by Laws of their own Making, Substituting Payments in State Paper-Money Securities, instead of Sterling money of Great Britain.
5. The opposers of Taxes; which must come on, if a Power is set up, to exact the Payment of the French and Dutch Loans to the Congress, with what was borrowed from Home Creditors; or is due to the American Army—Debts, which in 1782 amounted to Forty odd Millions of Dollars—not disclosed

to the Multitude till the year 1783—then heard with astonishment—and since increased, and increasing by the non Payment of the Interest, stated to be the first year at near Two Millions and a half of Dollars. See the Requisition of Congress of 27 April 1784 for 3,812,539 Dollars—near a million Sterling for the Interest of Debts & (?) without the Principal.

6. Whole Provinces averse to any Establishment, tending to Check their Claims to exorbitant Boundaries; relying upon their Superiority, over the Colony they mean to invade, abridge or ingross.

7. Such as Tremble at the Retrenchment of their Limits, by the Intrigues of a discontented District; which a *general Sovereignty*, may from Motives of Policy be inclined to favor: or at the Idea, so subversive of the Projects of many, that Congress is vested with the Crown Rights to the Waste Lands, *provincial & extra provincial*.

New York has at Stake 6 or 7 million of acres, by the Defection of Vermont that is filling with Loyalists, *in the neighbourhood of Canada*. Pennsylvania is weakned [sic] by a Party in it. countenacing the Title of Connecticut. Congress to confine New York, to the Letter of Charles the 2nd's grant to his Brother in 1664, have so late as in October last, bought the Indian Title to the Western Lands on the Mohawk River, and all beyond it into the Country of the Six Nations—and Congress must undoubtedly be at variance, with such of the Provinces, as claim their Breadths thro' the Continent to the South Sea. They wish their immense Land Stock to be at their Disposition.

8. The Possessors of confiscated Estates; who are in Consternation at the prevailing Principle, of an envious Majority in all the Provinces, that the Forfeitures are due to the Continent *at large*; and are not at the Disposition of the *Separate* Sovereignties; who have usurped authority to distribute the confiscated Estates to a *Few* of their Friends, or rather to parcel them out to such as happened to be in Power, at the moment of the respective British Evacuations.

9. The partial Advocates for severed sovereignties, from commercial views of Preheminence, natural or adventitious.

10. The apprehensions of such of the Provinces, as being in Default for the Expences of the War, look forward with abhorrence, to the Day of Account and Repartition.

11. The Proselytes to Discontent from the Loss of Trade by the Exclusions of the British—by the Jealousies of the Spaniards, and the French Partialities; and from the Obstructions to the Mediterranean Trade by the Algerines—in Consequence of which the American Merchants now learn that without the ample credit they had from Great Britain the Resources of America cannot be brought into use—and that it was to this they owed the Improvement and Cultivation of the Country.

12. All that have suffered Damage by the War whose Hopes of Compensation are extinguished by the (unfeeling?) Resolve of Congress of the 3rd June 1784.

Such and so innumerable, the Seeds of Discord and Debility! How fallacious then the Ideas of the Republican Speculatists of Europe, who are painting America as the Hope and Refuge of Humanity! Visionaries, who tho' *an Equality* of Estates is the Soul of their System, are at the same time inattentive to the diversified Distribution of Mankind, ordained by Heaven itself that will admit of no such Equality—Utopian Dreamers! Philosophers as they are called perhaps but uninformed benevolent, and the Dupes of Politicians who urge to Schemes that are impracticable, to *divide and destroy.*

America alass! seems to be (devoted?) to the wildest confusion. Blood has been already spill'd at Wyoming on the Susquehanna in the contest between Connecticut & Pensilvania; and not to forsee a Deluge of it in other Places, is to know Nothing of the Country and the People, the Magnitude of their Disputes, their contradictory Views, the Incitements to Passion, the Temptations to offend, and the Facility of offending.

These are however only Hints, of the *main Obstacles to a general Commonwealth.* Every Province has its own Parties, upon Points of local strife and Division:- and as certainly as there are, who draw hope from such a constitution, there will be others as eagerly to oppose it. The oppressed overtaxed Southern Half of New York are already become indifferent to the Ruin of the Rest of the Colony and foment the claims of Vermont and New England.

What Prospect then that Thirteen Sovereignties, with twice that number in contemplation, who formed out of the wilderness when claims are adjusted, can be persuaded to any *essential* augmentation of the *Congressional Powers!*— Short of authority to govern in commerce—to raise money—form armies and direct their operations, Congress (as France and Holland find by the Non Payment of their Loans, and England by the Disregard of the Treaty) is in Fact subordinate to the *Assemblies*—But possessed of these Powers, will be *supreme*—nor can—nor will suffer control.

Not all the Terrors of the War, extracted so mortifying Cessions as forming the League or written Confederation, in the desponding moments of the Congressional Flight from Philadelphia to York Town in Nov. 1777—*What I have said assigns the Causes.* They advanced not a step farther, than to unite in council for a Defence against the Mother Country, and the League was calculated to gull the Powers they courted for their Allies—Can it be expected that those sovereignties, *then so wary and artful,* will consent to their own Annhililation, now the war is over & the motives to the Bond of union, are changed into interested objections, to any general Subordination and Restraint.

America, 'tis true, can't exist without a general Government, and is verging swiftly, to worse Scenes of misery, than she has hitherto witnessed.

Such as doubt it, are taught a Lesson by Testimony they need not distrust— Washington in his circular Letter to the Colonies, of the 18 June 1783, informs them, that without a Constitution of Energy, all their Victories and Labours were worse than in Vain—That Letter deserves the greater Credit, for being written under Embarrassment to conceal from *Europe*, what it was his Design to inculcate on the Americans, and among these also there were many that might be and in Fact were disobliged. It was his aim to acquire the applause those Sentiments might have merited if revealed early enough to prevent the War, or to close it by a generous Conciliation. It was conceived with ambitious Designs—had (?). Deliberation, underwent many alterations by the advice of Friends and was ventured at last with Trepidation from its Tendency to excite popular Jealousy & expose the weakness of the Country to G Britain and the Internal adherents to her Cause.

This manageable Debility however of the old Provinces, will last no longer than until their Calamities, compel their Democracies, as they must very soon, to Submit to a *Depotism*; or excite them to prevent it by the Choice of a Constitution, *similar to that of the Mother Country*—a constitution, which in the Comparison of their *present* with their *former* Condition, they never think of without Regret.

Of these two Events the last perhaps has the most inauspicious aspect to Great Britain, from its Influence upon her Factions and overtaxed Inhabitants, and its conformity to their Habits and Taste, and it will be her Fault, if she does not instantly meet the Preparatives to the Revolution whatever it may be; and by a wise Policy turn it to her own advantage, either for the Recovery of what she has surrendered, or the Security of what she has (reserved?); and as *conducive to both Ends*, to place the latter, without Delay, upon the only Basis, that can render remote Colonies, safe and useful to the Parent Dominion.

It will be Blindness indeed, not to discern the approaches of some such change in America; and a great Error, in forming the intended Establishments, to be unmindful of the Causes of the *original Revolt*—Superficial observers think they have found them, in the Stamp Act, Duty Acts, & Tea Act; but an enlightened Discernment perceives these to be rather Consequences and Effects of a general and more remote Cause.—Matches to a Train laid *long before*, in a neglect of the Colonies under arrangements, once indeed competent to the Condition of infant Plantations, but by their Growth and Opulence, Education and Spirit, become inadequate to their Government—The Statement of Rights by the Congress of 1774, the least immoderate of any, may shew this; and an Idea of the requisite model for the common Tranquility, was communicated to England, years before the war; and if offered to America, had been embraced at any Moment of its Duration. What? when the terms of 1778 were rejected?—Yes—for these excited Suspicion by their Extent; and were abortive, because the Powers of the commissioners, were neither equal to their overtures, nor decisive & irreversible—Parliament reserved authority to confirm or reject, what they should have come out *unalterably to conclude*. There were Americans in arms and in office for the Congress, always averse to the Separation of the Empire; perceiving greater Safety to their Country, and honor to themselves, by the Settlement they waged War to procure; and it was in that conviction that one of their Governors, (offended?) at the Treaty for the Separation frankly owned it to have been his Hope that the Party for Independency would have been broken & ruined by Propositions for a generous and lasting Reunion, which unfortunately never had been properly authorized & promulged.

Canada and the British Possessions, to be now a Temptation *to the Americans*, to shelter themselves under the same protecting Power, or by that Power to be influenced or restrained, must not want any Privilege, which it consists with the *general utility* to grant them; for every unfavorable Discrimination, not induced by Necessity, must inevitably be the Spring of Inquietude, and preserve the union no longer, than until with the Loss of their affection, they shall have abandoned their Fears . . .[3]

Celebrating Loyalist Heritage (1884)

Introduction

In 1789, six years after the Peace Treaty, Lord Dorchester, the governor general of British North America, proposed to recognize loyalist sacrifices and single out loyalist families by putting a "mark of honour upon families who had adhered to the unity of the empire and joined the royal standard in America, before the treaty of separation in the year 1783." He declared that all true loyalists should be distinguished by having the letters U.E.L. (United Empire Loyalists) affixed to their names. On July 3, 1884, one hundred years after the Treaty of Paris, descendants of loyalists in Toronto gathered to remember their Anglo-Saxon ancestors. The excerpted speech shows the pride in the British empire and the emphasis on the bravery and character of white loyalist immigrants.

In every part of this wide Dominion may still be found some of the descendants of that noble band of whom a Canadian poet has so worthily sung, that they—

> Loved the cause
> That has been lost; and scorned an alien name,
> Passed into exile, leaving all behind
> Except their honour and the conscious pride
> Of duty done to country and to King.

As the chairman has reminded us, just one hundred years ago did the Loyalists of America, abandoning home, property, every worldly gain and advantage, rather than forego their allegiance to the British Crown, and in the face of hardships and trials, such as might have daunted less brave and resolute hearts, come to what was then a wilderness, and become fathers and founders of what we now so proudly call the Dominion of Canada. It concerns us; not, upon this occasion, to inquire into the merits of that unhappy quarrel which cost Great Britain the American colonies. Ample justice has been done by the writers and historians of that day, and down to the present time, to the motives and actions of the successful revolutionists. More than justice, in fact, for too many of the chroniclers of these events have not been satisfied with exalting the actors on the one side, and ascribing to them every virtue, but have most unjustly and ingeniously depreciated and misrepresented those whose greatest crime was that they were "loyal and true to their sovereign, and willingly sacrificed every worldly possession rather than sever their connection with the Empire." The United Empire Loyalists of one hundred years ago valued liberty as much as the revolutionists, but they would have secured the redress of their grievances by other means than by severing the tie which bound them to Great Britain, and when the party of revolution became the stronger and the die was cast, and the ultimate appeal made to the sword, then they drew it for the king, and never sheathed it until the struggle was over, when, rather than preserve land or possessions, or secure an immunity from persecution and ill-treatment by the abandonment of their principles, they determined upon that grand exodus which we commemorate this day, and manfully set their faces toward the wilds of New Brunswick, Nova Scotia, and Canada, to become the first founders of what is yet, thank God, an integral part of the Empire, the fairest jewel in Britain's Crown. The history of the cruel persecution and unjust legislation of which the loyalists were made the subjects in most of the States of the American Union after the close of the struggle and the establishment of the Republic, were it only more generally known, would astonish those even among our own countrymen who have so much admiration to bestow upon the successful revolutionists, and but little sympathy for the heroism and endurance of those who remained faithful to the cause, as they believed it to be, of loyalty and honour. Undoubtedly the revolution, owing to the bitter animosities engendered by the struggle, frequently led to cruel reprisals and deeds of bloodshed on both sides; but that could not justify the cruelty and persecution with which hundreds were visited who had taken no active part in the strife, or the expatriation of the many thousands whose only crime had been their refusal to renounce their allegiance to their king . . .

. . . As you all know, in order to reward the loyalty and to relieve the present necessities of the Loyalists and their families, as well as to provide for their future subsistence, the British Government made liberal grants of land in Upper Canada. . . . The new settlers were provided with farming implements, building materials, and provisions, and some clothing for the first two years. . . . And now one hundred years have passed away since that honour roll was drawn up—the Loyalists of that day have passed to their rest, but far and wide throughout the Dominion their descendants may still be found glorying in the name and the traditions they have inherited, and by our gathering here today we desire to show that, as did our fathers in those days of old—so do we desire to preserve the unity of the Empire, and shall ever honour the memory of those who cheerfully risked every worldly gain or advantage, aye, even life and liberty, to preserve unbroken the ties which bound them to the Motherland. Nor can we forget, on an occasion like the present, how nobly the old Loyalist spirit showed itself when Canada subsequently became the battlefield during the war between Great Britain and the United States. It has been well remarked that the true spirit of the Loyalists of America was never shown with greater force than in the conduct of their descendant, during the war of 1812-14. As their fathers willingly risked life and fortune to maintain their connection with the Empire, so the sons were ready at the first trumpet call to leave wives and little ones' come forth from their homesteads, and acquit themselves like men in resisting the invaders who strove to wrest their adopted country from the British Crown. Sir, it is a just subject of pride to us Canadians that, thanks to the loyalty and the pluck of the militia and volunteers of those days, without distinction of class or nationality, the Canadas, with a frontier of more than 1,000 miles, and aided only by a few regiments of regular soldiers, resisted the whole military power of the United States for two years, at the end of which not one inch of Canadian soil was in possession of the invaders . . .

. . . Mr. Chairman, I am persuaded that the same spirit that characterized the Canadian militiamen and volunteers in 1812 and the Loyalists of 1784, breathes in their descendants now, and that my countrymen would be ready and prepared now, as then, if occasion should unhappily require, to defend not only "their rights and property," but the "safety and glory of this Dominion, as one of the most highly favoured portions of the British Empire." True, we do find a certain class of writers in our midst attempting to decry loyalty to the Crown and attachment to Imperial connection as inconsistent with true patriotism and pride in our country as Canadians. I yield to no one in my love for my native country. The very soil of Canada is dear to me. I love her lakes and forests, her mighty rivers, her broad and fertile fields. I am proud of the past history of my country, of the wonderful progress it has made not only in material prosperity, but in all that contributes to the higher life of a nation; its advancement in education and culture, the fitness our people have displayed for free and constitutional government, and that observance of law and order which is the noblest characteristic of the Anglo-Saxon race. But all this is entirely consistent with a deep and abiding love and attachment to the Motherland, whose glorious traditions we inherit, and which are the common property of every subject of the empire. Is there anything servile or unpatriotic in the feeling which makes the pulse beat more quickly and the heart swell, as we recall the glorious deeds of Britain's heroes on land and sea—whether in the old days of Wellington and Nelson, Waterloo and the Nile, or, coming down to our time, to Balaklava or Inkerman; or but yesterday, as we read of the rush of the Highlanders upon the foe at Tel·El·Kebir? Is there anything servile or unpatriotic in that feeling of reverence and affection for all that is great and noble in the lives and characters and works of the long array of statesmen, philosophers and poets, of men of mark in Church and State, that have made Britain's history the proud and glorious one that it is? Is there anything servile or unpatriotic in that sentiment of deep and chivalrous loyalty to the sovereign which takes out of self and makes men dare to do and die from the highest motives of faith and duty? Sir, are not all those feelings which elevate and ennoble a people? And if it is good for us to recall today the loyalty and patriotism, the bravery and endurance of our Loyalist forefathers, shall we abandon the rich heritage of centuries, and cut ourselves and our children adrift from the glorious memories and associations which now belong to us Canadians as members of the one great United Empire? I am persuaded of better things of my countrymen, The old Loyalist spirit is not extinct, It may not babble as loudly of its loyalty as some do of their independence, but the stream runs deep, though noiselessly, and that time, I trust, will never come when Canada will cease to be a part of the Empire, and when we shall cease to bear the proud name of British Canadians . . .

THE UNITED EMPIRE LOYALISTS.

> In the brave old Revolution days,
> So by our sires 'tis told,
> King's-men and Rebels all ablaze
> With wrath and wrong,
> Strove hard and long;
> And, fearsome to behold,
> O'er town and wilderness afar,
> O'er quaking land and sea and air,
> All dark and stern the cloud of war
> In bursting thunder rolled.
>
> Men of one blood—of British blood,
> Rushed to the mortal strife;
> Men, brothers born,
> In hate and scorn
> Shed each the other's life.
> Which had the right and which the wrong
> It boots not now to say:
>
> But when at last
> The war-cloud passed,

Cornwallis sailed away;
He sailed away, and left the field
To those who knew right well to wield
The powers of war, but not to yield,
Though Britons fought the day.

Cornwallis sailed away, but left
Full many a loyal man,
Who wore the red,
And fought and bled
Till Royal George's banner fled
Not to return again.

What did they then, those loyal men,
When Britain's cause was lost?
Did they consent,
And dwell content
Where Crown, and Law, and Parliament
Were trampled in the dust.

Dear were their homes where they were born;
Where slept their honoured dead:
And rich and wide
On every side
The fruitful acres spread;
But dearer to their faithful hearts
Than home, or gold, or lands,
Were Britain's laws, and Britain's crown,
And Britain's flag of long renown,
And grip of British hands.

They would not spurn the glorious old
To grasp the gaudy new.
Of yesterday's rebellion born
They held the upstart power in scorn
Britain they stood true.

With high resolve they looked their last
On home and native land;
And sore they wept,
O'er those that slept
In honoured graves that must be kept
By grace a stranger's hand.

They looked their last and got them out
Into the wilderness.
The stern old wilderness!
All dark and rude
And unsubdued;
The savage wilderness!
Where wild beasts howled
And Indians prowled;
The lonely wilderness!
Where social joys must be forgot,
And budding childhood grow untaught;
Where hopeless hunger might assail
Should Autumn's promised fruitage fail
Where sickness, unrestrained by skill,
Might slay their dear ones at its will;
Where they must lay
Their dead away
Without the man of God to say
The sad sweet words, how dear to men,
Of resurrection hope. But then
'Twas British wilderness!
Where they might sing,
God save the King!
And live protected by his laws,
And loyalty upheld his cause.
'Twas welcome wilderness!
Though dark and rude
And unsubdued;
'Though wild beasts howled
And Indians prowled;
For there their sturdy hands,
By hated treason undefiled,
Might win from the Canadian wild
A home on British lands.

These be thy heroes, Canada?
These men of proof, whose test
Was in the fevered pulse of strife
When foeman thrusts at foeman's life;
And in that stern behest,
When right must toil for scanty bread,
While wrong on sumptuous fare is fed,
And men must choose between;

When right must shelter 'neath the skies,
While wrong in lordly mansion lies,
And men must choose between;
When right is cursed and crucified,
While wrong is cheered and glorified,
And men must choose between.

Stern was the test,
And sorely pressed,
That proved their blood best of the best.
And when for Canada you pray,
Implore kind Heaven
That, like a leaven,
The hero-blood which then was given
May quicken in her veins alway;
That from those worthy sires may spring,
In number as the stars,
Strong-hearted lions, whole glorying
Shall be in Right,
Though recreant Might
Be strong against her in the fight,
And many be her scars;
So, like the sun, her honoured name
Shall shine to latest years the same.
KINGSTON, Ont.[4]

Notes

1. Brook Watson to Joshua Mauger, July 12, 1783; and between January and July 1783; Mauger Papers, Gilder Lehrman, New York Historical Society.

2. George Athan Billias, ed., *Winslow Papers, A.D., 1776–1826* (Boston: Gregg Press, 1972), 187–95.

3. Oscar Zeichner, "William Smith's "Observations on America, *New York History* XXIII (1942): 328–40.

4. George Athan Billias, ed., *The Centennial of the Settlement of Upper Canada by the United Empire Loyalists, 1784–1884* (Boston: Gregg Press, 1972), 52–65.

Index

About the Author

Ruma Chopra, PhD, is associate professor at San Jose State University. Her first book, *Unnatural Rebellion: Loyalists in New York City*, examined the American Revolution through the loyalist perspective. Her next project titled, "Enemies of Britain in the Atlantic World, 1750–1800," explores the political deportations that came out of the British Atlantic experience of imperial rivalry, military conquest, and cultural mixing.